KILL SWITCH

KILL SWITCH

BILL SHAW

headline

First published in 2011
by HEADLINE PUBLISHING GROUP

1

Cataloguing in Publication Data is available from the British Library

Hardback ISBN 978 0 7553 6245 5
Trade paperback ISBN 978 0 7553 6246 2

Typeset in Adobe Garamond by Palimpsest Book Production Limited,
Falkirk, Stirlingshire

Printed and bound in the UK by
Clays Ltd, St Ives plc

Headline's policy is to use papers that are natural, renewable and recyclable
products and made from wood grown in sustainable forests. The logging and
manufacturing processes are expected to conform to the environmental regulations
of the country of origin.

HEADLINE PUBLISHING GROUP
An Hachette UK Company
338 Euston Road
London NW1 3BH

www.headline.co.uk
www.hachette.co.uk

*To Liz — always waiting for me with a
warm smile and loving arms*

This book is based on my recollection of events, which may not be exactly as others recall them. Where conversations cannot be remembered precisely, I have recreated them to the best of my ability. Where people need to be protected or to avoid offence, I have altered names. Any mistakes are my own.

I've paid my dues
Time after time
I've done my sentence
But committed no crime . . .

'We Are The Champions' – Queen

Prologue

The prison gate slid open and then slammed shut behind me. The sound of metal against metal jarred my ears. The Commandant had promised to put me with the only other 'Englishman' in his custody, which I assumed meant a two-man cell. That was until I saw what lay ahead of me within the forbidding walls of the Kabul detention centre that rainy afternoon in March 2010.

It was immediately clear to me that the place where I was about to be wrongly incarcerated was unfit for human habitation. The walls were cracked, the floors pitted, and the entire building smelled of decay, and poor sanitation. The twenty-five metre long corridor that stretched before me was flooded and yet so overcrowded that scores of Afghan and foreign inmates had no choice but to huddle along it. The majority stood in striped uniforms or sat draped in old blankets, while others lay in dirty puddles, their eyes staring out of faces gaunt with hunger, despair – or both.

After three decades as a proud member of Her Majesty's Royal Military Police, I now knew for the first time what it felt like to be behind bars. Despite four years' front-line private security experience in Afghanistan and Iraq, I'd become the unexpected 'guest' of the Central Police Prison at Tawqeef, dominated by watchtowers and barbed wire. Part of a sprawling colonial-style complex that also housed the police headquarters, this beating heart of Kabul's law enforcement was a place I'd previously done well to avoid.

Many on the payroll in the Afghan National Police had been variously accused of murder, trafficking offences and money laundering. Criminal gangs and terrorists were said to collude with officers whose ID cards, vehicles and uniforms frequently played a role in the kidnapping of foreign businessmen. In spite of their long-suspected connection with the Taliban, their building was a regular target for random bombings and rocket attacks, including one a few months earlier in which many were killed. Having spent a lifetime serving my country before leaving the military to guard senior diplomats, it beggared belief that I'd ended up in such a place surrounded by terrorists, murderers and thieves.

'You, come.' The colonel of the prison guard beckoned me deeper into his lair. Determined not to show any emotion, I picked my way through the vagabond crowd until I reached where he stood waiting by the first door on the left – cell No. 1.

'Hold it together, Billy,' I told myself. 'You'll be out of here in no time.'

Stepping inside, I found myself in a room four by four metres in which sixteen Afghans lived, ate and slept. Chipped metal bunk-beds were screwed to the walls in two tiers, giving ten sleeping spaces, and the concrete floor was covered in grubby grey blankets. Carrier bags of personal belongings hung on hooks screwed haphazardly into cracks in the mud walls. Boxes and baskets were crammed under bunks. Men slept, stood or sat wherever they could. High up on the opposite wall was a small window with three metal bars that looked not outside, but onto another room.

Two fluorescent tubes glared stark white light onto my new quarters, picking out each green globule of sneeze or spit. It showed up every stain on clothing, bedding and blankets, and illuminated a mouse nibbling stale bread. A small television in one corner broadcast an image of an imam reciting passages from the Koran. The flickering TV's blaring volume reminded me of my headache after nothing to eat or drink for nine hours. The pain behind my eyes wasn't helped by the pall of cigarette smoke and a loudspeaker that crackled to life to reel off a list of names. Half-hopeful, I listened out for mine.

Mindful of the customs, I removed my shoes and placed them amongst the assortment of sandals and flip-flops just inside the door. Then I stepped further into my cell. The colonel introduced me to the room 'leader', Abdul Wakil, who had an enormous belly and who I privately dubbed 'El Gordo', The Fat One. Paying my respects, I said, '*Salaam Alaikum*,' (Peace be upon you). El Gordo responded in kind but not everyone else did. Two mullahs, distinctive by their longer beards and white turbans, seemed especially wary.

The colonel left me then – friendless, unprotected and alone. I heard the main gate clang shut behind him. Many of the prisoners in the corridor, including those whose appearance told me they were Taliban, crowded the doorway to glare at the Westerner dropped like a lamb into their midst. Keeping my back to the wall, I hastily assessed my surroundings. I was grateful that most of my cellmates were middle-aged and, I hoped, less likely to be hotheads. One approached me and said, 'My name Assam.'

I responded cautiously and pointed to a thin blond man in his thirties lying on a lower bunk with his back to me. 'The Englishman?' I asked.

Assam nodded but said, 'He no words. No mix.'

I made my way over to the sleeping man and shook him awake. 'Stone the crows!' he said, when he realised I wasn't an Afghan. 'Welcome to the nuthouse.' My fellow 'countryman' turned out to be an Australian in his thirties named Robert Langdon. I was keen to find an ally in those confined quarters, but Rob wasn't overly warm and I sensed there was more to him than met the eye. 'Good luck, mate,' he said as he turned his back to me once more. Disappointed, I found a space on the floor and sat down to gather my thoughts.

Everything had happened so swiftly that I found it hard to believe I was in prison in Kabul. In the blink of an eye, I'd gone from being an upstanding member of the community to a common criminal. My so-called crime? To tell the truth. Being honest, open and fair had served me well my whole life, but in this ravaged country I was soon to learn that truth was just another commodity – one that could be bought and sold.

One

I can only have been about six years old when I was first sent by my mother Edith to buy a military blanket from the army surplus store in Cross Lane Market, Salford, Manchester. It wasn't cheap at ten shillings, but winter was coming and Mam saved the money from the welfare she received from the State.

Neither of my parents had held down a job in years and with seven children they lived on their family allowance of about eight shillings per child per week. My father, who'd been inside for theft before being crippled in a road accident, had been 'on the sick' for as long as I could recall. Any cash he could get his hands on was spent down the pub.

The army surplus store on the corner of Eccles New Road was a cornucopia of delight for a scrappy little kid with a vivid imagination; cram-packed from floor to ceiling with every kind of military kit from jerry cans to uniforms. It was the closest I'd ever come to a Santa's Grotto. I could have stayed in there all day. In an atmosphere pervaded by the smell of rubber and camphor, I wandered around, mouth open, staring at the water bottles, tents, survival packs and thick-soled boots. There were masks, helmets, trench coats, WWII battle dress, camping gear and mess kits, as well as Swiss army knives, hurricane lamps and mosquito nets. I wanted to be a soldier from the minute I first stepped over the threshold.

'I can let you have this blanket for eight shillings,' the owner told me. 'Tell your mam there's still some wear left in it.' Triumphant, I struggled away with it in my spindly arms. A few hundred yards along the road, I stopped to rest outside the drill hall of the old Lancashire Fusiliers barracks, from where I could hear the beating of a drum. Curious, I went to investigate. Through the half-open doorway, I watched teenage members of the cadets marching up and down with ramrod backs.

'Left right, left right, left right! About turn!' the moustachioed officer barked. 'Straight and tall, lads. Square to the front!' I found myself pulling back my own bony shoulders. Clad as I was in scrappy rags with shoes so tight they disfigured my toes for life, I desperately wanted to be one of those smart young men with slicked-down hair in crisp uniforms and shiny new boots.

Not a trip to the surplus store went by after that when I didn't stop at that drill hall and silently march in time to those pacing up and down inside to a drumbeat. The military was my future; I knew it as clear as day. Most of the boys I grew up with were headed to jail as were many of my family. For some reason, I had a sense of moral responsibility which kept me out of trouble, chiefly because I didn't want to end up like the rest of them. It was eight years before I was finally old enough to sign up as an army cadet but that was my first step towards a life that would lift me from poverty and crime.

I think my chief motivations were that I wanted to be different and to make a difference. Throughout my early childhood living in a two-up, two-down council slum in Brindle Heath, my clothes marked me out as the poor kid compared to the rest of my schoolmates in their grey sweaters and ties. I could never do PE because I didn't have any kit or clean underwear. I had to wait in a corner for my free meals while those who paid sneeringly took their fill. While other kids went on summer holidays, I stayed home and worked on a market stall. That is, until I found out about the Salford Poor Children's Holiday Camp in Prestatyn, Wales, which I went to four years on the bounce. From the age of eight, I walked six miles to Salford Town Hall on my own to book it myself. Even then, I was the only one at the camp without any pocket money; the boy who couldn't afford sweets at the tuck shop, and the only kid without swimming trunks.

Not that I cared. I had the time of my life. One year when I was there, Prince Charles came to Rhyl as part of his investiture at Caernarfon Castle. We were taken by bus to see his helicopter land and I pushed my way right to the front. With sores on my face and my head closely shaved because of nits, I waved my little paper flag wildly and was so excited to see our future king. I never for one moment thought I'd meet his family one day or be invited to Buckingham Palace.

Going home after a week playing in the Prestatyn sand dunes was always tough. Christmases were especially bleak. There was never a tree and crêpe paper decorations dangled from drawing pins stuck in the ceiling all year round. We rarely had visitors but if we did, we'd tell them we'd decided to put the decorations up early that year. On Christmas morning in 1968, when I was ten, I woke hoping to find the usual squashed satsuma or a Brazil nut or two in the holey old sock I'd tied a knot in to hang it on the mantelpiece. Mine was the only sock out of seven that my parents hadn't remembered to fill.

'Oh, bugger, Bert, we forgot our Billy,' was all my mam said, a cigarette stuck to her bottom lip as she prepared our scrawny turkey and ash fell onto the stale bread stuffing. Dad just shrugged and headed back down the pub.

My father was a strict disciplinarian who used to lay me and my sisters across his knee each night to whip us with his leather belt. 'I'll tan you now because you'll only create once you're upstairs, and you know I can't get up there because of my gammy leg.' He'd beat us so hard that we'd have to sleep on our tummies. Tears stinging my eyes one time, I called him a pig and ran away. He went mad and yelled, 'Come back here, you little f****r!' only to give me another hiding. Every other word began with an 'f' or a 'c' with my dad. I actually thought my mam's name was 'Edith, You Daft C***!' until I was old enough to know better.

A white mongrel with two black patches appeared at the door of our home one day. My father was in hospital then, encased in a body cast after he crashed the truck he was driving, so the dog I named Rover was allowed to stay. Thin as a rake, he had to fight for scraps like the rest of us but I always found him something. That mutt came with me whenever I ran away from home – usually to avoid a beating from my dad. I'd see my father limping off the bus and be so stiff scared that I'd scarper. One day Rover and I hid in the cellar of an old Victorian boarding house across the street. We stayed there for hours until the police came because Mam had reported me missing.

My father had always warned us, 'If you ever bring a policeman to our door, I'll kill you!' When they came that night I first ran away, I heard him going bananas and realised

I'd better get home. He started on me the minute he saw me. 'Come here, you bugger!' he yelled, grabbing me by the ear.

'Leave the lad alone!' the policemen said. To my amazement, he did. I ran away two or three times after that but as soon as the police arrived I knew it was safe to go back.

Coming back from Prestatyn one summer, I found Mam waiting at the bus stop. 'I've got some news, our Billy,' she said, as we headed home. 'Now that you've got a new baby brother, the council have given us that bigger place they promised us at the Ladywell Flats.' She paused. 'There's no pets allowed.'

I stopped in my tracks. 'What about Rover?'

'Your father's taking care of that.'

Our new flat was clean and modern, with an indoor bathroom and hot water; a dramatic improvement from before, but I was too worried about Rover to appreciate any of it. When Dad came back from the pub, there was no arguing with him as he told me to loop a piece of string around the dog's neck and follow him to the vet. Rover was laid in a basket with some poisoned meat. 'He'll bite into it and then just fall asleep,' the vet said, which is exactly what he did.

From an early age, I realised that a life of structure and discipline within the military would give me a way out. I didn't want to be just any old soldier, though. I'd set my heart on the Parachute Regiment. I don't know what it was about the 'Paras' that so attracted me – maybe their distinctive red berets or the fact that they had the best kit and most extensive arsenal. The Paras were real-life versions of the Action Man I'd always wanted but could never afford. Either way, I was dead set on joining their ranks. Taking myself off to an

Army Open Day at Tatton Park at the age of ten, I spent the whole day climbing thirty feet up a parachute stand, wriggling into a wire harness, and jumping off. It was there that I learned that the Para airborne assault force *was* the best. They'd turn a little urchin like me into a member of a feared and respected regiment ready to fight for Queen and country. That was my destiny, and I couldn't wait.

From the minute I joined the cadets at fourteen, I took to the military like a duck to water. While my mates were out joyriding or taking drugs, I was at the drill hall two nights a week and every weekend. 'Square to the front, Shaw! Left right, left right!' Mad on soldiering, I lapped up everything they taught me from battlefield craft to weapons training and map reading. I was so keen that, by fifteen, I was promoted to corporal and sent to teach weapons training to 4 Para Territorial Army cadets at the Oldham Army Cadet Force. That same year, I attended a two-day course at a Recruit Selection Centre in Harrogate.

'I want to be a member of the Junior Paras,' I announced proudly.

'Sorry, sonny, so does everyone else. There are no vacancies. You'll have to join the Royal Regiment of Fusiliers.'

There was no budging them so on 10 September 1974, I attended Bassingbourn Barracks in Royston, Hertfordshire, to train as a Junior Fusilier. Sixteen years old, I traded in my hand-me-down clothes for a combat uniform and flew through basic training. It wasn't nearly stimulating enough for me, though, mainly because there was far too much sports and hanging around. I wanted to learn combat skills and forced marches, military exercises and weapons training. I longed to be a foot soldier, armed and ready for combat. I pleaded once more to be transferred to the Paras but there were still no places so I quit. 'I'll come back and sign up at eighteen and join the Paras as an adult,' I told the senior officers defiantly.

So in January 1975, I handed back my combats and the next day put on a white coat and brown striped apron as a teenage apprentice at Dewhurst's butchers in Eccles. My weekly wage was £14, half of which I gave to my mam. I also took a couple of cut-price chickens home every week for the Sunday joint. To keep my hand in with the military, I continued in the drill hall at weekends. My cadet uniform was immaculate – I made sure to take care of that myself. I'd wash and dry it, then neatly fold it and put it on the window-sill in the bedroom I shared with my brothers; the only room in the house that wasn't filthy because I kept it clean myself. 'Keep your grubby hands off my kit!' I'd warn my younger siblings.

After a year of cutting up joints of meat, I presented myself at the Army Careers Office in January 1976. 'I'm set on the Parachute Regiment, Sir,' I insisted to my interviewing officer. He promised to recommend me and sent me to Sutton Cold-field for a two-day Adult Selection Course where I had to take a series of exams including maths, English and psycho-metric testing. Having left school at sixteen with only one O-level in home economics, I thought I'd be out of my league, but somehow I passed.

What bothered me most was the medical. Nervously, I waited with the other recruits in the corridor. Just before it was my turn, I hurried to the toilet and took off my under-pants. Dirty and full of holes, I stuffed them into my pocket.

When the doctor asked me to drop my trousers, he asked, 'Why haven't you got any underwear on?'

'I don't wear any, sir.' I was too embarrassed to tell him the truth.

We were shown a series of films about Army life, one of which featured the Royal Military Police working in the Far East. I liked the idea of living abroad and noted that their berets were similar to the Paras. Just before my final interview, I was required to fill in a form stating which regiment I wanted to join and why. 'It has been my lifetime ambition to be a member of the Parachute Regiment,' I wrote confidently. Asked to give two other choices, I was stumped but then I remembered the 'Red Caps', so I put down the RMP. All I could think of as my third choice was the regiment I already had a connection with, the Fusiliers.

During my final interview, a captain went through my test results and pronounced me good at English and spelling. Then he said, 'You'd clearly be best suited to the military police, Shaw.'

'No, Sir!' I cried, almost jumping out of my seat. 'You don't understand. I want to be a soldier, not a policeman!'

He peered at me over his spectacles. 'I can assure you, Shaw, that the RMP are soldiers through and through and are deployed as part of the Army around the world. In fact, they have a distinguished military history going back many centuries with unique operational responsibilities in and out of the field of conflict.'

'But I want to be in the Paras, Sir,' I protested. He told me then what people had been telling me for years. 'Sorry, but there are no vacancies.'

Seeing my expression, he added more gently that once I was in the RMP I could apply to the Para Provost (the RMP element of the Fifth Airborne Brigade). 'They parachute in with the foot soldiers and support their brigade on the ground,' he said. 'It may be the closest you'll get, son.'

Deeply disappointed, I wondered what I'd let myself in for as I boarded a train to Chichester and the RMP training camp. I soon met up with several other recruits heading to the same base and we quickly discovered that none of us had wanted to join the military police – we'd all been the victims of a recruitment drive. Furious, I intended to complain and attempt to get into the Paras one last time, but from the minute I arrived at the Roussillon Barracks, I was hooked.

The regimental motto for the RMP is *Exemplo Ducemus* – 'By Example We Lead'. I was delighted to learn that military policemen had to be even smarter than the troops and wear their best brown uniform at all times (not just for parades like regular soldiers). I couldn't believe how slick I looked in my No. 2 dress uniform with its red beret and I relished the pride I was expected to take in both. I loved keeping my kit shipshape and I was gobsmacked by our accommodation, which was so much cleaner than home.

The RMP taught me how to drive and paid for me to take my motorcycle test – sparking a lifelong interest. There was plenty of soldiering and I didn't even mind being back in a classroom. I won the right to wear the blue and red 'Recruit of the Week' sash so often it was almost embarrassing but I was part of a good squad with no bullies. We were all in it together and I made some lifelong friends. Being in the military police was perfect for me. I never regretted not joining the Paras, and I never once looked back.

That was, until I was incarcerated in a Kabul prison cell thirty-four years after I'd first pulled on my RMP uniform. Only in Tawqeef, with time on my hands, did I reflect back on the events of my life and the circumstances that had led me to that point. In a vermin-infested jail, unshaven and unwashed, it was hard to imagine that I was still setting an example to anyone. I knew I was innocent and that the most important people in my life – family, friends and colleagues – were fully behind me and would do everything to get me released.

But as I waited for that day, I couldn't help but realise the irony of my situation. Despite doing everything by the book and having a better military career than a skinny Salford kid could have imagined, I'd ended up on the wrong side of the law anyway. Sitting on an old grey blanket similar to the one I'd first bought in an army surplus store forty-five years earlier, I could have laughed out loud.

Two

I sat on my own that first afternoon, feeling dazed, vulnerable and incredibly alone. I was also bloody freezing. All I had on were the clothes I'd put on that morning at the secure compound where I lived and worked on the outskirts of Kabul.

In the privacy of my steel-clad quarters on the Anjuman base, I'd donned some cargo trousers, a polo shirt and a black fleece. It bore my company logo G4S (for Group 4 Securicor) where I was the commercial contracts director for Afghanistan. G4S had recently bought out my former employers Armor-Group to become the largest and one of the most respected private security companies in the world, with operations in over a hundred countries. Even with a jacket as an extra layer, I was chilled to the marrow in that cold, damp place.

Every time the main prison gate opened and a guard came down the corridor, I looked up, hoping he'd come for me. He never did. Whenever names were read out on the public address system, those who'd been called gathered in the corridor to be chained at the feet and wrists. Their handcuffs were then locked to the front of chains wrapped around their waists, severely restricting all movement. It was like something from the Middle Ages. Once shackled, the prisoners were led away in pairs, hobbling awkwardly, presumably bound for court hearings or visits from lawyers or relatives. I couldn't understand why I hadn't been summoned yet. There'd been no word from my company or from the British embassy, both of whom had promised to get me out of there as soon as they could.

The hours dragged and at around 18:00 hrs an evening meal arrived, carried in buckets by a skinny kid who did the cooking and cleaning in our cell. His name was Marbat and he prepared the food in a grimy corner before tipping it out onto a large metal platter. He placed that on a plastic mat rolled out onto the floor which everyone gathered around to eat. Not a morsel had passed my lips all day but I wasn't hungry; in fact my stomach was in knots. I was even less inclined to chow down when I saw the rice, potatoes and beans piled in a greasy clump. A large cob loaf was handed round but the bread was so hard that it took effort to break a piece off and even then they could only eat the centre.

The Australian, Rob, remained resolutely on his bunk so I asked, 'Don't you eat this?' He grunted and shrugged his shoulders. Then I noticed he was tucking into some military rations of his own. That would be a 'No' then.

One by one, my cellmates reached into the plate to scoop food into their mouths. As a rule, the Afghans use their right hands for eating and their left hands for cleaning themselves in a country where toilet paper is a rarity. Nonetheless, their 'eating' hands still picked spots or noses, pressed nostrils as they snotted out bogeys, and wiped phlegm from their lips. No wonder Rob didn't join in.

When El Gordo beckoned me to the meal circle, I edged forward gingerly, scraped up a handful of rice steeped in cold lamb fat, and forced a smile. 'Good,' I said. 'Thank you – *Tashakur.*' I managed to get away with just a few mouthfuls.

After the meal, prayers were said to Allah. My only prayer was that nobody would slit my throat before I was released, so I held my palms to the heavens too, figuring it was the same as saying Grace. Marbat placed the leftover food in a small cupboard with a little door. Cockroaches spilled out whenever the door was opened and rats and mice scurried back and forth along the wall, hunting for crumbs. Other cockroaches dropped from the ceiling and occasionally landed on me, which sent me into a frenzy of brushing them off to make sure none were in my hair. To add to the irritation, flies buzzed me repeatedly.

I was only distracted from swatting insects when a siren sounded and a dozen of those in the corridor shuffled in for roll-call. These men seemed to 'belong' to our cell because Marbat had given them a share of our food. When everyone was accounted for, a second siren sounded and people moved back to their own spaces or out to the corridor to ask a guard for a light. Those who didn't smoke the pungent cigarettes chewed the rough Afghan tobacco instead, which they wrapped in small pieces of tissue and packed in their gums, staining their mouths green. Others huddled near the TV for the 'Koran Channel', while the rest sat cross-legged on the floor playing chess or draughts. Some listened to transistor radios quietly while their neighbours curled up to sleep. Rob had a small iPod and lay in a foetal position watching a film on the tiny screen.

I was deeply reluctant to leave my cell but my need for the toilet grew pressing and eventually I could hold on no longer.

Assam indicated where the ablutions cell was so I got up and headed into the corridor. Vigilant but with my head down, I pushed through the strangers, passing several cells on my left and some sort of open courtyard to my right accessed by a gate. I tried not to look around too much or draw any attention to myself. I was only halfway along the corridor when the stench of ammonia and excrement began to assail my nostrils. The number of flies doubled. By the time I reached the ablutions cell, my eyes were watering.

With one hand over my mouth, I stepped inside and quickly looked right and left. Several men stood with plastic bowls, towels and razors queuing for the use of what could loosely be termed the 'facilities'. Puffing on cigarettes, they all turned to stare at me. Their smoke was the only thing that prevented me from gagging. Checking the room for a weapon, I clocked a broken metal broom handle on a high window ledge I could use to defend myself if necessary.

The floor beneath my feet was sticky with spit and sneeze, discarded rubbish, used razor blades and dirty syringes. Three basins were loosely attached to the right-hand wall but they had no downpipes so the water gushed onto the floor. The sinks were cracked and filthy, as were the walls. Each plughole was bunged up with human hair sheared off by those who obsessively shaved everything except their faces as part of their religion. Above the sinks were three mirrors blinded by scratches. On the opposite wall were two broken shower cubicles, with bare copper pipes spouting cold water.

To the left were four holes in the ground surrounded by cracked ceramic bases. There was no flushing facility; just a jug of water to throw down. The holes were overflowing and

I had to watch my step and hold my breath even to approach. There was no loo paper and the only privacy was provided by a little metal door which I pulled shut behind me. Holes the size of saucepan lids had been drilled through each one at waist height which meant that as I squatted I could see out and anyone else could see in. Needless to say, my insides were blocked and I couldn't do more than take a Jimmy Riddle. My stomach distended, I abandoned my efforts and got out of there as soon as I could.

Back in my cell, I felt sick and exhausted. How could I have ended up in such a place? It reminded me of my earliest years sharing a mattress on the floor with two of my brothers and only clothes or blankets as bedding. We had no heating or hot water and we filled our disintegrating shoes with cardboard. We ate watered-down baked beans straight from the can and then drank tap water from the tins. Without toothbrushes or toothpaste, we rubbed our teeth with salt, Ajax or soot. Usually the last in to the monthly tin tub, I washed in cold black water and dried myself off on a rank old curtain. I'd hoped never to feel as dirty as that again.

The unwelcome memories of my childhood were interrupted by Marbat appearing to make us all *chai* or tea. He brewed it up from a metal flask and served it in chipped cups or little glass beakers. He also brought a few bananas, broken into pieces and shared out. When I was growing up, bananas were a luxury and we only ever got 'burnt' ones – black, soggy and discarded from the market. Grateful for small mercies in Tawqeef, I took a little fruit, sipped my *chai* and longed for a proper brew.

Every minute that passed then felt like an hour, but by around 21:00 hrs, El Gordo indicated where I could sleep. I'd half-expected to be kicked out into the corridor along with the poor lads in puddles, but instead he pointed to an unused corner of the cell – a spot about two metres by one where the blankets didn't quite reach and next to the rubbish and slops bins. The area was buzzing with flies and other vermin but I didn't care. That corner was exactly where I wanted to be – with my back to the wall, a few feet from Rob, and in direct view of the door.

One by one, my cellmates took to their bunks or arranged their blankets on the floor. I sat in my 'bed space' and tried to acclimatise to my situation. 'It's okay,' I told myself. 'Someone from the embassy will turn up any minute to demand your release. This'll be a cracking story for the folks back home. Oh God. The folks back home. What would Liz be going through? She'd only imagine the worst.' Looking at the sea of bodies around me in this Afghan dungeon, I wondered whether my wife of over thirty years could ever have imagined me somewhere like this.

Most of my cellmates fell asleep surprisingly quickly. Despite my mental and physical exhaustion, I was determined not to close my eyes and was relieved that the lights stayed on. Using my jacket as a pillow, I tried to get comfortable but found it impossible. Apart from the cold that crept up through the floor and in from the courtyard, I was like a coiled spring. Anyone who wanted to hurt me would have to climb over the rest of them first but I had to remain on my guard. When one man crawled towards me I flinched, until he handed me a blanket which smelled of my childhood. Nodding my thanks, I folded it neatly and sat on it to cushion my bones.

'Won't be long now, Billy,' I said to myself over and over in my head. 'You'll be out of here tomorrow. You'll see.'

Three

I didn't sleep a wink. Not only was I incredibly cold but whenever I did doze off, I woke at the slightest sound. I've always been a light sleeper and any movement disturbs me. The sixteen men sandwiched all around me in bunks or on the floor snored, farted, twitched and groaned; a few cried out. Each time anyone even shifted their weight, my eyelids snapped open.

In my most relaxed moments of fitful semi-consciousness, I imagined myself with Liz in happier times. I'd first met her soon after I joined the RMP in 1976 and was posted to the largest Army garrison in Europe at Catterick, North Yorkshire. Liz, too, had become a 'Red Cap' after years of wanting to be a police officer. From the minute I first set eyes on her, I was smitten. Aged eighteen, she was 5ft 4in, sporty, slim, with short dark hair and an impish, freckly face; she had an infectious wheezing laugh that reminded me of Muttley the dog sidekick to Dick Dastardly from the cartoon *The Wacky Races*.

Painfully shy, I didn't think a rough Salford lad like me stood a chance with someone so popular and good-looking, but I was wrong. My dazzling opening line was something like, 'Hi, I'm Bill Shaw. I've heard a lot of good things about you and gather that you come from Leeds. I have an auntie who lives there.' Amazingly, it worked. The young woman whose pet name became 'Lily' so that we became Billy and Lily, seemed just as taken with me. She was even prepared to put up with my family and my obsessions for neatness, punctuality and even numbers. The latter stemmed from my childhood when I decided 4 was my lucky number, and everything from kisses to checking something had to be done four times.

We were engaged within six weeks and married the following May, 1977, in Horsforth, Leeds. On our wedding day I was a naïve nineteen-year-old in platform shoes and my first ever suit, complete with flared trousers. Liz wore a second-hand dress she bought from a friend of her mother's for £25. My youngest sister Ruth, then eight years old, was a bridesmaid in the first dress she'd ever had made for her and looked like a little princess. We had a reception for a hundred guests at the Horsforth ex-serviceman's club. It was the day of the FA Cup Final – Manchester United against Liverpool. As we left the reception we heard on the car radio that Man U were 2-1 up, so I jumped out and screamed, 'We scored!' Liz laughed and told me, 'Stop it, Bill, or they'll think you've just scored!' Our honeymoon was one night in a B&B in the Lake District followed by five nights in Liz's aunt's Blackpool boarding house. We felt like a king and queen.

Liz fell pregnant soon after and had to leave the RMP, as was the custom back then (even though she'd have loved to have stayed in). Soon after, I was posted to bandit country – the IRA's stronghold in County Armagh, Northern Ireland. Liz, baby Lisa and I moved into a mouldy property on a soulless estate in the town of Craigavon. On my wages of

£40 a week, by the end of each month all we could afford to eat was potato pie but Liz never once complained. She turned that horrid little house into a cosy home for me and Lisa while I patrolled the streets with the various artillery regiments during two of the most dangerous years of 'The Troubles'.

Each morning when Liz kissed me goodbye, she never knew if she'd see me again. Doorstep shootings were a real and present danger back then, and we lost a lot of good people from the RUC and allied services. We lived and operated alongside people who were 'carded' – known members of the Provisional IRA and Sinn Fein. I saw them every day on the streets and they knew exactly where we lived. My only consolation was that they didn't target families in those days. That came later.

Car bombs had long been a favourite weapon of the IRA, who'd rather kill remotely than face a gun battle or the chance of getting caught. As the twenty-one-year-old corporal in command of a four-member patrol known as a 'brick', I took my responsibilities very seriously. We'd spend hours clearing the streets and waiting for bomb disposal squads to check out any suspect vehicles. Day to day, we just didn't know where Death was lurking. It was all a game of chance.

Team morale was badly sapped on August Bank Holiday, 1979, when events took a turn for the worse. As me and my platoon were enjoying a day off in Port Rush thirty miles away, a three-vehicle convoy of Army trucks was driving past a lorry laden with straw bales near Warrenpoint, County Down, when it was detonated by a remote-controlled device.

While we innocently strolled around the seaside town, six members of the Parachute Regiment stationed not far from us. lost their lives. Half an hour later, just as the site of the killing was swarming with soldiers and medical staff, a second bomb went off claiming ten more lives from the Parachute Regiment and two from the Queen's Own Highlanders. It was the British Army's greatest loss of life in Northern Ireland since The Troubles began.

On the same day in a peaceful bay off County Sligo, Lord Mountbatten, his fourteen-year-old grandson, and two others were killed by another radio-controlled bomb detonated on his fishing boat. Three others from Lord Mountbatten's family were seriously injured. When we heard the news, we felt physically sick. Packing up, we headed back to the base to comply with what we knew would be a massive security lockdown and to offer what help and support we could. As with all such senseless killings, everyone within the military relied on each other and we eventually bounced back. That was tough though, even with the black humour that gets everyone from soldiers to undertakers through what cannot otherwise be faced, the sense of a new and dangerous threat was ever present.

It was in Armagh that I really became a man. This was what I'd signed up for and I loved the work, despite the dangers. The camaraderie was like nothing I'd ever known, from watching each other's backs out on the cruel streets, to the daily rituals of tea and cakes, known as 'stickies'. It was during my first two-year tour of Northern Ireland that I decided that I wanted to do the full twenty-two years' service in the RMP and not just the six years I'd originally signed up for. Liz was completely behind me and our decision to spend our lives in the Army as a family team.

It wasn't always easy working in what was effectively a war zone. I tried to instil in the men and women in my unit that there was good and bad in everyone. 'It's important to try to see the difficulties faced by the various factions and reason with them whenever we can,' I said. Not everyone agreed with me, I'm sure, but by keeping lines of communication open with the people we were there to protect, we managed to avoid any serious casualties.

The downside was that Liz and I still lived in constant fear of our lives and especially of IRA roadblocks. 'If ever we come upon one when we're all together, then don't worry because I'll jump out of the car and run so that they'll only come after me,' I told her. 'They won't touch you and Lisa. Just drive away as quickly as possible and leave me, okay?' I could tell from the look on her face that there wouldn't be anything 'okay' about that at all.

Once a week, Liz had to take Lisa to Legahory Post Office to collect her family allowance and was always careful not to speak in case someone picked up on her British accent. Whenever she went into Lurgan to do some shopping, she was fearful of seeing me patrolling the streets in case Lisa called out 'Daddy!' She told our growing daughter that I'd get into trouble with my boss if I spoke to them. We tried to make a game of it but there was nothing funny about what we were facing. When we left Northern Ireland it took us a while to get used to living without that level of fear. Liz even found it strange walking into a shop without being stopped first to have her handbag searched.

Sleeping on the floor of a prison cell a million miles from the life we'd made for ourselves since then, I could have kicked myself for putting her through that kind of anxiety again. I pictured her lying awake in our bed at our holiday home in Spain, almost certainly worrying herself stupid about me, the silly sausage. Finding our peach-painted holiday villa on a hillside an hour from Valencia had been the realisation of a lifetime dream for us both – even if paying the mortgage meant I had to keep working in countries like this. After more than three decades of living in sub-standard married quarters around the world, we'd finally found somewhere we could settle one day. We'd always had our home in Leeds but were looking forward to the time when we could retire to the sunshine.

Our three children were grown now and scattered all over the UK so we had a choice of places to stay whenever we went home. Usually, it was with Lisa, our 31-year-old daughter, a teacher married to Marcus, a Major in the 2 Scots. We are a family who use nicknames so Lisa, known as 'Bear', has two adorable kids, Madeleine (known as 'Moo-Cow') aged seven, and Caius ('Chunky Monkey'), who was four. Our two sons Craig ('Fat Boy'), 27, in commercial real estate, and Lewis ('Blue Lew'), 19, a senior aircraftsman with the RAF, were in Lincoln and Northumberland, and not yet hitched.

In Spain we had plenty of room for them all, a swimming pool, orange trees and our own small olive grove. I'd learned Spanish when I was seconded to the Spanish infantry in 2002, having already picked some up on a UN Military Observers' Course in Argentina two years earlier and in Colombia where

I'd helped train embassy security staff in Close Protection work. Liz's Spanish was catching up fast. We'd made good friends with our neighbours Salva and Amparo and our kids loved coming to stay. We planned to keep hens, grow vegetables and plant a flower garden.

Liz especially loved roses – she'd had red ones in her wedding bouquet – but we'd never lived anywhere long enough for them to get established. A Spanish builder was about to erect a pergola for us on the back terrace and I planned to plant roses all around it for her – it was the least I could do after her years of putting up with my miserable face.

I must have dozed for a bit because I was awoken from my reverie at around 04:30 hrs. It was a misty, cool morning and the oldest mullah in my cell got up, stepped into the corridor and began the *adhaan* or Muslim call to prayer. His raspy, tobacco-stained voice was surprisingly melodic. Like the music of a snake charmer, it lifted the heads of the men all around me and they shuffled sleepily to their feet, coughing and retching, to wash themselves before they answered his call.

The gates to the courtyard at the core of the detention centre were unlocked by the guards and everyone began to trickle outside into the milky dawn. I got up too, my back stiff and sore. Limping like an old man, I followed the last of them out and stood in the shadows, watching through an open gateway as they assembled in front of a lean-to mosque fashioned out of plywood. Hundreds of Afghans of every age, size and type knelt as one, praying to Mecca as if their lives depended on it. To their minds, they probably did.

Seeing that they were preoccupied, I decided to grab the chance to use the ablutions room. Holding my breath, I urinated into the overflowing trap but once again was unable to do more. My throat was dry and scratchy and my skin felt tight with tiredness. My lower back ached. I longed for a hot shower, some soap and a steaming mug of Yorkshire tea. Instead, I splashed my face with cold water and slicked down my hair with the one personal possession I had left – my comb. Being allowed to keep it had felt like a small but important victory. I hoped to look less dishevelled when someone from the embassy came to get me.

Prayers lasted for fifteen minutes and then everyone swarmed back into their cells to recite passages from the Koran before dispersing into the corridor or outside. Tentatively, I followed. Stepping through one of the gates I found myself in the large open courtyard surrounded on all sides by cells. The roofs were topped with tin and their guttering fringed with thick rolls of barbed wire, making any chance of escape impossible.

In the distance I could see the mountains of the Hindu Kush, from whose snow-capped peaks cold air pours onto the plain of Kabul almost 2,000 metres above sea level. Military helicopters clattered back and forth in a clear blue sky and a Hercules dipped its wings before landing at the airport just a few miles away. To the west, I could see 'TV Hill', where only a few months before I'd supervised the erection of a new communications mast for the British embassy before sharing a picnic with my men. Eating a chicken drumstick and drinking Coca-Cola as I looked down over the city and the shabby Tawqeef compound, I never imagined in a million years that I'd soon be locked up within its walls.

It began to rain lightly but no one took much notice as they sat on their blankets in groups. Others hung their washing out on lines slung between rusty metal brackets holding up the barbed wire. Most wandered between little stalls set up by enterprising prisoners selling *chai*, fried eggs, tomatoes or hot water tapped off from a 20-gallon pot heated over a Calor gas burner. Other inmates sold toiletries and all kinds of items. I wasn't surprised – the Afghans could flog a deep freeze to an Eskimo. There was even a laundry of sorts – a large bucket filled with soiled clothes which were then hung out in the rain to dry.

Everything cost 20 Afghanis (around 30 pence) although some of the stallholders who spoke a little English told me, 'American dollar? Good!' As I didn't have a cent or even a *pul* on me, I couldn't have bought anything if I'd wanted to. One young man had a camera and walked around offering to take photographs, which astonished me. He showed me some he'd taken previously. With Christmassy borders or 'jingly' (cheap) decorations around the edge, they looked like postcards. I could just imagine Liz's reaction to receiving one from me with the message, 'Greetings from Afghanistan!'

I kept to the periphery on my side of the courtyard, walking slowly up and down to loosen my stiff joints. It was an effort to avoid the discarded rubbish, stale bread and ever-present globules of green spittle congealing slowly in the weak morning sun. All eyes were on me and I felt exposed and vulnerable, so when my cellmates wandered back inside at around 07:30 hrs, I did the same.

After the second roll-call of the morning, Marbat brought in some boiling water from the courtyard and made us all a morning cup of *chai*. It was strong, dark and overly sweet, but it tasted surprisingly good. Best of all, in a place where I didn't intend drinking the water, *chai* was relatively safe and quenched my thirst. Holding out my cup to Marbat, who averted his gaze from my Western eyes, I asked for some more.

The plastic meal cloth was laid out on the floor again and Marbat fetched the hunk of bread from the cupboard in the wall. It was even harder than the night before and only edible if small pieces were chipped off and dipped into tea. Other prisoners rummaged through carrier bags and baskets and brought out small items of food they'd saved. Everything was shared out equally in the meal circle – apart from whatever Rob had, which must have been sent into him specially. Once again, he ate alone and in silence.

This breaking of bread and sharing of food was clearly part of the cell ritual and I took note, although I declined to eat anything and drank copious amounts of tea instead. A pregnant cat swaggered in, meowed weakly at a mouse, and wandered out again. I thought of our pet beagle, Trotsky, and how he'd give them both a run for their money.

My mind was filled with thoughts of home once more, worrying about everything from who was walking the dog to whether the grandchildren were missing talking to their 'Pop' on Skype. I wondered if I'd be allowed to make a telephone call and then realised that I didn't even have any numbers with me – they were logged on my mobile phone, which I'd had to leave behind. Frustrated and angry, I reminded myself that it would only be a matter of hours before my situation was sorted anyway. I didn't need any numbers. I didn't even need to get acquainted with any routine. I just needed to stay alive.

One of my fellow prisoners offered me his towel and a bar of soap. He wore a white skull cap and his name was Sadiqi. I slipped my shoes on and went with some reticence to the ablutions cell. I knew from years of working in multicultural environments that it was considered impolite under Islamic law for a man to show any part of his body to another so I stripped to my T-shirt and trousers and splashed my face and armpits. It wasn't easy to do in a stinking room full of men waiting for the traps and with a basinful of soapy water gushing out all over my feet. I dried myself with the borrowed towel, combed my hair, and went back to my cell to wait.

The opening of the corridor gate at around 08:00 hrs made my heart rate quicken and I looked up hopefully from where I was sitting. 'William! Mr William!' I heard the guard shout. Nobody had called me William in years. His frame filled the doorway and he beckoned me with his finger. Eagerly, I jumped up. Rob turned and half-looked at me over his shoulder. I caught his eye and grinned but he turned back to face the wall without saying a word.

This was it. My moment of release. Thank God it was over. It was Thursday morning and the Afghan weekend began at lunchtime. Nothing would move in the city until the Saturday so this was the last chance to get me out before then. I couldn't wait.

Scooping up my shoes, I hurried after the guard who was

leading me to the main gate and to freedom. Sure enough, a friendly face was waiting for me. It was Azim, my right-hand man and the best procurement officer I'd ever worked with. One of my four-hundred strong Afghan staff (separate from the additional five hundred or so Gurkhas in my employ), Azim was a typical middleman who supplied us with everything from ammunition and vehicles to old Russian weapons. He even found us a Swedish stove for the sauna we'd had installed at the base. Azim was a veteran haggler and must have negotiated his way into the detention centre.

I reached for his hand through the locked gate and said, 'Azim! It is *so* good to see you!'

'Mr Bill sir,' he said, tears spilling down his cheeks as the guards pushed me back to prevent us from physical contact. 'I'm sorry. So sorry.'

Waving my hand at him to indicate that none of it mattered now, I waited for the guard to slide open the gate. Azim said something sharply to the guard on his side which I assumed was to press for the same. Then he did something that filled me with cold, hard dread. He reached down into a box at his feet and, through the bars, began to push personal items towards me – first a toothbrush and some toothpaste, then a shaving kit and a bar of soap.

'But, Azim—' I began before closing my mouth.

In silence, I accepted the items he passed me as he negotiated vociferously with the guards to allow the rest of the box in as well. I could see it contained sweets, a sleeping bag, a towel, some bottles of water and a change of clothes. The guards agreed but told him to hurry.

'What about getting me out, Azim?'

'Yes, yes. Sorry but I have no news, Mr Bill, Sir,' he told me, shaking his head. 'The company main office is dealing with your case – Mr Spandler, Sir. I have no further information for you at this time.'

'Please, Azim,' I said, through gritted teeth. 'Go back to the office straight away and tell them that they *have* to come and get me out of here.'

Azim nodded emphatically. 'Yes, Mr Bill, Sir, yes. I promise. I will see them immediately.'

'And send a message to my family. Tell them I'm okay.'

The guards pushed Azim away and he backed off slowly with a doleful expression on his face. Once he'd gone, they rifled through the box, took what they wanted and waved the rest through. The gate opened and the box was dumped unceremoniously on the floor.

Walking back to my cell with enough provisions to keep me for a week felt like a particularly cruel form of mental torture. Head down, I found my place in the corner and sat with my face turned to the wall. None of the other prisoners approached me. No one asked for anything. They left me alone to my disappointment.

Four

The unfortunate series of events that led me to that hell-hole dated back five months earlier to Friday, 9 October 2009, when I'd despatched two Afghan Close Protection operators to collect our G4S director Mark Spandler from the international airport.

Being the weekend, the traffic would be worse than usual so I'd sent the men early in an armoured Toyota Land Cruiser, codenamed 'Foxtrot 2', one of our registered fleet of thirty. The vehicle with a mid- or 'B6' level of armouring had recently been checked over and refuelled and had its air filters blasted clean of the all-pervading dust. The last thing you wanted in downtown Kabul is a breakdown.

The route my men would be taking was the old Silk Road between Kabul and Jalalabad – the largest city in the east of Afghanistan. Codenamed 'Route Violet' by the military, this was soon renamed 'Route Violent' by those of us who used it. The Americans call it the 'J-Bad Highway'. Damaged by years of war and neglect, it was known as one of the most dangerous roads in the world, and had long been a favourite target for insurgents. It wasn't just IEDs (Improvised Explosive Devices), drive-by shootings or suicide bombers that made it so high risk. Originally designed as a B-road for animal-carts and light traffic, Route Violent became a six-lane racetrack as drivers mounted verges and the dusty central reservation to navigate around potholes, people, cars, mules, or the 'jingly trucks' covered in shiny metal chimes that jingled together noisily. The frequent squealing of brakes only added to the cacophony of car horns and the yells of angry drivers.

In the two years since I'd first arrived in Afghanistan, I'd travelled along Route Violent dozens of times. It was some-where you couldn't avoid, like the feared 'Route Irish' out of Baghdad which I'd also managed to survive unscathed. What made the Jalalabad Road even more unsavoury was the stench. The city's open cesspits lay either side of it and truckloads of excrement from communal latrines were emptied into them daily. The antiquated system of sewage ditches frequently overflowed into neighbouring fields and streets. The stink was almost unbearable in the summer.

An hour or so after my men had left I received a call on my mobile from our team leader in the Ops Room. 'There's a problem, Bill,' he told me. 'The 4x4 you sent to collect Mark has been seized by the authorities.'

'Why, damn it? On what grounds?'

'It's a Snap VCP by the NDS. The lads say they've locked themselves in the vehicle but it's chaos down there.'

I let out a sigh. Snap VCP referred to a random vehicle checkpoint. The NDS or National Directorate of Security, the decade-old intelligence agency of Afghanistan, was fast becoming a law unto itself. Its 5,000-plus members, who report directly to President Hamid Karzai's government, were widely feared. Recently they'd turned their attention to the growing numbers of foreign private security companies (PSCs), especially those that rode around like cowboys and gave the rest of us a bad name. The locals dubbed such mavericks 'the Toyota Taliban'.

The NDS didn't appreciate that we not only provided essential security for diplomats, aid workers and development agencies but that – by doing a job others were unable or unwilling to do – we brought money and employment to the economy. Many in the NDS especially resented our well-paid Afghan staff and seemed to enjoy making the lives of any who worked for a PSC as difficult as possible. We at G4S had a better relationship with the NDS than most because they respected our reputation in protecting the American, Canadian, Norwegian and British embassies, as well as the European Commission Police. They also trained on our base so they saw us daily. This was the first time in a while that they'd interfered with our work in what was becoming a routine dance for some of our counterparts. They'd confiscated weapons in the past but as soon as we produced the correct operating licences they handed them straight back. I fully expected the same thing to happen with the Land Cruiser.

'I'll go and sort this out myself,' I told the Ops Room as I grabbed a folder full of documents stamped by the Ministry of Interior as part of its archaic bureaucratic process. 'Mark's stranded and we've got to get him back.' My journey along Route Violent that Friday afternoon would take me past the Indian embassy, which had been targeted by a suicide bomber the previous day. We'd heard the explosion from our base and went into immediate lockdown. Almost eighty people had been killed or injured and to take a run out on Kabul's 'suicide alley' so soon after that attack was an unwelcome risk. Even with a 9mm Glock pistol in my holster and a couple of AK47s in the footwell, it was not a place I'd ordinarily choose to go.

'Maiwand? Can you come with me, please?' I asked one of our newest interpreters. 'Arm yourself.' In his mid-thirties and single, Maiwand Limar was thin and scruffy. Trained in Close Protection, he was friendly enough, though, and I did my best to like him and understand his broken English.

We set off in a Land Cruiser codenamed 'Oscar 4'. The heavy Friday traffic had turned the highway to dust. Customers at the makeshift shops that lined the road held hands and scarves over their mouths as they jostled for space with bicycles, wheelchairs, mule carts and passing 4x4s. Men, women and children could be seen carrying on with their lives in the shells of buildings and bombed-out apartment blocks. It was impossible to keep our distance from all the other vehicles, as security protocol dictates. Surrounded on all sides, I prayed no one rear-ended us and detonated a bomb, as had happened recently with some Italians. There were no survivors. The most dangerous areas were near the embassies and military camps but we never knew where or when a contact might come and we couldn't escape if we were stuck in traffic.

Armoured vehicles are not only high profile and overtly Western; they weren't damage-proof. Our Land Cruiser's 6mm-thick ballistic steel plating only went so far in protecting against low-velocity weapons or long-range fire. The preferred methods of attack usually involved jumping in front of a target to detonate a bomb vest, but a new type of IED was proving popular, one that could stick magnetically to any steel surface and do considerable damage. Even in the height of the Kabul summer when temperatures could reach 40 degrees centigrade, we always kept the windows rolled up. The rule was never to open them wide enough for a hand-grenade to be thrown in.

As we neared the scene of the VCP, I realised that there was very little traffic coming back towards us. 'The NDS must have blocked the road,' I told Maiwand. It was just as I'd suspected. 'Look at that!' There were about twenty NDS officers in six pick-up vehicles, spread across one of the carriageways, many carrying RPGs (rocket-propelled grenades). Bolted on top of two of their command Toyota Hiluxs (undoubtedly donated by Washington) were 12.7mm Dushka heavy machine guns, their barrels facing the oncoming traffic.

The NDS officers in their distinctive olive-green uniforms and AK47s slung loosely across their chests strolled nonchalantly between cars. Some were smoking but most stood staring vacantly into space. Beyond them, the traffic stretched back to the airport with frustrated drivers leaning on their horns. Many had abandoned their vehicles and marched up to the VCP to protest. Shopkeepers who sold wares out of old sea containers along that stretch of the road weaved among the crowd offering *chai*, fruit and biscuits. Women in full burkas, children, stray dogs, old men – all of life was there.

I spotted our Land Cruiser parked to one side, and was disappointed to see that two more armoured vehicles had been confiscated as well. Their drivers were nowhere to be seen. Checking all around, I had to assess the risk of stopping in such a 'hot zone'. The minute you leave your vehicle you're away from your armoured bubble and if it is a trap, you're in trouble. Just as in every warzone from Bosnia to Iraq, the MO or *Modus Operandi* is to keep driving or at least stay locked in your vehicle if you have to stop. 'Push on through,' I'd tell my lads and lasses. 'Never leave yourself unarmoured.'

In this situation, though, I had no choice. Cautiously, I parked our Toyota a little way back and got out of the car with Maiwand.

'Be careful!' I warned him as we pushed through the crowd to look for my men, Mohammad and Qais.

They found me first. 'Mr Bill! Mr Bill! The NDS aimed many weapons at us. We had to unlock and they refused to recognise our documents. So sorry, sir!'

'Which is the commander?' I asked. They pointed to a weather-beaten Afghan in his forties, standing beneath the barrel of one of the machine guns. I watched him for a moment and noticed he was acting strangely, maybe even drunkenly, which would not have been unusual. He was aggressive to everyone and his men were following his lead, pushing and shoving everyone around.

The commander spotted me (the only Westerner) in the crowd and then his eyes rested on my vehicle. To my dismay, he gestured to his men to confiscate that as well. Furious, I hurried forward. 'No! No!' I cried. 'Maiwand, tell him that our vehicles are properly registered under the current system.' My interpreter did as I asked. 'Remind him that we have the contract to guard the British embassy.' I showed him our licences from the Interior Ministry written in Dari and English. He didn't even look at them and carried on barking orders to his men.

'He with country accent,' Maiwand remarked. 'Maybe he no read.'

'I read and speak English well!' the officer snapped before

waving me and my papers away. Refusing to give up, I raised my voice in order to make him pay attention. He didn't like that and at one point we were nose-to-nose. It was then that I saw that his eyes were bloodshot and his pupils enlarged. Blinking, he bared teeth stained green with tobacco juice and then he turned his back on me, refusing to enter into any further dialogue.

I suppose I could have collected my men at that point, got back into my vehicle and driven back to the base. But I had a duty of care to my company, and to my boss who still needed collecting from the airport. I couldn't just let the NDS confiscate our vehicles unlawfully – those Land Cruisers were worth around $150,000 each. It took months to get them into the country and even longer to get them registered. We needed every one.

Irritated, I marched back to my vehicle, reached inside and activated the kill switch to immobilise the engine. I then did the same with the first vehicle. If the NDS couldn't even start them up, I hoped that they might just leave them. With the help of our Filipino mechanic, Joseph, I'd had kill switches fitted to all our vehicles to prevent them from being stolen. Joseph devised different switches for each car; some were rigged so that the radio had to be switched on; others only worked when the seatbelt was engaged. With these two vehicles, I had to flick the sidelights on in one, and press my finger to a steel plate under the dashboard in the other. Having done that I walked away as two NDS men raced past me and jumped into the drivers' seats but the engines wouldn't even turn over.

They went mad then; running up to me and shoving me

in the chest. Then they began waving their weapons around. My Afghan staff hurriedly translated that unless I started the vehicles immediately they'd shoot them all dead. 'Mr Bill! Mr Bill! They'll kill us!' There were suddenly six AK47s pointed at us and my men lifted their hands in surrender. 'Start the engines – quickly please!'

Further NDS pressed in, adding to the tension. I'd been in situations like this before in flashpoints from Armagh to Basra and knew how quickly things could escalate. Sure enough, the barrels of both machine guns swivelled in our direction. Life came before property and I wouldn't risk the lives of my men so I shouted, 'Okay, okay! Calm down!' My men translated but the NDS continued to prod and shout.

'Stop that!' I insisted. 'Tell them I'll start the bloody Toyotas!' Annoyed, I walked back to the vehicles and deactivated the kill switches. Even so, the tension remained uncomfortably high. The traffic on our side of the road remained at a standstill as more drivers complained only to be roughly jostled away. Curious pedestrians pressed towards us in even greater numbers as my men tried to keep them back. We were all fully trained in escape and evade techniques but I hoped we wouldn't have to use them.

Gutted, I watched as our vehicles were manoeuvred across to the other carriageway ready to be driven off to one of the NDS compounds. Inside each Toyota was around $25,000 worth of weapons and ammunition, tracking systems, trauma packs, first aid kits and the latest hi-tech satellite phones, and VHF and UHF radio equipment. I could only imagine the nightmarish paper trail that lay ahead of me to get everything back.

Stepping a few metres from the crowd, I began to place a call to my Ops Room to tell them what had happened but as I did so, I spotted three British Army Quick Response Force (QRF) vehicles approaching on the other side of the road. In the lead Land Rover were four armed soldiers, almost certainly on an embassy run with one of their senior officers. I recalled a recent conversation with Mark Spandler after a meeting he'd had with senior officers from the British forces. 'BritMil have assured us that the QRF will assist us in a crisis,' he'd told me, so I ran out into the road to flag them down. As they drew closer, I flashed my British embassy badge. 'We've got a problem here,' I yelled through the driver's window. 'Can you help?' The driver looked across at his commander sitting in the front seat and, on a nod from him, put his foot down and sped off. The other vehicles followed. They didn't even look back. I couldn't bloody believe it.

Just at that moment a shot rang out behind me. I ducked instinctively as people around me screamed. Women and children, dogs and men, all scattered. The few cars getting through on the opposite highway screeched to a halt, some rear-ending others. My men drew in close around me, as they were trained to do, while I spun round to see where the shot had come from. The NDS commander was standing a few feet away from us with a pistol in his hand. His gun was still raised and it wasn't clear if he'd finished shooting or was about to start again. Several of his personnel had pulled out their weapons too and were waving them in our direction. The man behind one of the Dushkas swivelled his weapon back and forth wildly, pointing it at us and then into the crowd.

If he opened fire, the injuries would be unthinkable at such short range.

I still carried my pistol but there were many more of them than there were of us. In any event, my military training had always taught me that opening fire was the last resort, even in self-defence. Everything else comes first – assessment, negotiation, reasoning and diplomacy. I glared angrily along the road at the departing QRF vehicles, hoping they'd heard the shot but they carried on. That's when I knew I was on my own.

At that moment the NDS commander raised his pistol parallel to the ground at waist height and, without even blinking, began firing indiscriminately into the crowd of spectators, and then at us.

Bullets whizzed past my ears. 'Run!' I yelled, grabbing Maiwand and herding Mohammad and Qais towards the nearest sea container. The shots kept coming, pinging the ground all around us and sending up little clouds of dust.

Diving for cover behind a wall of steel, we slumped together breathlessly as the shots continued to ring out. 'Has anyone been hit?' I asked, quickly patting myself for wounds. We were wearing body armour under our clothes but an exposed limb could easily have been hit and when the adrenalin starts pumping you often don't feel the pain. Amazingly, we were unscathed. How those bullets missed us, I do not know.

I reached for my pistol when my mobile phone rang. It was Mark, still waiting at the airport. Before either of us could speak, he heard the shooting and cried, 'What the hell's going on down there?'

'We're in contact!' I shouted back. 'The NDS are firing at us!'

The shots stopped as suddenly as they began but were replaced with yelling and screaming, thumping and engines revving. Mark could hardly believe his ears.

I peered around the corner of the container to see the unfolding mayhem. Cars were veering all over the place on the opposite carriageway as they tried to avoid the abandoned vehicles and the fleeing crowd. NDS personnel were rifle-butting the roofs and doors of the cars that had stopped. Drivers who'd run off were roughly dragged back and ordered to move on.

The commander stood silently in the middle of the storm, a smile spreading slowly across his face. It was as if he was waiting for everything to calm down before he let loose again. The minute he looked the other way, I ducked round the back of the container and ran out into the middle of the road where I felt safest in full view. Pressing my mouth to the phone, I requested immediate assistance.

'I'll send in the QRF!' Mark said.

'Don't bother!' I told the man I'd first met as an infantry officer in Basra. 'They were just here and wouldn't even stop.'

'Bloody hell! Okay, then we'll call a EUPOL (European Police) contract team.' Not even the NDS dared seize a vehicle with diplomatic plates. As he hung up, I suddenly felt uncomfortably isolated – the only white European in the middle of a highly volatile situation. I needed to extract myself and get myself to a place of safety, but how? Where? There was barely any movement in either direction and I was stranded in the middle of nowhere with a gun-toting commander who was almost certainly high on hashish.

Keen to minimise injury, I told my Afghans to beg or

borrow rides and get the hell out of there. As local nationals, they'd be relatively safe from attack. All three reluctantly left me as I waited for rescue. 'Come on, lads!' I murmured to myself as I watched for the EUPOL 4x4. 'Get me out of here soon!' My prayers were answered some thirty minutes later in the shape of a British embassy vehicle carrying diplomatic plates, which happened to be driving along Route Violent. Inside were two of my men. The driver slammed on the brakes the second he spotted me. He reversed at speed and his colleague unlocked the back door to let me jump inside.

'What the hell were you doing out there in the middle of all that?' they asked me, incredulously.

'Trying not to get killed,' I replied. As they drove me back to our base, I sat back and tried not to think of what might have just happened. I thought of Liz waiting at home, and of my children and grandchildren. What would they have done if I'd been killed by that crazy commander and for no bloody reason at all? I was only fifty-one. What if that had been *it*?

My palms were sweating so I wiped them on my thighs. Silly bugger, I told myself. Think of something else. How about a song? Yes, that's it. But the song that stuck like flypaper to my brain was by one of my favourite bands, Queen, which ends '*another one bites the dust . . .*'

Great.

Five

Whenever I have been at a low point in my life, I've tried to draw on my experiences as a soldier to pull me through. I'd had some interesting times in hot zones around the world where my courage had been tested along with my nerves. But, for me, probably one of the biggest personal challenges I'd faced had been getting through the notorious seven-week 'Senior Brecon' course before I could earn promotion and the chance to become an Instructor at Sandhurst.

In the Army, all infantry soldiers must attend 'Junior Brecon' and then 'Senior Brecon' (Platoon Sergeants' Battle Course) before they can be considered for promotion up the ranks. Failure to complete the intensive and arduous course is something of a career-stopper. Members of the RMP wouldn't normally be required to attempt it – and few would volunteer for such a 'beasting' – but as I'd decided to try for a place on the Sandhurst Cadre I had no choice.

Becoming an Instructor at Sandhurst would be a dream posting for me and a fantastic experience to boot. If I was picked, I'd be training the elite of the elite in the British Army at the Royal Military Academy's national centre of leadership excellence. I knew it wouldn't be easy as there were so many hurdles to jump first and I'd be up against fifty other senior NCOs (non-commissioned officers) on the selection cadre over six weeks. These wouldn't be just ordinary soldiers either

– they'd be the cream of their regiments; professional soldiers vying for thirty available posts, each with a two-year tenure. The competition would be fierce but I was determined to succeed. Failure was not an option.

Having been briefed by Joe Walker, a former Sandhurst Instructor and RMP friend, I began my physical and academic training several months before I was due to tackle Senior Brecon in 1988. I was a thirty-year old Platoon Commander based in Germany. As a Staff Sergeant, it had been fourteen years since I'd done any infantry or foot skills in the field and I knew I'd be weak. In preparation, I read as much as I could and attended a pre-Brecon course at Pirbright, Surrey. Joining Guardsmen and other infantry soldiers, that two-week course readied me for the pending induction phase and testing physical demands including foot and fighting patrols, defensive reconnaissance and trench-digging. Even though I was a veteran marathon and cross-country runner, to top up my fitness levels I joined recruit squads at the garrison where I was based for their PT runs. The difference was that I was carrying 35lb of weight and wearing full combat uniform. Then afterwards, I'd run the ten miles home.

The main Brecon course was in two phases, but I didn't have to complete the first for infantry firing and range qual-ifications because I'd already passed a Weapons Instructors' Course. Phase Two was the toughest part – an intensive seven-week course on the Brecon Beacons including the notorious Exercise Fan Dance – a twenty-four kilometre route march over six hours covering seven checkpoints carrying all personal kit and full platoon weaponry. It would be a test of endurance the likes of which I had never experienced before (and never wanted to again).

I arrived at the School of Infantry base at Dearing Lines in my bright red beret and No. 2 uniform and swapped it for the camouflage combat gear I'd once longed to wear as a Para. Walking to the administration building I was greeted with a yell of, 'Why are you walking?' and soon learned to do the brisk jog known as the 'Brecon Shuffle'.

We were split into platoons and then into ten sections of eight to ten personnel. My Instructor was Colour Sergeant Russ Bishop from the Parachute Regiment, an exceptionally well-built, mean-looking character with an indestructible level of fitness. A Falklands war veteran, he took no prisoners and had no favourites, regardless of cap badge. This was his last course before returning to his regiment and he expected the best. On the first day, Colour Sergeant Bishop took me to one side. 'This is going to be tough on everyone from start to finish,' he warned me. 'Many will fall away once they realise just how tough it's going to be. If you want to stay the course, you'll have to double your efforts. Do you understand me, Staff Sergeant Shaw?'

'Yes, Sir!' I knew he was right.

I spent that first evening packing all my ancillaries and making sure my personal webbing weighed 35lb. While others slept, I unstitched my oversized combat jacket which I'd taken in to look smart. The nickname for it was the 'battlefield briefcase' because its multiple pockets were essential for items needed on the hoof. A tight jacket was useless, no matter how much neater it might look.

My first test was to complete the Infantry 'two-miler'

carrying my webbing plus helmets, personal and section weapons, including heavy Carl-Gustaf MAW 84mm recoil-less rifles and 2-inch mortars. Platoons set off with a few minutes between each and we all had to complete the run in less than eighteen minutes. Colour Sergeant Bishop told us, 'Anyone crossing the finish line after me will fail,' before setting off at a jog which increased to a full run. If any one of us fell back there was much foul language and shouts of encouragement.

'Come on, lad! Keep f***ing moving!' he'd yell. 'You've nearly cracked it! We're almost there!'

When our platoon finally reached the finishing line, panting and puffing, I was certain we'd failed because Colour Sergeant Bishop crossed a few feet ahead of us. But then the Directing Staff (DS) congratulated us for passing because we'd done it well within the set time. He then turned to the thirty or so who drifted in after us and delivered some choice words about poor preparation, inferior regiments and bad soldiering. I was delighted but absolutely knackered and still had to jog back to the accommodation.

The next few days involved rigorous testing in weapons handling, combat radio skills, First Aid, Armoured Fighting Vehicle (AFV) recognition and basic military definitions and meanings of associated acronyms. I managed to pass them all. We then had to do individual night navigation across the difficult terrain of the Beacons armed only with a prismatic compass. I hadn't used the prismatic much and always relied on maps. This particular exercise had to be completed in less than two hours. We were each given a call sign before setting off in the dark using a compass bearing only. Once we got to our destination, a Gurkha would let us use his radio for our next bearing and so on. I eventually made my way back to the starting point and found only a couple of fellow soldiers heading in.

'Well done, Shaw,' the DS told me. 'You finished in just under two hours.'

The rest of the course was exceptionally physical with the focus on section, platoon and company skills. There were live firing exercises covering all eventualities including what to do in the event of nuclear, biological or chemical attacks (NBC) and Battle Inoculation. And the Exercise Fan Dance across challenging terrain in appalling conditions. We were beasted from morning until night. Colour Sergeant Bishop drove us to our limits with good reason; he was making sure we could handle the pressure of battle and be mentally and physically prepared for war. He did all the exercises alongside us and would often run out on his own, either before or after the day's events. All the instructors used aggression because they were teaching us to fight and kill, not pussyfoot around. It got to some of the lads and many packed and left, never to be promoted beyond sergeant. Some were injured and had to quit. I found it hard to keep up, but my new mates were fantastic and we were all in the same boat. Arriving back late from field exercises, we'd stay up most of the night writing our reports, with everyone adding their bit until we finally collapsed into bed.

As time went on, we lost more SNCOs, whose future hung in the balance. There were times when I didn't think I could go on either, and the relentlessness of the beasting started to get to me. But somehow, I dug deep and found it within me to keep going. 'You always wanted to be a Para,' I reminded myself. 'This is your chance to prove that you could have done it.'

At the end of the seven weeks, those of us left standing were physically and mentally drained. Shattered, we assembled in the gym to learn if we'd passed or failed. When I heard the words, 'Staff Sergeant Shaw: Pass!' I could hardly believe it because so many good men had failed. Secretly, I was really chuffed.

One of the most important things I learned on Senior Brecon was how much my colleagues and commanding officers came to mean to me. The Army had provided me with some much-needed structure in my life. It had allowed me to develop my leadership qualities and then use them to the best of my ability. Being among like-minded soldiers 24 hours a day, seven days a week, I'd learned the importance of discipline, teamwork and action. Not to mention the rituals of living, working and eating together to create a common ethos. Having morning coffee or afternoon tea and 'stickies' wasn't just Army etiquette or a matter of keeping traditions alive; it was a vital part of the bonding process. This Salford kid who used to eat cold beans from tins and hardly ever used a knife and fork, suddenly found himself in the rarefied atmosphere of the Mess. With the help and encouragement of my peers, I rose through the ranks to become not only an officer but an Instructor of officers. That's what the British Army did for me.

Perhaps because of my background, I'd always striven to be fair and just. I believed in giving everyone a chance, regardless of their history. The average British soldier is a bloody good sort; they're usually only trouble when they've had too much to drink or become misguided. Most of the arrests I made in my career were for fights and assaults, a few for burglary and one for attempted rape. There was rarely a really bad egg. The first arrest I ever made was outside Gaza barracks in Catterick. Fresh out of training, I found a member of the Royal Signals drunk and leaning against a tree. Going by the book, I arrested him, took him to the guard room, and reported him to his unit. I had to write a lengthy report after which he was hauled over the coals and fined. I felt bad then because he'd done no real harm and all the boys were 'on the pop'. I just wished I'd handed him over to his mates and said, 'Do me a favour? Put him to bed.' After that I always gave drunks the benefit of the doubt. I'd put them in a taxi, pay the fare and tell the driver to take them home. Some of my fellow RMPs thought I was crazy but this seemed fairer to me and once or twice, I even got my cab fare back.

I think everyone has leadership skills, it just depends whether they're in a position to use them, or indeed choose to use them wisely. Sometimes they are unaware they possess any. My own personal leadership skills were greatly enhanced by my experience at Sandhurst where we carried cards to remind us of the most important qualities of leadership – Integrity, Knowledge, Self-Discipline, Courage, Humility and a Sense of Humour. With these in mind, I strove to have a good relationship with all my charges. Most were very loyal and I got them doing all sorts, including charity marathons and enrolling for the Duke of Edinburgh Awards scheme. Whether they liked me or not didn't matter as long as they were dealt with equally. I tried to get my recruits onside because they wanted to be, and not because I'd beasted them into it. I also showed compassion and understanding by asking how I'd feel in their shoes. The answer always told me which route to take.

What I couldn't stomach were bullies. I'd seen enough of that as a kid. I'd also been bullied in Hong Kong when my youthful enthusiasm for my job alienated me from those who wanted an easier life. I once watched a Staff Sergeant ask a fellow patrolman (who he disliked intensely for some reason), 'It's your birthday today, isn't it?'

'Yes Staff.'

'How old are you?'

'Twenty-one, Staff.'

'Twenty-one, eh? Well take your f***ing hat off and put your head down.'

The patrolman duly removed his hat and bowed his head. The Staff Sergeant then hit him on the head with the magazine from his rifle twenty-one times, counting each one out and adding, 'Twenty-two, for good luck!' An SLR magazine is not a light piece of equipment when filled with bullets. At the end of his unprovoked assault, Staff said, 'Happy f***ing birthday! Tell me, you weren't born Caesarean were you?'

His victim, who was trying not to whimper as bumps began to rise up through his hair, replied, 'No, Staff – Scorpio.'

The Staff Sergeant sighed and said, 'I rest my f***ing case!'

On their first day on the Sandhurst parade ground, I'd line up my latest batch of thirty officer cadets from all walks of life – infantry, guards and cavalry. Pointing to my fellow Instructors making themselves hoarse by screaming at their men in true, '*You 'orrible little lot!*' style, I'd ask quietly, 'Do you hear that, gentlemen?'

They'd nod.

'Do you want me to talk to you like that?'

As a man, they'd shake their heads. 'No, Sir!'

'Very well, gentlemen. Be assured that if you step out of line or mess up you will be in trouble, but I promise you that if you do as I ask and in good order then I will never raise my voice to you in that way and I shall never swear. Do we understand each other?'

Clearly relieved, they'd shout, 'Yes, Staff Sergeant!'

I kept my word and, during the two years that I was there, I got them all through. The hours were long and I usually worked seven days a week between recesses but it was so rewarding, I didn't count the time. At the end of my tour, I was selected to help run the next Cadre for potential Instructors. This was indeed an honour to be even thought of as a DS for the new course and it proved to me that all my hard work had paid off.

In prison in Afghanistan, there were times when I felt as mentally and physically challenged by anything I'd experienced on Senior Brecon, at Sandhurst, or elsewhere. I'd got through those challenges with perseverance and determination and I knew the key now was to remain focused, maintain my regime of exercise and mental stimulation. I had to keep believing in myself – no matter what. It was a matter of personal pride to clear my name and prove that I'd acted honestly throughout, as expected of a member of Her Majesty's armed forces. I wasn't always successful in fighting my demons in jail and I'm ashamed to say that there were times when I let my situation get the better of me. Overall, though, I like to think that all those who'd encouraged me to push on through on Senior Brecon would have been proud of me.

Noises outside the prison and in the city beyond would frequently jolt me awake. The still night air was filled with the sound of sporadic gunfire and the occasional explosion in nearby streets as insurgents continued to harry international forces. I lay awake feeling helpless and vulnerable in a place that I knew had already been the target of attacks. What if we took a hit now, with so many bodies crammed together? There'd be carnage and I couldn't imagine the prison guards risking their lives to help any of us trapped inside.

My aversion to loud bangs and even family fireworks stemmed from an event fourteen years earlier, when I was second in command of 175 Provost Company RMP at Thiepval Barracks in Lisburn – the biggest military base in Northern Ireland. It was a two-year tour and Liz and the kids stayed home in Leeds for safety while I lived within the heavily fortified compound.

I was at the base on the afternoon of Monday, 7 October 1996, standing in a corridor talking to the OC and RSM. I was due to have a check-up at the dentist in the garrison's medical centre that day but had to cancel because of work commitments. All of a sudden there was an unexpected freezing of the air, a strange momentary vacuum, and then . . . *Bang!* I knew instinctively what was coming but there was no time to act before an enormous explosion shook the whole building, shattering glass and throwing pictures off the walls. In the immediate aftermath, there was complete silence as the lights failed and then several of the civilian staff started screaming. It was clear that a bomb had gone off within our perimeter fence.

'All right everyone! Stay calm!' I shouted into the darkness. 'You know the drill. Assemble in the corridor. There'll be a lockdown until we've established what's happened.' Soon afterwards, the lights flickered back on and the PA system crackled to life and ordered an immediate evacuation to the leisure centre. It would normally have been the rugby field but it was cold and raining that bleak autumn night.

Placed in charge of more than a hundred evacuees, I led them outside across an open car park towards the leisure centre, which was close to the Intelligence Headquarters and Medical Centre. There was a strong smell of cordite in the air as a further two hundred or so staff began converging on the same path from elsewhere. 'Move along as quickly as possible, please,' I urged them. 'Let's get everyone inside safely and quietly, okay?'

Suddenly, there was a bright flash of orange light between the two buildings as another car bomb went off. The massive explosion sent out a shock wave of hot air and debris that knocked me – and everyone else – clean off our feet. Glass and bricks, metal and fire rained down on us from above. For a moment I lay flat on my back on the ground, completely dazed. My ears were ringing so loudly that I couldn't hear a thing. Getting up and dusting myself down, I looked around in the thumping silence to see dozens of people lying bleeding from shrapnel injuries or staggering around in shock. The medical centre – where I should have been sitting in the dentist's chair – had been completely demolished.

'Is everyone all right?' I shouted. My voice sounded to me

as if I was underwater. 'If you can, keep moving. There'll be medical staff on hand at the leisure centre.' I assisted the walking wounded and kept the lines of people moving in case another bomb went off. It took a while but we got everyone to safety. Twenty-one soldiers and ten civilians were injured that fateful afternoon. Warrant Officer James Bradwell, forty-three, a married man with children, died three days later of his injuries. Having helped those affected by shock into the leisure centre I managed to make a quick call home and leave a message for Liz. I knew the story would hit the news and I didn't want her to worry.

The rest of that night was spent helping evacuate the most severely injured to hospital and providing those made homeless with sleeping bags and food. It was the early hours of the following morning before I managed to get back to my own quarters, negotiating my way through broken buildings filled with debris. In my room I found that a mirror had been blown off the wall and lay in jagged shards across my bed. A wardrobe and chair had been blown over, and books and magazines were scattered everywhere. I shook the glass off my quilt and climbed on top of it but my ears were still ringing. Lying in the half-light, I was filled with sudden fury at the cowards who'd planned maximum casualties as people left work or – with the second bomb – were en route to the medical centre.

My frustration at being behind bars in Kabul while the men who'd set off those bombs were still free somewhere was only fuelled by my memories of Lisburn. Needless to say, I tossed and turned in my concrete corner that second night in Tawqeef. Even my ears felt to be ringing again from the explosion which had almost ruptured my eardrum and left me partially deaf in one ear. Irritable and cold, I tried to shut out the white noise in my head while I lay there waiting for the dawn.

Six

It wasn't just distant memories my mind preyed on. More recent events – those that had led me from Sandhurst to Tawqeef – weighed heavily on my thoughts. Chiefly, my company's decision to pay a $25,000 'release fee' demanded by the NDS for the return of our confiscated Land Cruisers. Then to lodge a formal complaint about the whole damned business.

I was against paying them from the start but I also accepted there was little other choice as we were struggling to fulfil our obligations without a full complement of vehicles. 'This'll just give them a licence to print money,' I told Mark Spandler with a sigh.

Then I thought of those who'd warned my company not to pursue our complaint against the NDS. 'If I were you, I'd advise G4S not to rock the boat,' one colleague had said. 'Be careful this doesn't backfire. If anyone starts pointing the finger, jump on the first plane out,' offered another. Some of my lads ribbed me about how I was going to be thrown into Pol-e-Charkhi, the infamous prison on the outskirts of Kabul which housed some of the most senior Al-Qaeda detainees from Guantanamo Bay. I laughed along with them at such a preposterous idea.

Our interpreter Maiwand, who'd worked with the NDS, offered to help and eventually brokered a deal with an NDS officer whose name was Eidi Mohammad. It shouldn't even have been me that delivered the money to Mr Mohammad that day in October 2009, but the new finance manager had only just arrived in Afghanistan so I was sent in his place. Once I'd received the vehicles back and handed over the cash, I told Eidi Mohammad, 'We'll need an official receipt, for our accounts.' Through Maiwand, the smiling man in mirrored sunglasses assured me we'd be sent the proper paperwork, but we never were. The longer we waited, the more we feared we'd been the victims of some kind of sting. Corruption was endemic in Afghanistan and '*baksheesh*' (a tip or bribe) was expected for almost everything. When the NDS confiscated three more of our vehicles, and demanded $10,000 each for their return, it was clear something had to be done.

Then President Karzai announced that he'd clamp down on the corruption that had tainted his government, leaving us wondering what this would mean for those of us in the PSC sector. Karzai's ministers were the only ones allowed to buy and import unplated second-hand armoured vehicles from places like Dubai. They then leased them to foreign PSCs for around $200,000 a year each. Only then could the vehicles be registered with the Ministry of Interior and receive an operating licence. To get official number plates could take years of red tape and cost a further fortune in import tax.

Karzai's new Anti-Corruption Unit was set up in the basement of the grand villa that housed the Attorney General's office. The complex sat bang in the middle of an area of so-called 'poppy palaces' because their construction was believed to have been funded by the opium trade. With the backing of Scotland Yard and the American law enforcement agencies, however, the new anti-corruption drive encouraged us to go further.

Mark and I summoned two senior NDS generals to our base in January 2010. They took *chai* and listened when we told them that we either wanted our money back for the cars that had been unlawfully confiscated or an official receipt. Mark told them, 'We simply can't afford to operate if this kind of thing carries on.' The generals confirmed that no such 'release fee' existed. We followed up our complaint by informing the Ministry of Interior and the Private Security Company Association of Afghanistan. We also updated the British embassy. The ball was rolling.

During a call home around this time, I told Liz, 'Don't worry, darling. It's the company making the complaint, not me. My name's only on the report because I was the courier that day.'

'But does it have to be you who sticks your neck out, Bill?' she asked.

My neck was well and truly exposed by the time I sat waiting for the *Saranwal* or Prosecutor on my final visit to his office to follow through on our complaint. Even my interpreter Ishmael seemed anxious; with good reason. The English and US mentors who oversaw the Anti-Corruption Unit had warned us that as Eidi Mohammad had fled and Maiwand blamed me, I was now their chief suspect. I couldn't believe it and went straight to the British embassy.

'We can't advise you,' was all they said.

'But we're the complainants, for goodness sake!' I protested. 'We only warned them what was happening within their own organisation. How can they turn that against us?' The officials for whom my company arranged 24-hour protection said they'd assist if I was detained but other than that I was on my own.

Liz wanted me to fly straight home then, but I knew I couldn't. 'That would only make me look guilty,' I told her. 'I'd be unemployed and unemployable. The Prosecutor might go after the company instead and that could cause all sorts of problems for it and my men. I have to stay.'

G4S hired me a lawyer and secured a letter from the Attorney General that stated under no circumstances should I be detained during the investigative process. I emailed Liz daily to keep her updated. '*There really shouldn't be a problem,*' I wrote, '*but if they do hold me for some crazy reason then I expect the embassy to kick in . . . I will be fine so not to worry . . . if anything happens you have the numbers you need to call . . . Love ya mills and squills xxxx*'

Liz had replied. '*I will dream of you tonight, my love and think of you all day til I hear you are back safe.*'

My confidence that common sense would prevail was dented the moment I arrived at the dingy basement office at the Afghan Anti-Corruption Unit that rainy Wednesday afternoon in March. Mohammad Ibrahim Ghafory, a grey-haired man with a hunched back and a reedy frame, had always greeted me warmly in the past. The day of my arrest, however, he was decidedly frosty. No *chai* was proffered and he stalked out of his office almost as soon as I'd arrived.

After waiting almost an hour for his return, a young Afghan came in and sat down behind me. I asked Ishmael who he was and he replied, 'He *says* he's a driver.' Sensing danger, I stood up. The Afghan got to his feet too and fixed me with a glare. I was trying to decide how best to get past him when the Prosecutor returned and beckoned me to follow him. The Afghan followed closely. I couldn't tell from his clothing if he was carrying or not.

At the gated courtyard at the top of the stairs, Mr Ghafory gestured for me to get into the back of a small, white, unmarked Nissan. Standing by the open back door was a uniformed policeman armed with an AK47, its loaded magazine attached. It was raining hard and I drew my Gore-Tex jacket around me as the Prosecutor pointed to the car again.

'What exactly is happening here, Ishmael?' I asked.

Sweet Ishmael looked pale. 'He says you are being arrested and taken to a detention centre.'

I could feel my anger rising. 'What for?'

Ishmael translated but there was no reply. Mr Ghafory just pointed at the car again.

'No,' I told him. 'I'm going to use the toilet.'

The policeman looked to the Prosecutor and then back at me, his finger on the trigger. Ishmael said, 'I think you must wait. I'm sorry, Mr Bill.'

'I'm going,' I insisted and walked away. To my relief, no one tried to stop me. The Anti-Corruption Unit was familiar territory to me, and I quickly made my way to the office of my project manager there Steve Howe. When I told him what was happening he was visibly shaken. Steve, who was ex-Royal Artillery, had become a good mate; we trained together in the gym at the base most mornings. I used his phone to call the British embassy and was put through to Tim Miller, the overseas security manager.

Tim sounded calm and told me to do as the Afghans asked.

He said the embassy would find out where they were taking me and promised someone would come as soon as they could. Putting down the phone, I considered my options. G4S provided the security for the entire compound. Its thirty-four guards were in my employ and devoted to me. If I ducked past them none would try to stop me but I didn't want to get them into any trouble.

Taking a deep breath, I began handing my personal belongings to Steve. I took off my body armour and gave him my pistol, holster, spare ammunition and my mobile phone. I noted the time on my watch – just before 14:00 hrs – as I handed him my wallet with my passport and cash.

'You'd better get someone to call Liz,' I said. 'Tell her not to worry. The embassy has promised to sort this out.'

With Steve at my side, I went back to where Mr Ghafory was waiting. If the situation wasn't so serious I could have almost laughed. Me – a military policeman – a man who'd made countless arrests in my almost thirty years of unblemished military service, was about to be arrested and charged with a crime I didn't even commit. The irony wasn't lost on me.

Steve walked those last few steps with me, my mobile phone clasped in his hand. By the time we reached the car ready to cart me off to jail I was angry and indignant. 'This is a complete farce!' I protested. 'I've been a military policeman all my life and am well aware of the law. I've received no indication of official charges nor have I been given any rights or cautions as recognised by statutes protecting international human rights.'

My mobile phone rang. It was Mark Spandler. Steve asked

if I wanted to speak to him but I was too emotionally charged. 'Bill's being arrested,' Steve whispered. 'He can't talk to you right now.'

'This is a mistake!' I said, before reluctantly slipping into the back seat. Sandwiched in the middle, I was flanked on one side by the armed Afghan and on my right by the man who'd been sent to watch me. Up front were the driver and the Prosecutor's interpreter. The door was slammed behind us and the car lurched off.

I craned my neck as we drove out of the compound gates, looking back over my shoulder as the symbolic villa at the core of President Karzai's pledge to bring justice to his country disappeared in sheets of Afghan rain.

Seven

They say that the most evocative trigger of memory is smell and I believe that to be true. It was never more so for me than in Tawqeef's ablutions cell. The overpowering stink of ammonia, which clung to the mucous membranes, took me straight back to the 1960s and my father's piss-pot.

Dad would lie in bed every morning doing the crossword and smoking acrid Park Drive untipped cigarettes. As he recovered from his latest session at The Odd Fellow's Arms, he'd bang on the door with his walking stick, calling out for one of us to make him a cup of tea. The sound filled us with dread and we'd fight about whose turn it was. More often than not, my sisters made me. Fearfully, I'd creep towards the bedroom where he'd be lying with his scarred leg on full view. Next to it would be his specially built-up shoe, which was filthy and stank. Grumpily, he'd point to an old washing-up bowl full to the brim with his urine and spit. Cigarette ends floated in it. Holding my breath, I'd carry it out as carefully as I could and empty it down the toilet basin, fighting the urge to retch.

Squatting over the trap in Tawqeef each morning evoked such vivid memories of those days that it's no wonder I was unable to function. On occasions, the smell got the better of me and I'd bring up what little I had in my stomach, splattering it over walls covered in years of spit and other bodily secretions. Wiping the bitterness from my lips, I'd reflect that I hadn't thought of my father in years. He'd died in 1997 after cancer and two strokes, the first of which my mother didn't even notice for three weeks. By then the two of them were living and sleeping in front of the telly, the air around them thick with smoke and alcohol. They never went to bed or washed. They hardly even spoke.

When his body finally packed in after years of abuse, I'd just returned from another tour of Northern Ireland and was in Cyprus to set up the first joint Army/RAF police unit. It was quite a challenge to get the two services to cooperate but we managed it in the end. I flew home to arrange and pay for the funeral. At the crematorium in Salford, I stood over Dad's coffin and tried to think of one kind thing that he'd done for me in forty years, but nothing sprang to mind. All I remembered were the senseless beatings, the piss-pot and the drunkenness, the squandering of any money we ever had, and the mean way he treated us all. My sisters were forced out of the house as teenagers because of his violent assaults on them. One was sent to a home which led to a spell in prison and an early death from alcohol poisoning. The other two, thank God, escaped and found happiness.

I'd always been the 'white sheep' of the family – the one who'd made something of my life – and yet, here I was, bringing up bilious memories in a prison thousands of miles from home. I think I hated Tawqeef most for the way its pervading smells of urine, cigarettes and body odour messed with my mind.

My chief concern, as always, was for Liz and the rest of

the family. I couldn't help wondering how she'd reacted and what she'd say to the kids. I kept reminding myself that I'd be out long before she had to spread the news. I even imagined my next email to her: '*This'll make a short chapter in my autobiography one day, he he!*'

Time passed in a kind of grey fog. I remember wandering out into the courtyard and walking around the periphery where it quickly became apparent that certain parts of the prison were exclusively for drug users. The ground was littered with syringes and razor blades and the paraphernalia of addiction. One young man, clearly high, was handcuffed to the railings while going through some kind of trip as saliva dribbled from his mouth.

A stocky young Afghan made a bee-line for me and introduced himself as Idris. In his early twenties with wavy black hair, he spoke reasonably good English through large front teeth. Pointing to the corridors where the drug offenders lived, he told me, 'They no good. Stay here.'

I was wary but he persisted.

'Idris want learn English good,' he told me, smiling broadly. 'You help Idris and Idris help you, yes?'

I couldn't trust anyone in Tawqeef but realised that this young man could at least answer some of my questions about the detention centre for my own protection.

'Manchester United?' he asked, with a grin. 'David Beckham?'

I nodded and began to ask questions as Idris happily gave me a crash course. He explained that Tawqeef was originally designed for 150 inmates but currently held almost four times that. The building comprised four corridors around the inner courtyard; each with five cells housing twenty or so prisoners. There were just three ablutions cells with twelve toilets for the five hundred-plus inmates. Where people lived depended on their status, wealth and crime. The lowest of the low slept out in the corridors or on the floors of overcrowded rooms. Idris lived in cell No. 3 along my corridor with twenty young men charged with anything from kidnapping to people trafficking. Cell No. 4 had seventeen older men but Cell No. 2, Idris said, housed only five men including a police general, government official and a junior politician. 'They have every good thing,' he said, shaking his head. 'Phone. Food. Family come. Guards no look.'

I asked him about the men in my cell, especially the mullahs. He knew nothing other than that they were charged with corruption and passport offences. The older one was strict but the younger one, Ali, seemed more open. Like all religious devotees, they had long beards which they weren't allowed to cut and would oil every day to keep from drying out. Ali had a good sense of humour which I found out after a couple of days. My friendly cellmate Assam surprised me by telling me that Disney cartoons were popular in Afghanistan. '*Quack, quack!*' I replied, mimicking Donald Duck as he laughed. A few minutes later, the young mullah called out, 'Mr William?' When I looked up, he said, '*Quack, quack!*' and then laughed so hard at his own impersonation that he fell to one side. Both mullahs were a good influence on the rest of the prisoners. In the courtyard with others watching, they couldn't be over-friendly to me but whenever we passed they'd nod and acknowledge me, which in itself offered me some protection.

Idris said the rest of the detainees were awaiting trial for anything from murder to prostitution, visa offences to traffic violations. Several poor sods from Sri Lanka, Nepal and India, who'd been tricked into buying dodgy visas, had been in there for months without a hearing. I tried not to think about that. They had little or nothing and, looked down on by the rest, had no choice but to sleep in the corridors. 'You well luck, Mr William,' Idris added. 'Cell No. 1 good.'

I asked Idris then what he'd been jailed for. Without hesitating, he said, 'My woman betray me,' and made a sudden slashing movement diagonally across his face with an imaginary knife.

For the rest of the day, Idris followed me everywhere, chatting endlessly. He introduced me to his friend Wasir Khan, who worked for Supreme Food Service (the company that supplied most of the expats in Afghanistan) and had been arrested after a road accident. The two of them stuck to me like glue and I didn't kid myself it was for my sparkling Mancunian wit. Any Westerner in Tawqeef would undoubtedly receive food and money from outside. Idris had probably already heard that I'd had a delivery from Azim. Unless some Taliban with a hatred of all Western 'infidels' decided to kill me, I'd be a valuable commodity. I took a little comfort from the thought.

At about 16:00 hrs, the main gate slid open again and a guard walked into the courtyard. I looked up and then away, hardly dare hoping. Then I heard him calling my name. He nodded in my direction so I followed cautiously. To my surprise, the guards unlocked the gate and ushered me through. Was this it? My spirits soared still higher when I was led towards the staircase to the Commandant's first-floor office. Standing there, armed and ready, were two of the Brits who worked for me – John and Dave, both ex-infantrymen. They were assigned to the Foreign and Commonwealth Office Close Protection contract which meant they were there escorting diplomats. Brilliant! Just as I thought, the FCO had finally seen through the whole charade.

'Bloody hell, lads,' I said, grinning broadly. 'Am I pleased to see you!'

They half-smiled and nodded and Dave patted me on the back encouragingly. It was clear these big tough men were upset to see me as a prisoner escorted by Afghan guards. I was grateful that I wasn't in handcuffs at least, especially when I came across two more of my boys, Mick and Lee, waiting at the Commandant's door.

'Great to see you too!' I said with genuine affection. They too hung their heads.

I was ushered into the office where consular official Jan Everleigh introduced herself and her colleague Tim Miller, the man I'd spoken to before my arrest. Jan began by telling me that visitors weren't normally permitted that late in the day but the Commandant had kindly allowed them in. Her words were translated as I nodded my appreciation.

I assumed this was all part of the opening formalities before Jan would explain that the Attorney General or British Ambassador or both had ordered my immediate release. But instead, she turned around, picked up a box similar to the one Azim had brought and presented it to me like an award. She said it was from the men I worked with, who'd all clubbed together. I glanced down to see books, a Thermos flask, sweets, a tube of multivitamins and some toiletries including mouthwash.

Swallowing, I could hardly find the words. 'You've not come to get me out of here?'

Jan looked at Tim and then back to me. She assured me they'd do all they could but said the British authorities could only monitor the situation and couldn't interfere in the workings of the Afghan legal system.

'But I've done nothing wrong and there isn't a shred of evidence against me! I thought you'd at least get me bail while you sorted all this out.'

Tim Miller shifted his weight as Jan reiterated that they had to allow my case to go through 'due process'. The most I could hope for at this stage was an early first court appearance, she said, which they would attend.

I stared at her incredulously as she went on to tell me that Liz had been officially informed of my arrest by a member of the FCO staff in London. Fighting the urge to raise my voice, I wanted to tell her that if I'd thought the embassy wouldn't be able to get me out straight away I might not have presented myself to the Prosecutor in the first place like an oven-ready chicken. I longed to point out that – if I wanted – I could persuade the four men guarding her to spring me from that place there and then. Instead, I held my tongue.

Jan pressed the box upon me as I fought to control my anger. Eventually I said quietly, 'I'm not daft. I understand your position, but I was led to believe that you'd help me out here.'

The visit was over almost before it began – less than fifteen minutes. As they went to leave, Tim Miller told me under his breath to check the tube of vitamins.

I left the Commandant's office carrying my consolation prize. My head down, I walked past my lads unable to look any of them in the eye. In the corner of my cell, I slumped to the floor feeling utterly dejected. God help me but I was stuck here until the Afghans got their act together and that could take weeks or even longer.

Miserably, I sifted through the box. Knowing of my passion for motorcycles, my workmates had thoughtfully put in a few bike magazines. There were also chocolates, deodorant and a towel with the letters ISAF for International Security Assistance Force, the body that first seized Kabul from the Taliban. Displaying its logo in the detention centre would have been akin to wearing a British military uniform, so I hid it.

In the tube of vitamins I found something stuffed into the bottom. Instead of a note from the embassy to tell me that they were secretly working to get me out, I found $30 worth of Afghanis. I stashed it in my pocket and stacked the paperbacks my mates had sent me in a neat pile in my little corner, hoping I wouldn't be in there long enough to read them. Then the depressing thought occurred to me that they obviously believed that I could be or they wouldn't even have sent them.

Once again, all I could think about was my family. Now that the weekend had begun, there was no way I could get word to them for a few days and there'd be no courts open before Saturday. Three more days. It would feel like three months – for us all. Not a day had gone by in the last thirty or so years when I didn't speak to, text or email Liz. Since I'd been out in hot zones like Iraq and Afghanistan, I made a point of also chatting with the kids at least once a week.

Just a couple of days earlier we'd played our usual game of trying to be the first in the family to say, 'Pinch, Punch!' for the first of the month. It was something that had been going on for years between us but I usually won in Kabul because I was four hours ahead. My daughter 'Bear' had beaten me the last time by timing her text to land in my mailbox at a few seconds past midnight.

Sitting in my cell thinking of them all, my mood swung from one extreme to the next. The injustice of my situation grated against all the principles by which I'd always tried to live. I'd not been formally charged with any crime. I had no lawyer or interpreter and no idea what rights I had, if any. No one had told me when my next visit from the embassy or the company might be. The rest of that night I sat in my corner. I barely ate, I hardly spoke. I'd never felt more alone in my life.

Deciding to try and get a better idea of what to expect in Tawqeef I went over to where Rob lay on his bunk and offered him some of the food I'd been given. 'So, what are you in for?' I asked. It took some coaxing but he eventually told me his story, which wasn't easy listening, not least because it was peppered with his colourful views about the Afghans every few sentences. An ex-soldier turned private security contractor, he'd been working for an American PSC guarding a convoy thirty miles outside Kabul when he had a row with an Afghan guard. Claiming he acted in self-defence, Rob shot him and placed his body in a truck which he set light to after throwing in a hand-grenade. The Gurkhas with them reported him back at their base and Rob was arrested at the airport trying to flee the country.

Having been sentenced to death by hanging in January 2010, Rob was transferred to Pol-e-Charkhi prison, but persuaded his government to lobby for him to be returned to Tawqeef. He didn't elaborate and I wondered what Pol-e-Charkhi was like if this place was preferable. His best hope was his family could raise enough money to persuade the victim's relatives to show '*ibra*' or forgiveness for his crime, so that he could serve the rest of his sentence in Australia. He wasn't hopeful and I soon realised that compared to his predicament mine was hardly worth talking about, so I went back to my corner.

Shivering with cold, I piled on some extra layers and zipped myself into my sleeping bag. The floor was as cold and unforgiving as ever and my back was still aching from the previous night. The sooner I went to sleep, the sooner the time would pass. I was beginning to understand why Rob lay in bed all day in his own little bubble. The rough grey blanket I put my head on chafed but I didn't care. I just wanted to get home.

Eight

As a commander of men, I'd always had to keep my wits about me. I had to not only set an example to others but give the younger ones guidance. That had been drummed into me from Chichester to Basra, Armagh to Hong Kong, Munster to Colombia. Instilling *esprit de corps* was one of my key strengths as a soldier, and I'd mentored many a young recruit through the rigours of military life.

Keeping my wits about me in Tawqeef was going to be my toughest challenge yet but I had a lifetime of experience to draw on, as well as a wealth of memories – good and bad. Living and working in Iraq during the Second Gulf War and then later with my previous employers, ArmorGroup, had provided me with some of the most valuable lessons in survival in a hostile climate. Not least was the fear that you didn't know if death was just around the corner.

Soon after I arrived in Kuwait in 2003 as company commander of 140 personnel attached to 102 Logistics Brigade it was clear that we'd be going 'over the top'. Our first job, though, was to get everyone else in safely. We were in Camp Arifjan south of Kuwait City – a massive American-run staging base. I deployed satellite platoons to the docks to receive vehicles and troops coming by sea and to the airports. They had to collect men, women and equipment and take them to their various bases – mainly Camp Coyote twenty kilometres short of the Iraqi border. There was a lot of contact with the enemy at that time, and every day brought fresh dangers. As soon as our troops had seized control of the southern Iraqi city of Umm Qasr in one of the first major military operations of the campaign, we'd be following to set up base there with responsibility for its port, as well as Safwan and Basra – scenes of some of the heaviest fighting.

None of us knew what we'd be facing, so the night before we went into Iraq I made the men and women in my care write a last letter home. 'I'll keep them safe and only send them if I have to,' I told them. 'Once we're done here and headed home safely, I'll hand them back to you to keep or destroy.' Then, for the first time in my military career, I sat down and wrote a last letter home too. I can't remember what I said but I do remember struggling to see the paper at one point. Fortunately, no one ever had to send it to Liz for me and I burned it before I got out. She knew how I felt anyway.

The worst thing for Liz at that time was that there was so much news coverage about the war that she could barely drag herself away from the TV. When we were in Safwan, especially, we were at the highest risk. We were based at what was known as Spaghetti Junction, the main crossing point into Iraq from Kuwait as well as the roads to Baghdad or Basra. There were many factions still fighting each other and taking pot-shots at convoys of British and American troops daily. Our vehicles would return riddled with bullet holes, but fortunately none of my people were hurt. I drummed it home to them time and again that they had to be constantly on their guard, even when they were in the relative security of the base. One night I found two of them asleep on duty at the police station in Umm Qasr and went ballistic.

'You can't trust anyone or you'll get yourselves killed,' I told them. 'And I'll be the bugger who has to send your letters home.'

The pressure in Iraq was relentless. One day, on what should have been a routine visit to a police station in Safwan to offer ongoing mentoring and advice, I received a call on the radio from one of my sergeants in charge of a section of eight men there. 'We're in contact, Sir!' he cried.

'Are you sure?'

'Yes, Sir. The Iraqis are firing at us!'

'Okay, but pay attention to what I'm saying Sergeant. Are bullets actually hitting the building?'

There was a pause. 'No, Major – I mean, Sir! They seem to be going over the top or around the side. But they're coming at us from all sides!'

'Okay, Sergeant. I'm on my way and I'll inform HQ and get a Quick Response Force team activated. But it sounds to me like you might be in the middle of a couple of warring factions, so just stay calm and cover all entrances. I'll radio again when I'm close.'

I instructed the driver of our soft-skinned Land Rover to put his foot down and get there as quickly as he could. Stopping a few hundred yards away, we listened and heard the distinctive rapid-fire rat-tat-tat of the ubiquitous AK47s. I radioed in and asked for cover before the driver accelerated away and drove me straight to the building. My men and the twenty or so Iraqi police officers inside were armed and standing in every door and window covering all arcs of fire and ready as we approached. With our body armour and helmets, we hoped we'd be safe from any stray bullets as we ran for the door. The sergeant was right; there was a lot of gunfire and it was close by too. But thankfully whoever was doing the firing wasn't interested in us.

Inside, I found the sergeant anxious and his men nervous. They were looking to me for guidance. I knew I had to remain calm and not to show any fear to these youngsters in what was potentially an extremely dangerous situation. 'The QRF are on their way and the brigade is alerted. If necessary, we can get backup from the division in Basra. We just need to sit tight, remain alert and wait and see what happens.'

The QRF would come in two armoured vehicles carrying sixteen soldiers. They'd have heavy machine guns and automatic weapons to supplement our pistols and standard infantry rifles. They'd also have plenty of ammo and grenades to last us for some time if we had to sit it out. What we didn't know was whether the fighting would escalate or which way it would go.

'Bring me a local interpreter,' I ordered. Within a few minutes a tall, thin man arrived chewing on a reed and staring at me with a bored expression. His name was Ibrahim.

'What's going on out there?' I asked him.

'Someone has been killed from one side and those from the other side are showing their displeasure,' he said, in excellent English. 'This is normal. As you say, tit for tat.'

'Are they likely to turn their guns on us?'

He shrugged and spat out the reed. 'Maybe. Maybe not.'

'So what do you think will happen here, Ibrahim?'

He looked up and smiled. 'They will run out of ammunition and go home to sleep.'

By the time the QRF arrived in a flurry of dust and men and we'd received the latest request for information from brigade HQ, Ibrahim's prediction came true. The firing dwindled and then stopped altogether. We'd been saved – well, that day anyway.

Within a few days I was summoned to the outskirts of Umm Qasr by the corporal who was in charge of another section. They'd been called by locals digging through rubbish who'd come across a body rolled up in an old carpet. 'I think we need to call in the SIB, Sir,' the sergeant said. 'This doesn't look good.' I decided to investigate the scene myself before alerting the Special Investigations Branch. There was a war going on and the SIB only got involved if British personnel were implicated in something. As the senior officer, I arrived and took control of the scene.

'Where's the body?' I asked the corporal, who looked pale and was sweating profusely. He pointed to a pile of rubble and rubbish in a ditch by the side of the road. Several Iraqis stood around, their scarves held firmly over their faces. I could see the feet of a body sticking out of one end and browned bloodstains seeping through the wool.

'Unroll the carpet,' I said, fighting the urge to place my hand over my own nose. It was a hot day and the hundreds of blowflies were irritated at being disturbed from their feast. Two of the locals unrolled the carpet and the headless body of a young boy rolled onto the rocks. In a carrier bag alongside him was what was left of his head, crawling with maggots.

My men and women turned away and one retched into

the ditch. They'd probably never seen anything like this and, truth was, neither had I, but I had to hold it together.

'It's a young boy,' I said, looking at the size of the body and the clothes he was wearing. 'He's not been here that long.' Turning to the interpreter I said, 'Ask them if they know who he is.' The locals told us then that a boy aged ten had gone missing from a nearby village a week or two earlier. They nodded and pointed and it seemed to me that this had to be the missing boy. I went back to my vehicle and retrieved a black zip-up body bag and disposable gloves. Focusing on anything but what I was about to do, I summoned the two Iraqis who'd unrolled the carpet and had them hold the bag open as I lifted the body in my arms and gently laid him inside, his head alongside him. Zipping the bag up quickly, I exhaled the breath I'd been holding and walked quickly away.

'Tell them to take him back to his village and bury him properly,' I said. 'Tell them we are sorry but there is nothing more we can do.' Moving my section on, I could tell from their faces that they were very shaken by what they'd seen but I was glad it was me not them that would have to live with the memory of that headless corpse in my arms. Back at the base, I threw away my gloves and scrubbed my clothes and took the first of several long hot showers.

I'd hoped that would be the worst me and my charges would have to deal with but within days two Army Land Rovers were shot up on Spaghetti Junction and – in the crossfire – a local was killed. About twenty of my lads and lasses, including some of those who'd been at the previous death scene, found the body of the Iraqi youth, riddled with

AK47 bullets. When they found out from some locals that the dead lad was from a nearby village, they radioed me to ask my permission to take his body home. I realised that they wanted to because this time they could.

'Okay, but be careful,' I told them. 'Keep a 360 and remember that everything potentially is a trap. I'll be there within the hour.'

When I arrived, though, I was horrified to find that they'd laid down their weapons to wrap the lad in a blanket and help with his burial. There were approximately forty Iraqi villagers around them, all weeping and wailing.

'Collect your weapons immediately!' I ordered. 'Where are your sentries? Who'd raise the alarm? We're in the middle of an insurgency area. Anyone could have picked up your guns and turned them on you. You can't just switch off like that, no matter how much you want to help.'

I think they must have thought me hard-hearted but I had to protect them and there was nothing more that could be done for the dead boy. I made them withdraw immediately, telling them angrily, 'I could have lost the bloody lot of you!'

Towards the end of our six-month tour, Tony Blair flew into Umm Qasr in a Chinook helicopter to meet the brigade. Only those troops wearing desert combats were allowed to be on parade for the Prime Minister, which was a shame because a lot of them still hadn't received theirs yet because of shortages, and had to watch from the wings. We were all briefed not to mention WMDs (weapons of mass destruction) under any circumstances. The PM arrived and stood on a dais to address the troops. He thanked us all for our work, and insisted the whole country was united in admiration for the job we'd done. He then wandered around the base to meet the various units. As Company Commander, I was the last to shake his hand before he moved on to his next PR stop at a local school. 'Good work, Major,' the Prime Minister told me as someone captured the moment in a photograph.

Within a few weeks our unit was sent to guard a much wider area including the MSR (main supply route) to Baghdad. Our brief was also to help train up the local police. We took over from our sister company, 156 Provost Company, some of whom were sent further north to the Basra and Al-Amarah region to do exactly the same job. We were all part of one big regiment – the same family.

On 29 June 2003, I took a coach load of my charges on a well-earned R&R trip to Kuwait City. It was the first time in six months we'd been able to relax and I thought a day away would be good for morale. We'd almost finished our tour in Iraq and I was proud of a good job done. We went to McDonald's, did some shopping, and played volleyball on a beach. It was there that my telephone rang. It was Tony Cooper, my RSM back in Rheindahlen, Germany.

'What the hell has happened, Sir?' he asked.

'What do you mean?'

'Six of the company have been killed, Sir,' he said.

'No,' I said. 'I can assure you they're all here with me or at Umm Qasr. Nothing has happened.'

'Men have been killed, Sir,' he insisted. 'It's all over the news. The wives are panicking.'

I placed an immediate call to Basra to discover that six RMPs had been on a relatively routine patrol at the police station in the southern Shia stronghold of Majar al-Kabir. Unbeknown to them, a firefight had broken out at the other end of town between a platoon of British Paras and local Iraqis when the soldiers arrived to carry out new weapons searches. An angry mob of some three hundred locals gathered in the town centre carrying stones and guns. Shooting erupted on both sides. Reinforcements were called in and a Chinook arrived to help extricate the Paras to safety. The mob then turned its fury on the only remaining Brits in their town (who wore red caps similar to the Paras) and stormed the police station.

They set light to their vehicle, which contained their only radio, leaving them unable to call for assistance. For two hours, the hapless RMPs managed to hold their ground, refusing to flee, but then they were overcome by the crowd who sprayed the building with bullets and then set fire to it. Cornered, they were executed in the worst single hostile attack sustained by British forces in more than a decade. It so easily could have been us. Those poor buggers were killed and we were not. It was the luck of the draw.

Gutted by the news, we packed up in near silence in Kuwait and went straight back. All the way home, I kept thinking, 'What if that had been my men?' My experience dating back to my childhood and honed on the streets of Armagh and by the IRA presence in Germany had taught me what we call in the service 'situational awareness'. I always hoped that me and my men would be able to keep out of trouble. I bollocked them endlessly to instil the same in them but they were young – they thought they were invincible – and it wasn't always easy.

'Read the situation,' I'd tell them. 'Constantly ask yourself what's going on here? What might go wrong? Remember to ask yourself – What if? What if? What if?' Now the 'What if?' had happened and the lives of six families back home would never be the same again.

At HQ my CO gave me the full details and all six names. They were all young lads; a lot of them had gone through training together and this had been their first unit. I put the company on parade and told them what I knew. Then I read each name out slowly. Everyone knew someone among the dead. 'Time for a prayer,' I said, as the military padre took over.

Liz had seen the TV news back home and feared the worst but she tried not to panic. She relied on her belief that if something ever happened to me she would know. I'd always told her, 'Until you actually hear that it's me then keep believing it isn't.' So she stoically held the fort for the other wives until I could put her mind at rest. As a Casualty Notification Officer for the duration of our tour, she'd attended courses on how to break bad news although she always said she'd be the first to crack. She wouldn't, of course; just like my good friend Bryn Parry-Jones, the OC of that unfortunate RMP company, who was back in England dealing with the bereaved families. He issued a remarkably composed statement although I don't know how he did it. I'm not sure I could have got through it if I'd lost six at once.

We left Iraq ten days later. The team who took over from us included Warrant Officer Colin Wall, 34, my old Staff Sergeant from Catterick. He was a good lad from County Durham who restored Land Rovers and had served under me for two years. When he first arrived he sought me out straight away to say hello, along with his new OC, Major Matt Titchener, 32, who I'd only ever spoken to on the phone before. 'Good to put a face to a name, Major,' he said, and I was equally as pleased to meet him. Within a week those two fine men and a Welsh corporal with them were killed in a drive-by shooting on a road we'd used daily. They were in a civilian soft-skinned Land Rover when gunmen sprayed them with machine gun fire before finishing them off with a grenade. With their deaths added to the toll, we'd lost nine people within a couple of months. I attended Matt and Colin's funerals, and Matt's was especially poignant as his pregnant wife read the eulogy and his two-year-old boy ran around the coffin in a football strip.

I thought about Matt's son on my third night in Tawqeef. He'd be nine years old now and probably wouldn't remember much about his father. I wondered how he and his mother were doing. Even with a sleeping bag and extra clothes, I felt the cold right through to my bones and hardly slept. I did nod off once, my eyelids leaden, but I was awoken by shouting. Sitting up, I listened to what sounded like a fight breaking out in one of the cells on the other side of the courtyard. Sure enough, the main gates opened and guards rushed in.

For several minutes, it seemed like all hell had broken loose. I could hear something or someone being slammed repeatedly against the metal gates and then the tell-tale clank of handcuffs. Someone screamed out in pain and guards barked orders while prisoners yelled their indignation. There was some scuffling and another cry. Afraid this might lead to a riot, I sat coiled in my corner. A few of my cellmates raised their heads blearily but then went back to sleep. Rob didn't even stir. My cell 'friend' Sadiqi batted his hand at me as if to say, 'Don't worry, this happens all the time.'

As I waited for the storm to pass, I thought back to the nights when I'd sit up in bed in our council flat listening to my parents fighting. One night, it was so fierce that I convinced myself Dad was murdering Mam. Jumping over my sleeping brothers, I flew down the corridor yelling, 'Leave her alone!' only to find my tiny mother beating Dad violently around the head with a chip-pan. Blood trickling down his cheek, he looked at me, then back at her as she swung for him again. Then he began to laugh.

There were no more incidents in the prison that night and I got up before prayers to see what the damage was. I found two of the culprits handcuffed to the courtyard gates in a crucifix position. Their arms stretched to the limit, their feet only just touching the ground, they must have been like that for hours. It was a chilly morning and one was wearing only skimpy clothing, his face covered in fresh bruises. The other was slumped forward, semi-conscious and mumbling. I longed to give them blankets and some water but knew that wouldn't be allowed so I had to leave them be. I was relieved when they were finally released later in the day.

After prayers and the first roll-call, one of the guards called me to the main gate where I found Azim waiting for me. As before, his eyes filled with tears at the sight of me and he promised to send reassuring messages home. Wearily, I asked him to bring my iPod so that I could listen to some music, as well as a bobble hat, some gloves and socks. His visit was even briefer than the last and once the guards had taken what they wanted from my supplies, I returned to my cell with enough food and water for several days.

I was able to offer my cellmates chicken sausages, cooked rice, tins of corned beef, fruit, hard-boiled eggs, fresh bread and grilled chicken breasts. None of them grabbed at anything and they all accepted with humility. I handed a few bits to Rob, who scuttled back to his corner with them. I watched the others tuck in but only picked at the food, my appetite gone. Peeling off a dollar from my stash and grabbing the flask the boys had sent me, I wandered out to the courtyard to buy some hot water from one of the stands. I took it to the ablutions cell and, after joining the queue of chain-smokers, washed myself through my clothes with handfuls of cold water topped up with that from my flask. I had no plastic bowl so I wasted more than I used. At least I had some proper soap and a towel this time but, with no mirror, I couldn't shave nor did I feel inclined to.

Feeling unbelievably tired and with a sore back, I returned to my cell and lay down for a while. The constant illumination pained my eyes and I covered my head with a blanket. Lying under it in the half-light, I sank emotionally as I contemplated my situation and tried to reason it all out in my head. 'This could take a while,' I told myself sharply. 'You'd better get into a proper routine and take better care of yourself. The people who know you will expect nothing less.'

I was luckier than most, thanks to Azim, who must have been bribing the guards to get in, which was ironic considering what I was falsely accused of. If I was going to be sleeping on the floor then I had to keep my body mobile during the day. I'd been as fit as a ferret since I was a nipper and then there had been all those marathons. I wasn't going to let up on my fitness now. The prison courtyard was about twenty-five metres wide by fifty metres long and I estimated that if I paced up and down it for an hour or more twice a day then that would be the equivalent of a five-mile hike. There was no time like the present so I pulled on my shoes and wandered outside.

Idris came rushing over the minute he saw me. 'Mr William teach me English now?' he asked hopefully. I shook my head and began what would become a daily ritual, marching the length of the courtyard as the sedentary Afghans watched, bemused. Idris paced with me at first, chatting, and then Wasir Khan, but the two of them quickly grew bored and slumped in a corner.

As I marched, I took careful note of my fellow prisoners. The Talibs, a group of heavily bearded men who remained in one corner, watched me with open derision. A few coughed up some phlegm and gobbed it noisily on the ground each time I passed. One glared at me with such open hostility that I made a point of averting my eyes. These 'long beards' were the ones I needed to watch.

The Asians were without doubt the poorest in the jail. Scorned by the rest, they fed on discarded food, which reminded me of 'midden-picking' as a kid – when we scoured through neighbours' dustbins. In their usual quiet way, though, the Asians kept busy, fetching and carrying or recycling scraps. Incredibly, they never stopped smiling and loved to talk to me about English cricket and football. Their cheerfulness humbled me.

The drug users kept to a group on their own – sniffing and scratching, coughing and fidgeting as they either came down off a high or began a new one. I'd seen the syringes and smelled the hashish, so I guessed the guards preferred them to stay stoned as a means of keeping them under control. The old men of the prison – the mullahs and grey-bearded sages – gathered in their own little groups to hold animated debates. Then there were the youngest of the prisoners, the teenagers who shared cell No. 3. Wide-eyed and skittish, they huddled together like skinny greyhounds.

The five immaculately groomed inmates of cell No. 2 stuck out a mile. Plump with good living, they'd wander into the courtyard and settle into comfortable corners prepared for them by underlings. Waited on hand and foot, they'd sit drinking *chai* and brazenly make calls on mobile phones that were banned for everyone else. They'd charge other prisoners up to $100 to make even a local phone call. I was tempted but I didn't want to do anything unlawful. I also was wary of leaving a trail of numbers that might be used in the future to hassle whoever I called.

One of the group seemed familiar. I was trying to place him when he came over to remind me where I had met him. He spoke very good English and his name was Alexei from Kazakhstan. The previous year he'd been employed by a specialist construction company that had done some work for G4S. Alexei told me he was awaiting trial on fraud charges (which he denied). He then invited me back to his cell for a coffee. Eager for a change from the sickly *chai*, I accepted.

Walking into cell No. 2 was like stepping into some kind of altered reality. It had recently been painted cream and had real carpets on the floor in vivid reds and blues. It was impeccably tidy and clean. The five bunk-beds that were in use had proper bedding with duvets and sheets, and there was an electric heater warming the whole space. In one corner was a huge television; there was fresh fruit in a bowl on a table, as well as tea- and coffee-making facilities. It looked like a plush living room. The fat general and the others soon joined us and I suddenly felt very uncomfortable. I thought of the poor lads sleeping in the flooded corridors without even a blanket, never mind carpets and a TV. It reminded me of a film I'd seen as a kid called *King Rat* set in Changi prison, Singapore. The 'rat' was the conniving American corporal and self-appointed head of the prisoners who had everything while the rest had nothing.

Alexei made some coffee and said, 'A man like you should not be in that filthy room next door, William. We would like to make you more comfortable. Please to move in with us. I'm sure we can find you a place.' He waved his hand expansively before offering me real milk and cane sugar.

My back certainly longed for something softer than concrete but then I remembered how the men in my cell had welcomed me, sharing what little they had. It would have been a betrayal to leave them. 'I appreciate your offer but I sincerely hope that I'll only be here for a few more days and I don't wish to offend the men in my cell,' I told them. I could tell they weren't pleased so I didn't linger. Whether they were hoping for a share of my supplies, or for even better treatment through their association with a Westerner, I couldn't say. Either way, they ignored me from that day on.

Back outside, I resumed my exercise routine and was quickly

joined by Sadiqi who asked me what had happened. My response seemed to please him because he grinned broadly and kept pace with me, saying, 'Exercise good. William good.' He only left my side when one of the 'long beards' barged into me deliberately, almost knocking me off my feet. Later, another of the Talibs came up to me, smiled, and drew his finger across his throat. I sidestepped him and carried on my way.

A few minutes later there was another fight in the druggies' corner which was quickly quashed by the guards. Unwilling to witness a beating, I went back to my cell. An hour later, the Commandant summoned me to his office. 'The Taliban are new arrivals,' he told me through his interpreter. 'They're trouble. They make people jumpy. Stay in your cell. The men there will protect you. Do not accept any food outside your cell and do not use the toilet alone.' I thanked him for his advice, but after a lifetime of restraining violent soldiers and a spell as an aikido instructor, I knew how to look after myself.

Our meal that day was supplemented by Azim's provisions. Now that it was edible, I ate a little to keep my strength up, and joined in the prayer of thanks. Sadiqi must have told the others about my decision to stay in cell No. 1, because my cellmates seemed pleased. One lent me his plastic bowl for my ablutions, and another pressed some fresh fruit on me.

The closer it got to night-time, though, the worse I felt. I knew that once everyone began to settle, I'd have no choice but to as well and I dreaded those interminable hours when sleep eluded me and thoughts of home crowded my brain. I found myself grinding my teeth for the first time in my life and the noise drove me crazy. Annoyingly, I didn't seem to be able to stop myself from doing it.

Lying on my blanket in all my clothes, my bobble hat, gloves and socks, Liz and the kids were never far from my thoughts. But I also found myself reliving my past – everything from the darker memories of Iraq to what was surely the proudest day of my life, in November 1996, when I received an MBE from the Queen with my family looking on.

I'd just been commissioned Captain from Regimental Sergeant Major and was back in Northern Ireland when my CO called me in to see him. This meant either a bollocking or congratulations and as I didn't believe I'd done anything wrong lately, I assumed he was going to thank me. It was probably for a recent trip I'd arranged to take a group of deprived youngsters to Ypres in Belgium to visit the battlefields. The poorest of the kids was a young boy from Aldershot, who'd never been away before and couldn't stop thanking me when I dropped him home with the souvenirs we'd bought him. I liked to think that he might have grown up to be a soldier, just like me.

Or I may have been summoned because I'd helped write a history of the military base at Worthy Down in Hampshire, or perhaps because I'd had some success in Malawi, Africa, where I'd been sent to help train up their military police force. To my surprise, it was none of those things. 'A former colonel of yours has nominated you for a medal, Captain,' my CO said, reading from a letter. 'You've been awarded the Most Excellent Order as a Member of the British Empire Medal for duties to Her Majesty's Service for your outstanding

contributions to work and the community. Congratulations.'
I'd already received Long Service and Good Conduct Medals
and one for operations in Northern Ireland. Later in my
career, I'd receive medals for my work in the former Republic
of Yugoslavia, the Second Gulf War, and Afghanistan. This,
though, this was the bee's knees.

At the Investiture at Buckingham Palace Liz, Lisa, Craig
and I were driven through the main gates in one of the RMP
Close Protection cars by Staff Sergeant Andy Joseph, an old
friend who'd volunteered his services for the day. I was only
allowed to bring three guests and five-year-old Lewis was in
school in Leeds where they held a special assembly to explain
what a big day it was for his family. In the inner courtyard
at Buckingham Palace we met up with other recipients of
honours, and were ushered inside. Lining red-carpeted corridors were members of the Household Cavalry standing to
attention. Looking for a familiar face, I wondered if I'd trained
any of them at Sandhurst. In the grand State Ballroom under
crystal chandeliers, I nervously awaited my turn, before being
ushered a few paces forward to stand before the Queen. I
bowed my head in respect as she smiled and asked me where
I was serving.

'Lisburn, Your Majesty,' I said.

'Ah, yes. Wasn't that the barracks that was bombed?' she
replied. 'Well, thank you for all you've done, Captain Shaw,
and take good care.'

I've always been a staunch royalist and her words are etched
in my memory for all time. Her Majesty then pinned the
medal to my favourite uniform of all, the navy blue ceremo-
nial officer's No. 1 dress with its dark tunic and trousers, and

distinctive crimson stripe down the leg. Standing before her with a ramrod back and probably the shiniest boots in the British Empire, that proudest of moments was more than a Salford kid could ever possibly have imagined.

Nine

When Azim didn't appear at the prison gate at 08:00 hrs the following day as I'd half come to expect, my spirits plummeted. There'd be no friendly face, no box of treats and no one to send a new message home. It felt like a kind of betrayal. Was this it, then? Was the company giving up on me too?

The weather echoed my mood, and it drizzled steadily for much of the day, making everybody tetchy as they crammed, coughing, into cells and corridors. Several fights broke out, which the guards quickly broke up, but the atmosphere was gloomy and I spent much of the day sitting alone in my corner.

I thought back time and again to the series of events that led to my arrest and why the decision to make an official complaint was probably doomed from the start. This was the Islamic Republic of Afghanistan after all – a strategically important country beset by civil conflict and military invasion since the time of Alexander the Great. Generation after generation had known war and foreign occupation, most recently by Russia and now by ISAF forces. Poverty, sickness and strife was the norm and many beleaguered Afghans had learned the hard way that survival depended on bartering and negotiating, begging and stealing from whichever power was in government at the time. You could hardly blame them.

The siren for afternoon roll-call got us all to our feet, and then the gates opened and two Westerners appeared accompanied by the Commandant. From their accents I could tell they were Americans and I immediately thought they must have come for me but they barely gave me a second glance. They wandered around for a while, peering into cells and then they left. Rob told me they were private mentors appointed by the United States to check on conditions. 'They come in, make sure no one's being tortured and then they bugger off,' he said. 'They ignore Westerners in case they're accused of favouritism. They're about as useless as tits on a bull.'

The PA system began calling out names. I was surprised to hear mine and then I realised that we were being summoned for visiting day. That's why Azim hadn't come! I pulled on my shoes, combed my hair, and hurried to get in line. Those of us without a prison uniform – the striped *shalwar kameez* overshirt and trousers – were handed them to pull on over our clothes. Heavy and made of rough cotton, there weren't enough to go round, so those who didn't have a visitor had to take off theirs and pass them on.

Suitably attired, some fifty of us were led out in single file to the guards' area and out through another gate. This led us into an oblong room about twice the size of our cell, at twelve metres by five. It was divided down the middle by a wall topped with a metal grille. On the other side, as tightly packed into their space as we were, stood an equal number of visitors waiting to see their loved ones. Many had queued outside for hours and as soon as we walked in everyone began pushing and shoving on both sides; some literally climbing over each other to get to the front. Hands were outstretched and elbows used to shove others out of the way to get to the grille and a small open hatch through which supplies could be passed.

The noise hurt my ears as men and women shouted to be heard. The PA system never stopped broadcasting as a young man in charge of the microphone stood yelling more names into it in one corner, his mike picking up every sound. My head throbbing, I looked around for Azim but instead spotted a familiar head towering above the rest. Its hair was blond and spiky and belonged to Kevin Stainburn, my human resources manager and friend.

Kev's nickname was KFP for 'Kung Fu Panda' because he was like a big bear. We'd both arrived in Kabul roughly the same time, in February 2008. Kev had served twenty years in the military, working his way through the ranks in the Royal Engineers and as an officer in the Adjutant General's Corps. In the early 1990s, I'd been his sword drill instructor at Worthy Down where my catchwords had been 'grace and accuracy' – neither of which he was particularly good at. At G4S, Kev and I worked in adjacent offices and got on very well. He was a good, loyal and effective worker. In his late forties, he didn't tolerate fools and could either badger or sweet-talk his way in or out of most situations. I was very pleased to see him.

Kev had only flown back from leave the previous day. Yelling to be heard, he said, 'How the hell did this happen, Bill? Don't worry, we're doing all we can to get you out.' What I didn't find out until later was that G4S had given my case a codename – *Operation Sierra*. He'd brought a couple of the lads in with him, Steve Howe and Wayne Arkley, a fellow soldier and MBE who was our facilities and logistics manager.

They meant well but I found that hard to handle and didn't want them to see me like that. I put on a brave face, though, and shouted, 'Thanks for coming!'

'We knew you were here from Day One,' Steve told me, as I cupped my hand round my ear to hear. 'When you were arrested I had two of our Afghans follow your car and they tailed you all the way here.' The memory almost choked me.

The lads brought me another box of food including some of my favourite chocolate digestive biscuits. Kev and I had to fight our way to the hatch for him to give it to me, along with a tracksuit and a pair of my reading glasses. As soon as I took the box I was elbowed aside as another prisoner reached through to hold his newborn baby being passed through the hole by its mother. The chaos and the crush and the noise all around me did my head in. All I wanted was to be somewhere private with them to find out how soon they thought I'd be released.

'Charlie Turnbull back in London has been in touch with Liz every day,' Kev shouted. 'She's coping well and sends love.' I was relieved to know that the family were being kept in the loop. Charlie was the operations director of Risk Management in London who'd served with me for ArmorGroup in Iraq. A good operator, it usually fell to him to inform the wives and families when any of our men were killed.

'This is Mr Osman,' Kev mouthed, pushing a diminutive Afghan to the grille. 'He's your new lawyer.' I strained to listen as Mr Osman introduced himself. He hardly spoke any English and in that crazy place where nobody could hear anything, he asked me to tell him my story.

'I can't possibly do that here!' I said. 'Go back to my office and read the statements in the file. They'll tell you everything. And go see the Prosecutor, too.' Talking to him was like wading through treacle. I wasn't even sure if he'd heard or understood me properly before he dropped back into the crowd.

'Bloody hell!' I thought. 'A lawyer who doesn't speak English or even know my case. Is that the best they can do?' I didn't even have a chance to question it because ten minutes after visiting began the guards shouted that it was time to return to our cells.

Frustrated and upset, I waved the lads goodbye and watched as they filed out to enjoy the rest of their weekend off. I imagined them going back to the bar to talk about how I'd seemed over a couple of beers. I thought of them sharing a meal together in the canteen. Wasn't Iliya, our cook, making curry that night? I could picture them in the gym, watching a movie, or calling their loved ones, free to come and go as they pleased. Behind bars, I had no choice but to return to my cell, where I threw off my itchy uniform that stank of BO and sat in my corner feeling like crap.

Not that I was left alone for long. Once the guards realised I'd be getting supplies, they began hassling me for their share, and then there were new demands – for cash. One by one, they'd seek me out, shake my hand and rub their index finger over my palm in a kind of freemason's handshake. I insisted I had no money and let them take their quota of rations instead.

When Azim appeared at the gate the following morning with yet another box of food, I had to ask him to bring less next time. Even after the guards had taken what they wanted there was still enough fresh bread, fruit, meat and eggs to share with my cellmates who greeted me with hopeful faces when I walked back in.

I was also relieved to have my iPod at last, although most of the guards had never seen one (Rob kept his hidden). 'It is not a phone,' I had to explain. 'Like a radio, but no sound, with headphones.' The Taliban allowed music occasionally but singing was forbidden and I didn't want to offend anyone. My iPod was a baby one I carried when I ran my five-mile circuit around the training ground at the Anjuman base. It came with a charging unit but I didn't have an adaptor so I used Rob's, spliced into a dodgy cable that hung from the wall and into which the television was also spliced. It was a health and safety nightmare.

Lying on the floor of the cell listening to music reminded me of when I was a kid. My only personal possession then had been a second-hand radio I bought for a couple of quid when I was fourteen. I'd saved the money from washing cars and working on the market. Every night I'd take it to bed and listen to Radio Luxembourg and DJs like Emperor Rosko and Tony Blackburn. The music of Genesis, the Rolling Stones and David Bowie lifted me away from my dingy council bedroom lit only by a street lamp because my dad had thieved the meter money again.

I only had 394 songs downloaded on my iPod, but they gave me 394 chances to escape from the confines of my predicament. Sitting in my corner, I turned it on, clamped the headphones to my ears and closed my eyes. 'Everybody Hurts', a song by R.E.M., filled my head: *When the day is long and the night, the night is yours alone, . . . Don't let yourself go . . . everybody hurts sometimes . . .*

In my mind, I was no longer in a cockroach-infested hole but was slow-dancing with Liz around the edge of our clear blue swimming pool. The sun was sinking over the Valenciana hills, the Rioja was breathing, and the candles were flickering on the table. I ached to hold my wife in my arms, kiss her and tell her how much I missed her and our life together. What do they say? Absence makes the heart grow fonder? The last time I'd seen her had been in January when I'd flown to the UK for ten days with her and the kids. We'd stayed with Bear and the grandchildren in Dover and then Lewis came back to Spain with us for New Year. Liz was my anchor; she always had been. From my first few days at Catterick – when I'd finally pulled myself out of the muck of my childhood – I'd never stopped loving her. I only wished I'd told her more often.

My usual work rota was nine weeks on, three weeks off. Although I really enjoyed my job, I was mentally and physically exhausted by its relentless nature and had already told the company that I needed to take some time off. 'I'm knackered, mate,' I'd told Mark Spandler. 'I've done four years solid with just a few weeks' off at a stretch and I always work on leave anyway. If I spend summer in Spain with the family, I can come back refreshed in September.'

It was this same determination to maximise my time off that had led me to turn down a lucrative job offer the previous year. A rival PSC had head-hunted me for a contract with a better salary, working from the far less hostile environment of Dubai, with trips back to Iraq and Afghanistan. But with less leave, I turned it down.

I was due to fly home in just over a week – from 16 March

to 5 April – and my sons Lewis and Craig were flying to Spain so we could spend some 'Lad's Time' together. They were both busy working full time and I hadn't seen Craig in months. We planned to do some jobs around the house and garden and then take some hikes in the hills before sinking a few beers. Trying not to jobs whether or not I'd be freed in time to see them, I spent most of that day plugged into my iPod, listening to U2, The Carpenters, Dido, Robbie, Queen and Steve Harley. The music had the capacity to lift or sink me, and the emotions it sparked were not always welcome, but the distraction it provided from my surroundings was invaluable and I was so grateful to be allowed to escape – in my head at least.

Sitting up after a while, I asked Rob if I could borrow a pen and paper. Even though I knew Charlie and Kev were reassuring my family, I wanted to write them a letter myself. Huddled in my corner I rested the paper on my thighs. I didn't know what to write and I didn't want to say too much, in case the guards read it. I thought long and hard about how to express my feelings but even trying to put my situation into words got to me. This would clearly take time.

In all the years I'd been with Liz, I'd only ever written that one letter in Iraq to be opened 'in the event of . . .' I'd always felt that to do so would be tempting Fate. We joked about it a lot when I'd tell her to 'dust off the paperwork', but we never went into details. We'd made our wills and my departure was always so rushed, there wasn't time to say more – or maybe we just chose not to. Being killed never really crossed my mind – our philosophy was that we would deal with it when it happened. Our dear friend John Ingham died in a light aircraft crash in 2008 and his widow couldn't believe it; she always thought she'd be the one comforting Liz, not the other way around.

In spite of my bravado, it was never easy to go away and harder still if I didn't know exactly what I was going into. It must have been worse for the family because I was always so busy and eager to get on with it. Liz and the kids took consolation from knowing I was in a job I loved and that going to hot zones was what I was paid for, but that didn't stop their tears. I couldn't help but reflect each time that I might never see them again but we'd lived with that since our first days together in Armagh. Nonetheless, it was always difficult to say goodbye.

Alone with my thoughts in Tawqeef, I put the pen and paper away until I could decide what to say. Instead, I lay in my bed space and deliberately played songs that had special meaning to me and my family. There were numbers like Terry Jacks's 'Seasons in the Sun' which I'd always loved. 'If anything ever happens to me, play this at my funeral?' I told Liz in one of our rare discussions about the possibility when we were first married.

'Not bloody likely!' she replied.

'Why ever not?'

'Because the lyrics are all wrong – *Goodbye papa, please pray for me, I was the black sheep of the family*? You, Bill, are most definitely *not* the black sheep of your family!' To this day her righteous indignation makes me laugh.

Then there was our wedding dance song, Barry White's 'You're the First, the Last, my Everything' and Gilbert Becaud's 'A Little Love and Understanding' which Liz liked me to sing as a lullaby. I took Rod Stewart's *You're in my Heart* with me when I was deployed on two months' exercise with the Queen's Own Highlanders to New Zealand. Despite our chequered history having to sort out their frequent brawls in the bars of Wanchai, Hong Kong (where they were known as the 'Queen's Own Hooligans'), those men treated me as a brother. Some of them had seen their mates killed at Warrenpoint in 1979 and they taught me the utmost respect for the Infantry. I'd play them Rod Stewart at night to remind us all of home.

I also tuned into Beyoncé's album *I Am . . . Sasha Fierce* because it reminded me of Liz. 'It's about a powerful wife and mother, always waiting at home for me, even after all these years,' I'd told her. The words to 'Halo' seemed even more appropriate as I lay there thinking of the woman I loved. '*I can see your halo . . . hit me like a ray of sun, burning through my darkest night.*'

I fell asleep with that playing in my ears.

Ten

By the dawn of my sixth day in the prison, Monday, 8 March, I was probably at one of my lowest points. Thankfully, Azim arrived with a smile. His latest supplies included a few things I'd specifically asked for like a jar of coffee, a plastic bowl to wash in, and some more bottled water so that I could brush my teeth without risking the tap water. He also pressed a small brown envelope into my hand which I later found contained $500 – no doubt of his own money. Bless him.

'You will need this, Mr Bill,' he told me. It was far more than I could possibly need in Tawqeef and I feared it would only mean more hassle from the eagle-eyed guards who spotted the exchange, but I took it gratefully and stuffed it into my pocket.

Then Azim made another suggestion. 'Why don't you pay them off, Mr Bill, sir?' he asked. 'This is the way of our society. I could speak to the judge.' He would have taken care of it, I'm sure, but I shook my head.

'No, Azim. Leave it,' I said. 'We need to do this properly.'

I'd already been advised by Sadiqi and Idris that it would probably have taken $15,000 or so to bribe someone to get me out, but what they didn't understand was that to do so would be flying in the face of all I stood for. There were no guarantees, anyway. I'd heard of one man in Pol-e-Charkhi whose brother had paid off the judge and then complained.

Soon afterwards he was arrested and sent to the same prison for 'corruption'.

Azim clearly thought me crazy not to want to pay someone to get out, but he nodded his understanding. I'd always treated him like one of my Sandhurst officer cadets, making sure that he was looked after and happy in his work. Humble and kind, he repaid me tenfold. Keen to improve his English, he and his assistant Jamshed picked up on some of my most common expressions like, 'How you diddling?' (meaning 'How are you doing?') or calling them the 'horse's cock' or 'elephant's tadger' if they'd done something good. Now Azim was truly an elephant's tadger, making my life behind bars that bit easier.

His previous boss had been our accounts manager Richard Adamson, a former Royal Marine who'd lived in Afghanistan for years and was fluent in Dari and Pashto. In August 2007, Azim drove Richard into Kabul for a regular bank run. Having collected a couple of hundred thousand dollars for wages and other necessities, their soft-skinned Toyota 4x4 was stopped at a police checkpoint. The men in uniform demanded they hand over the money but Richard refused so they shot him in the leg. He still refused so they shot him in the neck, seized the money and fled. Azim rushed Richard to hospital but he died soon afterwards.

Azim was still traumatised by what happened when I arrived six months later. Now his new boss had been thrown in jail and he was just as upset. Although he'd always have an important role in the company, everything had changed for him; it showed on his face.

I went back to my cell and split the cash he'd given me into small amounts. I rolled the majority into a wad and put it in my sleeping bag which I kept rolled up under Rob's bed. I handed a few dollars to Abdul Wakil because I'd seen others do the same. Rob and Sadiqi had explained that these 'subs' not only covered the cost of our food and the services of our *chai* boy Marbat, but also paid the bearded bouncers who slept in our corridor to take turns guarding our cell. It was a system El Gordo had set up so that our belongings and supplies were never left unsupervised. When I saw the lack of cohesion and discipline in some of the other cells, I was grateful that I'd been placed in cell No. 1.

Later that morning, a guard called my name and told me to follow him to the Commandant's office. My first thought was, 'What do they want now?' I was relieved that I only had seven dollars in my pocket. Then I wondered if the Commandant was going to warn me to stay in my cell again because of death threats. I couldn't do as he asked or I'd have gone crazy but I'd thank him for his concern.

To my surprise, I opened the door to his office and found Kevin accompanied by a woman in her mid-thirties. She introduced herself as Kimberley Motley, an American defence lawyer, and shook my hand firmly. In an instant, my life improved. With a soft Southern accent she told me, 'I'm going to represent you from now on.' I felt as if a massive weight had been lifted off me.

'What about Mr Osman?' I asked.

'Forget the other lawyers,' she said. 'They've been terminated.' I hoped not literally.

'I'm now in charge of your case. These accusations against you are ridiculous and I'll do all I can to get you out of here as quickly as possible.'

Kev explained that Kim specialised in helping foreigners ensnared in the Afghan criminal justice system. She'd heard about my case and approached G4S directly, offering to represent me. I was immediately impressed and although I realised it would take a little time to sort out, I felt I was in far safer hands.

As the guards stood brazenly ogling Kim (a former Miss Wisconsin, as I later discovered), she asked me about my case. 'An Afghan called Mustafa who works for me will come to see you regularly for more information,' she added. 'Kevin here will accompany him.' I took this as a covert way of getting me more visits, for which I was grateful.

It was good to talk relatively freely and without the noise of the visiting room. I told her what I could, being cautious in the presence of the guards. Kim explained that Afghanistan had a three-tier court system. 'It can take several months to get a case heard at the first court and that depends almost solely on the lawyer chasing the judge. If the Prosecutor and the defence agree on the result, then that's the end of it. Any disagreement and the aggrieved party pushes the case on to the next and then to the final Supreme Court. My aim is to get your case dismissed at the first hearing but if that fails, I'll push it to the next level as quickly as possible.'

I tried to quell all negative thoughts about how long that might take in a country where bureaucracy moves at a snail's pace.

'The company will provide every assistance to Kim,' Kev interjected. 'They've also decided to keep you on full pay and cover all supporting fees.' This was a great comfort to me.

'Have you spoken to Mark Spandler yet?' I asked Kim. 'He knows as much about all this as I do.'

There was a pause. 'Mark's been sent out of the country,' Kev said. 'He spoke to the embassy and everyone thought it best.'

I looked up and stared at him for a moment, but said nothing.

'I'll be running the show here while Mark's in Dubai,' Kev continued, 'but he's in touch every day and he wants you to know that he's fully behind you.'

'Thanks, mate,' I told him, struggling to keep it together.

There was more to come, though. As Kim wandered over to distract the guards, Kevin pulled out his mobile telephone and held it out to me. 'I thought you might like to call Liz,' he whispered.

I hesitated. Although I wanted to speak to her more than anything in the world, I was nervous about phoning as I knew how upsetting it would be but before I knew it Kev dialled the number and passed the phone over. My hand was trembling as I took it.

Liz answered immediately and I blurted, 'Hi love. It's me.'

'Bill!' she cried. That was all it took. When we'd both composed ourselves a little, she asked, 'How are you, darling!?'

'I'm fine,' I lied. 'Really. You're not to worry. I expect to be released any day.'

'But I don't understand. What's going on? They said you'd spend a night or two in prison but then you'd be out. Why are you still in there?'

It was so wonderful to hear her voice, even though I could hear her stress.

'Things just take a lot longer out here; you know how it is. But everyone's taking care of me and I'll be home soon. How are the kids?'

'They're okay. Concerned. We all are, Bill. They send their love. Madeleine and Caius too.'

It was a struggle to keep upbeat but in the few minutes that we were allowed before the guards intervened, I was able to reassure her that I was being treated fairly, and she reassured me that she was coping. 'I'll write soon but I've got to sign off now. OK, luv?'

'OK,' she said, not wanting to let me go. Saying goodbye was so difficult. As with every phone call for years we ended with the German farewell '*Tschüss!*' Then the line went dead.

Later that day, I reflected on developments, though, and felt much happier. 'Finally!' I said, clenching my fists in victory. 'Things are moving!'

It's amazing how something as previously insignificant as a phone call or a personal visit comes to mean so much once you are no longer in control of your own destiny. I was secretly proud of the fact that I'd always been fair and just to those I'd had to put behind bars over the years – granting them special privileges if they behaved themselves. 'Do unto others as you would have them do unto yourself.' I'd never forgotten that maxim from Sunday school in Salford, which I'd only ever gone to each week for the free hot chocolate and biscuits.

Later that night, the meal mat in our cell was duly rolled out and the food divided into portions. Rob, as ever, sat on his bed eating one of his foil packets of American military MRE (Meals, Ready-to-Eat) that were brought in every few weeks by someone from his old company. I'd eaten MREs in Kuwait and Iraq and didn't much like them because they were too stodgy for my taste. The dishes like meatloaf or spaghetti

Bolognese came with a thin metal element that heats when put into hot water and warms the food instantly.

I'd come to realise that Rob had little or no social skills. He'd seen me interacting with our cellmates but always declined my invitations to join in. 'Come and have something to eat, even if only out of courtesy,' I'd tell him. 'They'll love you for it.' In all the countries I'd served I'd not only tried to socialise with the locals but encouraged my men and women to do the same. It wasn't just a question of winning hearts and minds, but of making the posting more enjoyable by learning new customs and traditions. Rob wasn't interested, though. It was like trying to coax a wild animal from its cave. He might have a quick cup of *chai* but he'd always go straight back to his bed space.

When he saw the amount and quality of the food G4S were sending in, though, I guess his hunger got the better of him and he decided to join in. I saw him eyeing a whole roast chicken one night so I waved him forward. He hesitated but then slid off his bed and sat close to me, as if for protection. He chatted for a while and then he got stuck in. My cellmates couldn't have been more delighted if I'd brought in a member of their own family to dinner. Clapping their hands together in delight, they laughed openly and patted me on the back. This silent, moody Australian who'd breathed the same foul air as them for the previous nine months but hardly spoken one word had finally cracked. As I watched Rob gobble up a piece of chicken (which made even the mullahs smile), I was grateful that at least one good thing had come out of me being in this godforsaken hole.

The next few days felt brighter one way and another, thanks

mainly to the efforts of those who were working on my behalf. Kev came to see me as often as he could, usually on a Wednesday and a Saturday in the unbelievably frustrating environment of the visiting area, which always did my head in. One day he brought in a lovely lad called Gary McDonald from Northern Ireland who worked on one of my projects. Gary had something he wanted to give to me personally. It was a religious charm from the Catholic shrine at Knock in Ireland; like a small St Christopher. I took it with thanks and when I got back to my cell I attached it to a piece of string which I wore around my neck and never took off. Every morning and night I kissed it four times and said hello to Liz and the kids. It came with a laminated prayer card, part of which read: '*Help me to remember that we are all pilgrims on the road to heaven. Fill me with love and concern for my brothers and sisters, especially those who live with me. Comfort me when I am sick or lonely and depressed . . . Pray for me now and at the hour of my death.*' Although I have never been religious, those words came to have great meaning to me.

Kevin arrived with the company medic later that week and the guards allowed us into what was euphemistically referred to as the 'sick bay'. A small cell beyond the main gate, it had an old bed and a scruffy screen around it. Once a week, scores of people queued in the corridor to see the prison doctor for anything from diarrhoea to drugs overdoses. There were many frail old men who suffered from breathing problems in Kabul's high altitude and their condition wasn't helped by that cold, damp pit of a prison. A few were taken to hospital and never seen again. One man had no legs and his friends would lift and carry him around. Others with missing or mangled limbs from landmines and IEDs were on crutches. Several had bad feet or skin problems and would be sent away empty handed. All that the doctor could prescribe for the most serious ailments were a few ineffective tablets.

The prison did have another medical man: an inmate called Dr Hussein who'd lived in Canada and spoke English. 'Many of these men die before they even get to trial,' he told me sadly. 'And not just the old ones – one kid hanged himself in the toilets a few weeks before you arrived. That's why the guards drilled those holes into the doors. I was called to see if anything could be done, but it was too late.'

The G4S medic, Mike Sizemore, was an ex-Special Forces American and a top operator. As he examined me, Kev filled me in on the latest beyond my prison walls. 'Even though G4S has got all its vehicles back from the NDS now, it has voluntarily impounded them all so that no more can be seized until your case is sorted,' he said. 'It's costing them a fortune but they're leasing fully licensed vehicles from Karzai's Ministers instead.'

'Maybe that's what the government wanted all along,' I replied, wryly.

Mike the Medic took my blood pressure, listened to my heart, checked me over and asked me how much weight I thought I'd lost. I normally weighed 13 stone which was about right for my 5ft 10in height, but we agreed that I'd probably lost about 10lb in Tawqeef. Fortunately, I was fully inoculated but told him about my heart palpitations and he gave me some mild tranquillisers. Although Mike could see I was exhausted and my joints were stiff, he pronounced my condition good and congratulated me for my exercise regime. He gave me some powder for the lice which were making my midriff red raw plus a stack of different pills. These included something to bung me up (the last thing I needed), as well as rehydration sachets, effervescent vitamins and headache tablets. I was like a walking pharmacy. He promised to get me some laxatives.

Back in my bed space, I examined what I'd been given and found a note from Mark Spandler, secreted in the tube of vitamins. He wrote: '*I'm doing all I can – rest assured . . . I hope all the kit, food etc has got to you – sleeping mat and pillow came from me. Can I get you anything else? Hang in there, mate. I will get you out and get this issue resolved. We are all supporting you here and will not rest until you're back. Mark.*' I really appreciated that, even if his note made me realise that the guards must have pinched the sleeping mat and pillow – neither of which I'd ever seen.

Once the Afghans in my cell spotted my stash of pills from Mike, they pleaded for relief for everything from toothache to a tummy upset so I gave them what they wanted. I could always get more and I only kept a few vital medicines back for myself. My biggest problem was the headaches that plagued me day and night. The cumulative effects of dehydration, bright lights, cigarette smoke, unpleasant odours and little or no caffeine built up pressure inside my skull. The only respite came in the frequent blackouts whenever Kabul's City Power plant shuddered to a halt. All of a sudden there'd be complete darkness which felt strange and alarming at first in an environment of 24-hour brightness. The guards would come hurrying in with torches and supervise the lighting of candles in every cell. The flickering light softened our surroundings and quietened everyone down. My headache would settle or even disperse and my little world seemed a kinder, gentler place.

It reminded me of the power cuts we had when I was a boy, which were usually related to how much money was left in the meter. We had very few electrical goods – no fridge or central heating – but we still ran out. My father would snap the locks off the meter, pinch the money and tell us to repeatedly feed through the one shilling he left us when he went down the pub. Once the electricity company cottoned on, they'd change the meters but he'd only break the glass and jam a piece of metal against the wheel to stop the movement but allow the current. Our sole source of heat was the open fire in the living room. Dad would send me to the Agecroft Colliery in nearby Pendlebury with a rickety old pram where I had to sneak through a hole in the fence and 'acquire' as much nutty slack as I could get my hands on. Now I had only the light of a sputtering stub of a candle, which glinted in the eyes of my Afghan cellmates as they sat or lay, waiting for the electricity to come back on.

When it did, I was finally able to finish the letter home. It was dated Thursday, 11 March, and part of it read: '*Hi love. Surprise! Firstly, I am so very sorry for putting you through this traumatic ordeal . . . We are going to see it through and you can clearly see all the support from London. Just exceptionally frustrating and heart rending stuck behind bars . . . I am not sure how long I am going to be here but I think we can forget my leave next week. No doubt we will laugh about it one day soon but for now it is not funny at all, he he not!*

'*I have got into a sort of routine as best I can . . . The night-times are the worst as I have images of you and the kids and all of us in Spain. At least when I get out we can do it for real without rushing back to work or checking emails several times a day. You have been very patient with all that and I thank you as ever.*

'You: I sincerely hope you are okay and coping well. I think you are stronger than me anyway . . .

'Me: Seriously darling, I am fine so no tears and no worries. At least I'm getting paid for being here and finding time to read books . . . Just need to get out now.

'Kids: I hope that all the kids are well and looking forward to Easter . . . Give them all my love . . .

'First night home in Spain we shall play 'Kingston Town' by UB40 by the pool at sunset with a glass of wine and dance together. I will then know I am home again . . . xx Well darling, I hope this has put you at ease a bit and made you feel better. They are treating me very well but it costs the odd ration or goodie. But that is the way of life here. I will sign off for now and write again next week. I love you with all my heart and looking forward to release day whenever that comes around. Thousands of hugs, kisses and cuddles for now and until we meet again . . . Love you very much. xxxx' (Always with four kisses, of course.)

I read the letter through one last time, but the words kept swimming in and out of focus, and not just because my dodgy glasses kept slipping off my nose. I folded the letter to give to Kevin. So, this was how it was going to be. Right then, I told myself. Treat this like another Army tour. It's just a new posting and a new barracks. Let's get on with it.

Eleven

It is amazing how quickly a human being can adapt to its surroundings, even difficult ones. Man is so resilient; so able to adjust to unfamiliar ways and fit in with those around him.

And so it was that I somehow grew accustomed to the peculiar life of a civilian after leaving the Army in 2004 at the ripe old age of forty-six. After my 'dining out' organised by my RSM and friend Tony Cooper, I prepared to hand my kit in to the stores. On Tuesday, 24 August that year, at the Rheindahlen Garrison near Monchengladbach, I signed over my ID cards, my combats, boots, helmet, respirator, denim trousers, jumpers and shirts. They were lined up on the stores table and I was told that I could keep what I wanted so I picked a couple of combat jackets and some boots for gardening.

I thought back to the previous night in the officers' mess, attended by friends from all ranks and regiments. With twenty-one-year-old Craig as my guest because Liz was stuck in England, we listened to Tony's speech charting my military career over the years with a few choice jokes thrown in. The next morning, his kind words were still echoing in my ears as I looked down at what represented a lifetime of service. The neatly folded pile of clothes, insignia and shoes didn't seem enough for the life I'd led. Every day in the Army had brought me something different. It had been all I'd hoped and more. I'd enjoyed a fantastic career. Each posting was great; there was never a bad one. There were new ranks and new challenges and Liz relished it as much as I did. Ex-military herself, she loved being an Army wife; hosting drinks parties, running netball teams, and supporting all the other families. We threw ourselves enthusiastically into any new posting not least because it was all we'd ever known.

I'd served six more years than the full twenty-two I'd decided to commit to back in Armagh. The variety of experiences during those twenty-eight years had never ceased and even the final period of my service had been full-on. I'd spent two years in Cyprus, six months at Divisional HQ in Bosnia, two years back at Catterick and two months in Buenos Aires on a Military Observers' Course. I'd been selected as a member of the Army Language Scholarship Scheme to learn Spanish at a military college in Beaconsfield, Hampshire. I'd spent six months in Northern Spain, attached to the respected *cazadores* of the Mountain Warfare Regiment. I was specially selected as a member of Close Protection Advisory and Training Team in Colombia to support the British Ambassador there. Then, in my final two years, I was promoted to Major, saw service in Iraq in the Second Gulf War, and was given a senior position in Rheindahlen.

A big part of me never wanted to leave the military, and I had planned to stay in until I was fifty-five; the latest I could remain if the rules allowed. Because of defence cutbacks, though, I was warned by my brigadier that there was a chance I'd be made redundant at fifty and before I made it to the rank of lieutenant-colonel. Then a former brigadier Ian Fulton, OBE, who I'd worked under in Bielefeld, Germany, in Malawi, and at Worthy Down, asked me if I'd consider joining him in the private sector. It occurred to me then for the first time that there was a life outside the military.

'You'd be perfect command material, Bill,' Brig. Fulton told me. 'We'd be lucky to have you.'

I wasn't getting any younger and I had my wife, children and grandchildren to consider. We'd lived in seventeen different homes in twenty-seven years. Our youngest son Lewis couldn't adjust to boarding school and needed a more settled home life. I'd earned my military pension and – before I got too old – I was being offered a chance to diversify and try something new. After much soul-searching, I decided to give it a go. I thought I'd be moving into a world where I knew what was going to be waiting for me around the corner. Little did I know.

What I also didn't realise was just how sorely I'd miss the action, the discipline and the camaraderie at first – even if I was to rediscover some of that later. When I walked out of that vast military base in Rheindahlen that warm summer's morning in 2004, I was a civilian for the first time since I was a teenager. Stepping through the high-security gates, I felt like a prisoner blinkingly emerging into the world. I didn't belong to the British Army any more. I was no longer an officer commanding. I was leaving everyone and everything I knew. It felt so strange to think that I'd never be allowed back onto that base without an invitation, or that I no longer carried the cards that had identified me as a man and a soldier for nearly thirty years. This was it, then. The future scared me.

Somehow, though, I adapted. It took a while but I fell in with being an employee in a private security company, first as Head of Officer Training Wing at the International Academy in Amman, Jordan, and then as Country Operations Manager for ArmorGroup in Baghdad. By the time I arrived in Kabul, the sights, sounds and smells weren't dissimilar to those of my previous three years. I'd picked up a little Arabic and Dari, come to enjoy the *mezze* food, and perhaps most importantly, learned how to live with the daily threat of death or injury from an IED, kidnappers or suicide bombers.

Locked up in Tawqeef, I learned to adapt again. I found ways of managing my disgust at the cockroaches and the mould, the mice and rats, the overflowing toilets and the lack of proper washing facilities. I learned how to fight for my place at the grille during the zoo of visiting hours and of yelling my innermost thoughts over the seething masses. I became accustomed to itching like hell from the lice that took up residence in my hair, skin and clothing. Having been fastidiously clean and tidy all my adult life, I was permanently unshaven, dirty and smelly. I hated that aspect of my incarceration with every fibre of my being.

What consumed me most of all though were my worries for the family. It was almost impossible to sleep and no matter how hard I tried to concentrate on reading or writing letters home, I couldn't shake off thoughts about what might happen to them if I was detained much longer. Determined not to go under, I decided that I needed not only a rigorous exercise regime but a military-style schedule to occupy my mind. Adhering to that routine became as important to me as marching in time or polishing my kit had once been.

Each morning I got up at 06:45 hrs and gave myself a strip wash while the others went into the courtyard to pray. After breakfast and the roll-call I'd wait for Azim if he was coming, allowing the guards to take their percentage. Then, depending on the weather, I'd head outside to start my marching which became almost like a daily meditation for me. Not that it was always easy in such a crowded space with the stalls and the mosque. When all 550 inmates flooded into the yard there were often too many bodies to be stepped over.

I deliberately avoided the dodgiest characters with drug habits or a history of violence. The ones that sought me out chiefly wanted to practise their English by talking about football, their relatives in Britain, or to ask if I'd been to Piccadilly Circus. The colonel who'd first taken me to cell No. 1 was thrilled to discover I was British, not American, as most Afghans assume all Westerners in Kabul to be.

'London!' he cried, grinning to reveal several gaps in his teeth as he gestured flying in a plane.

'Yes, yes,' I said. 'I'll meet you in London some day.'

'We drink whisky? In London? Yes?'

Most prisoners kept their own counsel and several sat preening themselves for visiting time. Obsessed with being hairless apart from their beards as part of their quest for Islamic purity and cleanliness, they shaved all their body parts (and I mean all) including their chests. I was fascinated to see many of them carefully applying black eyeliner to each other or painting their hands and toenails with henna.

Intrigued, I decided to learn more about their customs. It wasn't just a question of 'Know Thine Enemy', I was genuinely curious. In Malawi, I'd learned a few key phrases of Chichewa and some traditional songs. In Argentina, apart from practising my Spanish, I studied the country's history, visiting Eva Perón's mausoleum and Casa Rosada, the presidential palace. I picked up some German in Rheindahlen and in Hong Kong I went to night classes to learn Cantonese. Having flunked school, I was amazed how well I picked up that Far Eastern language and used every opportunity to exploit it. I was even able to put it to good use years later when I was RSM in charge of welfare and discipline of over five hundred personnel at Worthy Down.

One of my tasks there was to inspect the squads on the parade ground. Anyone found with dust on their shoes or uniforms, double creases in their uniforms, or other minor misdemeanours would have to go on what was called 'show parade' at 22:00 hrs. During one such inspection all the students were giving me their names and units in turn when a young male NCO shouted, 'Cpl Smith, Headquarters British Forces, Hong Kong, Sir!' The whole parade ground heard him, he was so loud.

Deadpan, I went nose to nose with him and said, 'Is that supposed to impress me, laddie? The fact that you're based in Hong Kong and I'm stuck in Worthy Down?'

Again he shouted very loudly, 'No, Sir!'

'Go on then, speak to me in Cantonese.'

'I don't know any, Sir!' he shouted back.

'How long have you been there?'

'Two years, Sir!'

'Two years and you don't know any Cantonese? You don't know *bejau* or *shooitao*? Beer and chips? The staple diet of soldiers?'

By then, most on parade were trying not to laugh.

'No, Sir,' the corporal shouted again, 'I hate them, dirty, smelly, horrible people!'

I put my face right close to his and said, 'My wife's Chinese.'

I could see the poor lad melting under the pressure.

'Not only that, but she's in a wheelchair!'

The two Staff Sergeants at the back doubled over.

'You can show yourself free from racial hatred tonight at 22:00 hrs,' I concluded.

He may have thought I was joking but I wasn't so that night he reported to the Duty Officer and duly shouted, 'Corporal Smith, Sir, showing myself free from racial hatred!'

In Tawqeef, I had several willing helpers happy to teach me about Afghan culture, most of whom seemed free from racial hatred. Dr Hussein was a pleasant companion who'd been arrested sixteen months earlier for a business deal that went wrong. He hadn't yet been to trial but refused to pay a government fine because he insisted he was innocent. 'I'll stay here as long as it takes to clear my name,' he told me defiantly.

Idris was never far away and I finally agreed to help him with his English. Having been an instructor throughout my military career, I took to my new role like a jingly truck to the Jalalabad Road. It was a far cry from the days when my father would clip me round the ear if he found me doing homework. 'You don't need an education, lad,' he'd say. 'You just need to get out and earn us some money!'

Idris became a model student, and Wasir Khan and others would join us on a blanket in the courtyard. I asked Kev to bring me in some A1 sketchpads and flipcharts for our lessons but the Commandant confiscated them. His translator explained, 'For your own security.'

I wasn't worried, although one of the long beards did march over to us one day to complain. He told Idris, 'Stay away from the American! You are not to associate with him and you are forbidden to learn English!' Idris just told him to go away.

In the absence of sketch pads, we used notebooks or scraps of paper. I began by drawing a human body and naming all the parts with arrows pointing out the eyes, hair, nose, ears, leg, torso or arm. Idris pronounced each word out loud so that the others could understand it; he then taught me the equivalent word in his language. I also learnt the Dari for gate, lock, handcuffs, fight and stop. I memorised numbers and discovered that the word for guard was *zorbed*. Perhaps the most important phrase I learned was *sedakuo tarjomaan*, which meant 'bring me an interpreter'.

There were a few old newspapers lying around so I used those too, marking up words like car, house, man, chair or tree. Idris would roll up the newspaper and take it to his cell each night to practise. Early next morning, he'd come running up to me and say, 'Test me, William! Test me!'

As Idris's English improved, so I came to understand a little more about his crime. The woman he'd harmed was a girl he'd dated at college, always in the company of a chaperone. She agreed to marry him when they graduated but then she told him she was promised to someone else. Infuriated, Idris slashed her across the face with a Stanley knife. Her injuries were so bad that she had to go to India for plastic surgery. Her father and brothers vowed revenge which meant that, if Idris was released, he'd have to move far from all he'd ever known.

After he told me his story he sat silently waiting for my response. I chose my words carefully. 'It isn't love to hurt someone you care about,' I said. 'You acted out of spite and you must never do anything like that again.' I think he understood. I only hope that he (and the poor girl) could pick up their lives.

I was soon befriended by another Afghan named Sadir, an educated man in his mid-thirties, married with two children. A very able English speaker, he'd worked for the Afghan telecommunications company Roshan and had a good job. One day, he was a passenger in his own car when his friend the driver knocked down two people, killing one of them. After the accident, the friend ran off. Because it was Sadir's car and he remained at the scene, he was arrested. His wife raised $1,500 (everything they had) and went to see the judge. He took it but told her that her husband would still have to serve at least eighteen months. Sadir was still waiting for his first court appearance and, with no money and no means to make any, he was destitute.

Sadir taught me much about Tawqeef. He explained that the stalls in the courtyard were under the direct supervision of the Commandant. There was also a small shop in our corridor run by prison guards and 'trustys' which sold fresh bread, cigarettes, biscuits and razors. I suspected the Commandant earned a nice little bonus out of all those twenty Afghanis and odd dollar bills – not that we'd complain. Without those little enterprises, the mood would have been rock bottom. They supplied us with hot water and cooked food. They gave us hobbies like threading beads and provided a means of income for those who worked on them. The Commandant even owned the prison camera, apparently. I posed for a couple of shots with Idris, Rob and some others, forcing a smile. I gave them to Kev to send to Liz in the hope that they'd stop her and the kids worrying quite so much.

Like Azim and several others, Sadir wondered why I hadn't bribed my way out. 'It is common to pay, William.' But then he told me of a mullah arrested for drugs offences whose wife was charged $10,000 for her husband's release by the judge, who also demanded sex. Even though she reluctantly did as he asked, he sent her husband to prison for eighteen years. Adultery is usually punishable by death in Afghanistan, so it's perhaps no wonder that the judge wanted the husband locked away.

When I asked Sadir why the men in cell No. 2 hadn't bribed their way out yet, he told me, 'The case against them will almost certainly be dropped. They are, how do you say in English, going through the motion?'

At Sadir's suggestion, I bought some beads and he and I sat together making bracelets and necklaces for the family; an occupation which was surprisingly absorbing and pleasurable. Sending them home to Liz, Lisa, Madeleine and Caius really cheered me up. As we sat threading, Sadir pointed out various prisoners and told me their stories. The more I learned, the more appalled I was; I have never known so many desperate people crammed into one place. The saddest were six Sri Lankans who'd come to Kabul as labourers, only to discover their work permits were forged. They were arrested but with no Sinhalese translators or anyone to help them, they were in limbo. Their families didn't even know where they were and would have been evicted from their homes without money for rent. I felt very sorry for them and would get up extra early each morning to meet them with a cheery, 'How you diddling?' When nobody was looking, I'd buy them some eggs or tomatoes, or give them money for hot water and soap (which they spent on food). We had to be covert or there'd have been a stampede.

They weren't the only ones who needed help. One day, I found Marbat trying to shave with a discarded razor so I gave him one of mine. A man I didn't much like in our cell snatched it off him so I berated him but he pretended not to understand. Later, when no one was looking I took Marbat to the shop and bought him another razor. It was just one small act of kindness for a destitute kid.

Sadir introduced me to another young lad of about twenty who'd recently arrived. His name was Babur and he'd been arrested for spending the evening with a prostitute, which was illegal – if widespread – in Kabul. Babur expected to spend about six months in prison but was surprisingly upbeat about it. 'I enjoyed myself!' he told me, grinning. 'Six months? I tell you William, it was worth it!'

I also became friendly with a group of Afghans from Kandahar, three of whom spoke English. Like me, they'd been arrested after they'd tried to expose corruption. Their leader was a softly spoken elder named Habibullah, who was seventy-six and treated me like a son. Whenever he saw me come into the courtyard he would order me some *chai* and invite me to chat. Or he might walk with me a while. When the Taliban threatened me, as they quite often did, he'd step in and tell them, 'Leave him!'

His English was impeccable and we spent hours discussing our different cultures. He told me of the many marriages he'd arranged, and the grandchildren he had. A devout Muslim who prayed frequently, he loved his country and never wanted to leave. We spoke of religion and westernisation and he told me how afraid he was of what would happen when the ISAF forces left. 'The Taliban will be back,' Habibullah said sadly, 'and then anyone who colluded with America or Britain will be treated most ruthlessly.' I learned more about Afghan tradition from that wise old man than I had in the two years I'd been living and working in his country. It was so refreshing to have a mature conversation without a fanatical rant.

Kev still came to see me at least twice a week and was able to pass personal messages between me and the family. It was so wonderful to finally have something from them to hold. He brought me some photos from my office including one of Lisa and the kids swimming in the pool in Spain. She was in a bikini so I had to put a sticking plaster over her body so that no one would be offended. There was a picture of my sister Betty's ten-year-old grandson Dylan (which some of the guards took special interest in, to my horror), and Kev brought me a calendar Bear sent at Christmas featuring different photos of Caius and Madeleine every month. Seeing their fresh, innocent faces smiling back at me in that stinking jail really brought it home to me how far away from them I was.

Liz's first letter came and I sat down quietly in my corner to read. My already misshapen reading glasses had been accidentally sat on by El Gordo and one arm was broken so I had to hold them onto my face. Liz wrote: '*My God, darling . . . how could this happen to you?? I am listening to all they tell me and know how hard everyone is working on your behalf but it is a total nightmare . . . We are all thinking of you day and night and know you will be back with us soon . . . Just take care of yourself in there and don't stress as everyone is doing all they can. Don't want you getting through all this and then your heart packing in!! . . . When you get home we will chat through it all and you can get lots of rest. I will find your requested music to have by the pool and dust off my dancing shoes . . . Do not blame yourself for any of this or for putting us through it as you say. We are a family and we stick together . . . We are as proud of you as always and just want you to keep smiling. As you say, one day we will look back on this and chuckle . . . although it may be a long time off yet!!*

'*Just know we are thinking of you day and night and long for your return. Love, hugs and a million tender kisses xxxx PS. Charlie tells me you still have a comb in your back pocket so it's not all bad news lol. xx*'

And so, the days passed. I didn't want to start marking them off because I couldn't have stood seeing them adding up. In any event, I was still determined that I'd be out of there soon. Every time the guards opened the gate and walked in I was still hopeful that it was me they were coming for. It never was.

I kept myself busy and tried to read some of the books the lads had sent in. Trouble is, they were all 'Boys' Own' kind of stories and I couldn't stomach anything about prison or violence. One book they'd sent me, however, really struck a chord. It was called *The Audacity to Believe* by Sheila Cassidy, a British doctor arrested and tortured by Pinochet's notorious secret police in the 1970s because she'd offered medical treatment to a wounded resistance fighter. That remarkable woman remained defiant in spite of the terrible time she had in her two months as a prisoner. I read with some sadness that the British embassy staff in Santiago visited her every now and again but repeatedly told her that they had to allow 'due process'.

Determined to help Rob if I could, I continued to try to reach him but his conversations were very one-sided and mostly involved bragging about how many people he claimed to have 'slotted' over the years. He sounded like a wannabe SAS hero. I tried to be sympathetic as his situation was undoubtedly a heavy burden and he was hopeless at communicating. In his deepest depression, he must have wondered a hundred times a day if the Afghans would really hang him. The Kabul government was supposed to have commuted such sentences to life imprisonment instead, but life meant life in Afghanistan and Rob would almost certainly die behind bars.

I'd try to cheer him up by talking about Manchester United or asking him which Australian football teams he supported but it was no use. He always came back to the same thing – weapons and killing and in the end I had to resign myself to the fact that we could never be mates.

On my tenth morning in Tawqeef, Wednesday, 12 March, I was in the courtyard as usual, pacing up and down, when I heard names being called – one of which was Idris's.

'No more English teach, William,' he said, when he came to find me soon afterwards. 'I go home.'

'Home? What do you mean? You haven't had a trial.'

'I go home,' he said, shrugging. 'It is decided. Maybe someone from my family go to judge.'

I was really chuffed for him but sad to see him go. Idris had been one of the first to befriend me and I'd miss his enthusiasm in English classes. 'Good luck,' I said, as he kissed me on both cheeks.

'I will practise my English and then I will visit my friend William,' he told me, with a broad grin, but we both knew he wouldn't. He never did.

Twelve

Like Route Violent in Kabul, the road dubbed 'Route Irish' by the US military had presented the biggest risk to life when I was working in Iraq. The eight-kilometre highway linking the Green Zone's government, diplomatic and military quarter with the International Airport was dubbed the most dangerous road in the world. It was certainly a paved path to Paradise for suicide bombers praying for martyrdom.

Working in Baghdad as Country Operations Manager for ArmorGroup between 2005–7 was a very different experience to when I'd been there with the British military forces during Operation Iraqi Freedom. What wasn't different was that me and my men were still considered open targets.

As someone with almost thirty years' military experience, I was thrown in at the deep end but the rules soon changed and new arrivals were sent on a two-week induction course to learn all about living and working in a hot zone. They'd be sent to the training camp at Al Hillah, south of Baghdad, to go through all the scenarios – how to drive safely within a convoy; how to give fire and support in 'Actions On'. While I spent time on the range 'zeroing' my weapons to make sure they were accurate within range, I'd see the new employees being taught what to do when an IED blows up and immobilises their vehicle and they had to get out just to survive.

I'd watch their panicked responses during exercises in which small arms fire was directed at them, or during what are called 'complex attacks' – a bomb followed by small arms fire when they left their vehicle. I made sure I was up to speed on my first aid skills and listened as a trauma medic talked us through how to treat gunshot wounds and loss of limbs. We learned how to tie tourniquets, inject morphine, elevate arms and legs to prevent blood loss and how to deal with a serious stomach injury. We learned all eventualities, even down to repatriating the bodies back from the scene, including making sure you scrape up all the body parts.

'It's a tough induction course,' one of the bosses told me, 'but most of those who leave here will have their first contact within weeks. What they learn here could save lives.' The course also gave the opportunity for the training team to confirm that each member was competent enough to go on the ground. If there was any doubt or a feeling that someone might be a liability then they would recommend that he be dismissed. We sent many people home, and others would come into the base after the induction course and tell us, 'I don't want to be here. I want to go home.' There was no disgrace in that and we'd bid them farewell.

Within a few weeks of arriving in Iraq in 2005, I lost someone in a situation that upset me badly. Being a senior manager, it was up to me to decide where the new guys would be posted to once they'd gone through induction. On Boxing Day, 26 December, two new men came to see me, both young ex-servicemen in their thirties. I sent one north to our bases at Buckmaster, an ordnance disposal camp east of Kirkuk which specialised in blowing up dangerous Iraqi ammunition. I sent the other to Umm Qasr. Six weeks later, the lad I sent to Buckmaster was killed by an IED. A single lad from the Parachute Regiment, he was the first man I'd deployed myself and it was my choice to send him there. I felt responsible for that. I made it my job to get his body back to Kuwait and then home. His was our first death of 2006 and I went to all the boys and the project managers and asked for money for a whip round; we raised around $4,000 for his family. My plan was to do that every time we lost someone, but within months the casualties came thick and fast and there was no way we could keep it up. We lost three in one convoy.

Under the guidance and friendship of my Country Director John Goreing, a former Major in the Paras, my unhappiest task was to deal with the recovery and repatriation of those who'd been killed and injured. My able Aussie deputy Cam Simpson, ex-Scots Guards, worked with me alongside the American and British military and our sister company in Kuwait. In the two years that I was there, I had to arrange the return of thirty-three men to their families. Most of them were killed along Route Irish or a similar road, Route Tampa. The surfaces of both were pocked with blast holes and the wreckage of charred vehicles. In the space of two months in 2005 alone there were fourteen bombs, almost fifty IEDs and over eighty attacks by small arms fire. Sixteen people died and scores more were injured.

Of the thirty-three men we lost during my tour, eighteen were Iraqis and the rest were expats, including Brits and

Aussies, New Zealanders, Fijians and a Gurkha. Many more were injured. Almost all were the victims of roadside explosions whilst driving or protecting convoys of goods, weapons and materials. The insurgents favoured crude bombs made from old artillery shells or shaped charges called EFPs (Explosively Formed Projectiles), whose devastation was astounding and deadly accurate.

Every time a convoy went out, we knew it was almost certainly going to be hit because they were often over a kilometre in length and necessarily slow. This gave the insurgents plenty of time to set up and pick off whichever lumbering vehicle they chose to target. The situation wasn't helped by rogue checkpoints where corrupt policemen telephoned ahead to let them know when a convoy was on its way.

After each new attack the convoy commander (or whoever else was able) would activate the 'Track24' panic button. This crisis management device sent a signal which sounded a loud alarm in the Ops room on our Victor Two base in Baghdad. As soon as we heard it we knew what to do, putting well-practised contingency plans into action. We'd make radio contact to try to confirm details of deaths or injuries, often listening as the convoy leader yelled something like, 'Two of our trucks have taken a direct hit! We have at least three men down. Repeat, three men down!' We'd hear their voices cracking across the airwaves and could only too easily picture the scene.

Once we knew exactly what we were dealing with, we'd liaise with our colleagues at the US Reconstruction Operations Centre (ROC) or Logistics Movement Control Centre

(LMCC), which would also have received the Track24 alarm. Between us, we'd coordinate whatever assistance was required. If they were able, the convoy commanders would bring the dead and injured back to the base. It was always a sombre task to have to identify those who'd lived and worked alongside us, and it wasn't always easy. It was my job to notify London immediately because news travelled fast and we didn't want families to learn accidently that they'd lost someone.

We'd arrange for the injured to be transported to the military hospital in the first instance and then, if they were non-Iraqis, to be taken by the US military to Landstuhl Regional Medical Centre in Germany where the company's welfare staff would be waiting for them. The dead would be flown to the mortuary at the US Camp Victory at Baghdad Airport. From there, the Americans would fly the bodies to Kuwait for us where ArmorGroup personnel would meet the coffins and prepare to fly them home. There'd be no solemn procession from military planes for these lads and no photograph of them on the national news. They'd been civilian 'guns for hire' in a foreign land. There weren't even any comprehensive statistics for how many non-military lives had been lost and their mourning was done privately.

The company insured us all heavily in the event of injury or death and the package was good, although I also kept up my military insurance. There were a few occasions when I thought Liz might need to use it but the closest up until Afghanistan was probably in December 2006 when I asked one of our drivers to take me to the US military compound

Camp Anaconda, about forty miles north of Baghdad. One of our armoured vehicles had been stolen from the compound and even though it had been badly damaged by an IED, the Ford F350 pick-up converted into a gun truck was probably salvageable. It was the day before I was due to go home for Christmas leave; I had no choice but to brave Route Tampa to interview the American military police about it.

On the way back down the main highway, we suddenly came under some heavy arms fire. Insurgents often lay in wait by the side of the road ready to take pot-shots at passing vehicles and that day it was our turn. There was suddenly a lot of noise as ammunition began to embed itself into our Land Cruiser (why do all my troubles start and end with Land Cruisers?). My adrenalin started pumping about the same time as the training and discipline kicked in. Grateful for my Kevlar vest, I watched as my driver kept his nerve, put his foot down and drove on through the hail of bullets.

I can remember sitting in the front seat as round after round thumped into the steel-plated passenger door inches away from where I was sitting and thinking, 'You cheeky buggers! I'm going on leave tomorrow!' It was only afterwards that we realised how lucky we'd been. The Land Cruiser looked like a colander, it had been hit so many times; the bullets had penetrated the skin but not the ballistic steel. I could so easily have been in the next coffin on my way to Camp Victory instead of packing my things to fly home to Liz and the kids. It was one of many occasions when I was thankful for proper armouring.

Four years later and I was in Tawqeef about to miss out on another much-anticipated home leave, only this time for a very different reason. Idris's release had come as a shock, and I was surprised by how much the thought of him walking free from the detention centre distressed me while I remained behind under lock and key.

Within a few days, there was an even greater shock when Sadir found me to tell me some news. 'Your friend is here,' he said.

'Idris is back?'

'No. A man named Maiwand. He arrived today.'

'Oh. Okay. Where is he?'

'He sleeps in the corridor on the other side of the court-yard.'

I wandered outside and scanned the milling crowd. Maiwand was sitting in a corner by the mosque talking to some others. He looked dishevelled and was sporting a beard. I walked purposefully over to him, held out my hand, and said, 'It's good to see you.' He looked up and, at first, refused to take it. With my hand still extended, though, he reluctantly got to his feet. We chatted for a while but the conversation was hard-going so I left him be.

Over the next few days, Maiwand's attitude gradually changed and before long he began to seek me out. He was angrier with Mark Spandler than he was with me, and blamed him for everything. I defended Mark unconditionally and reminded Maiwand that neither Mark nor I had done anything wrong. 'All we did was pay the NDS what it demanded.'

'We no pay the NDS,' he replied, coughing up a ball of phlegm.

'Of course we did. What do you mean?'

Maiwand then announced that Eidi Mohammad was not with the NDS at all but a private individual who'd offered himself as a guarantor. He said the NDS had released the vehicles for free, and that Eidi Mohammad had simply charged G4S $25,000 for the pleasure. 'We no pay bribe,' he added, flatly.

Stunned, I quickly rewound the incident in my head and recalled how Eidi had insisted I stay in my vehicle outside the compound gates while he and Maiwand went inside, past an NDS guard. 'Why did you tell us that he was NDS then?' I asked.

Maiwand insisted his explanation had been lost in translation, which was partially believable as none of us ever really understood him. Upset and angry at his announcement, I stayed out of his way as much as possible after that but it wasn't easy in such a small place.

Unfortunately, once Maiwand saw I was in a good cell with proper food, he began to hassle me to move in. 'No,' I told him. 'Our cell is already overcrowded. It isn't possible.'

Then, something happened that suddenly made it a possibility. On the morning of Wednesday, 17 March, Rob Langdon decided to have a shower. He put his soap and towel in the cubicle and went to get some hot water from the courtyard. While he was gone, a boy from No. 3 cell, who was from northern Afghanistan, wandered into the shower. When Rob returned, he went mad but the boy didn't understand so Rob manhandled him out and his bowl of hot water ended up all over the boy. The kid screamed and the prison guards rushed in. I heard the commotion but didn't know who was involved. Dr Hussein told me later what had happened. He tended to the boy's scalded legs and helped the guards carry him back to his cell.

Rob was handcuffed to a gate in the crucifix position. His feet could only just reach the ground and he was forced to stand like that for hours. Once everything had calmed down, I offered him some food but he turned his head away and wouldn't accept anything other than a sip of tea. 'Those f***ing Afghans! I hate the f***ing Afghans!' he kept saying.

'Sshhh!' I told him, 'Just keep quiet and play the game and then they'll forget all about it.' But he couldn't be subdued.

The mood in the detention centre that night was the blackest it had ever been. Blacker still in our cell. Everyone seemed disturbed by what had happened, especially because it involved Rob – who'd already murdered one Afghan, and now another lay injured. The guards eventually set Rob free around 23:00 hrs but then they made him sleep out in the corridor in handcuffs. One of the lads from our cell crept out and covered him with a blanket but I don't think he even noticed.

He was only allowed back inside just before dawn and went straight to bed. He ignored offers of breakfast so I told everyone to leave him alone. To help keep the peace, I visited the scalded lad with some chocolates although I winced when I saw his shin, which was blistering and red. I gave Dr Hussein pain pills and some dressings and hoped they might help. Tawqeef wasn't the kind of place you wanted an open wound.

Immediately after morning prayers, Rob's name came up on the PA system but he was asleep so Sadiqi shook him awake. 'Robert! Robert! They call you!' As he'd already been sentenced, this could only mean one thing – he was to be transferred to another prison. The guards never warned anyone if they were going to move them – they just called their names and they then had to muster themselves quickly, pull on a uniform and line up in the corridor. The whole thing usually happened within minutes.

A look of panic crossed Rob's face and he asked me to get Dr Hussein before the guards came for him. Sure enough, they arrived within minutes and gestured to Rob to go with them. He shook his head and Dr Hussein pleaded with them to let him stay. They were having none of it. 'They have a transfer order from the Commandant,' Dr Hussein said, shaking his head sadly. 'This cannot be changed.'

Rob asked quietly where he was being sent to. When they told him his face drained of all colour. The response was, 'Pol-e-Charkhi.' It was as if someone let the air out of him then. He slumped onto his bed, physically winded. The guards moved in and clamped handcuffs on his wrists. Then they shackled his ankles and wrists to the chains around his stomach. They urged him to hurry. When we complained that he couldn't pack like that they released one hand and we all pitched in to help. I pulled out a bag from under his bed and stuffed his iPod and charger into it. Despondently, he asked me to take out three letters he'd written and pass them on to his former colleagues if they came to visit.

'I will,' I promised. 'Good luck, mate.'

We watched in silence as the guards led Rob away, his chains clanking. It was a terrible sight. As I watched him go, I thought, 'Blooming heck! If that can happen to him, it could happen to me.' I never saw Rob again and nobody ever came to ask after him so I destroyed his letters.

An hour after he'd been transferred, the Commandant walked into our cell to ask the men what they thought of me. They told him, 'William is very good. William looks after us. William joins in.' Even the two mullahs said nice things about me apparently. The Commandant warned that if anyone caused any more trouble, I'd be sent straight to Pol-e-Charkhi too.

I shrank away from him physically and mentally at the thought.

Within a few hours, Maiwand sought me out in the courtyard, a big grin on his face. 'No. 1 cell no more full,' he said, defiantly. 'Now Maiwand come No. 1 cell.'

'No!' I said, a little too hastily. 'One of the men in our corridor will move in now. He's been waiting.' Maiwand looked at me with narrowing eyes before stalking off.

I hurried back to my cell and found Abdul Wakil. 'Please,' I told him through Sadiqi. 'If a man called Maiwand asks you to come to this room, tell him no. I cannot have him here.'

El Gordo patted my shoulder reassuringly. The last thing he wanted to do was upset me. I stored my food under his bed and soon discovered how well he deserved his nickname. In the early hours of the morning, I'd awake to hear him chomping on some biscuits or corned beef from a tin. In spite of his greed, he was good to me. Never more so than when he pointed to Rob's bed and said something.

'Abdul Wakil said you sleep there now,' Sadiqi translated happily. 'You are new best guest.'

I thanked him warmly. I'd recently inherited a pillow from another Afghan cellmate who'd been released. I moved it, my blanket and my sleeping bag to Rob's bed. I hoped the inch-thin mattress wasn't seething with lice as I was already scratching like hell all day, despite Mike's powder. I hung up my Afghan scarf as a makeshift curtain to dim the lights. Maybe now I could finally get some rest.

Better still, I had a letter from Lisa to read in response to one I'd written to her. 'Bear' started off by joking that I could retrain as a doctor with my handwriting. She told me not to be a *'soft, soppy sod'* by worrying about my fellow prisoners and made me laugh when she said she was struggling to get through my share of the wine back home. Then she brought a lump to my throat: *'We are all really proud of you for standing up to what was right in the first place, and also for not running away earlier. You are not the type of person who would have done that and that's why your kids are so proud of you. And one day, when the kids know about it all, they will have endless questions. Bit like POW stuff; you can embellish the details just like you did with your childhood Christmas stories . . . except this will be even more impressive!'*

The Commandant came back to our cell often to make sure there were no more conflicts. I came to the conclusion that, as prison governors go, he was all right. He had a lot of men to look after and a great deal of responsibility. It was he who'd set up the system of nominating cell leaders and he gathered them regularly to discuss conditions. Most of his guards were okay – if greedy – but the deputy commandant was a nasty piece of work; he was always on the make and Tawqeef would have been a very different place under his rule. The rest of the guards were scruffy and unshaven in their grey khaki uniforms, and wore anything from military boots to old flip-flops on their feet. Smoking and spitting constantly, they had one thing in common – they were a disgrace to their unit and would have been drummed out of my parade.

What I'm not sure the Commandant was fully aware of perhaps, was the level of violence within his walls – or maybe he just turned a blind eye. Most of the fights were over drugs, money or food. Every time one flared up, the guards would rush in. My training had always been that you only used violence as a last resort; when arresting someone, you restrained them as quickly as possible with minimal force. Having been trained in self-defence, I could handle most situations but even then hitting a prisoner wasn't an option. In Tawqeef, though, some of the guards had other ideas.

I regularly saw people being hit repeatedly with metre-long lengths of hosepipe, especially if they'd assaulted a guard. Once subdued, they'd be handcuffed to the gates of the courtyard and left there for hours in the favoured crucifix position. One young lad stayed chained to the gate for most of the day, every day. He came from a high-ranking family but had serious mental problems due to drugs. Daft as a seaside donkey, he was abusive and violent to everyone. He sang rude songs about the Commandant's wife and those of other guards.

After two or three attempts to get him under control, he'd be chained to the gate where he'd begin his abuse all over again. That's when he suffered the most. One or two of the guards lost it and really laid into him. Although I longed to intervene and tell them that this prisoner needed proper medical care, I couldn't. Instead, I blocked my ears against his screams and waited for the beating to end. Afterwards, he'd hang from the gate sobbing and then he'd shut up for a while, but before long he'd start up all over again. It was a vicious circle.

As I became increasingly familiar with the workings of Tawqeef, I began to notice something else that really bothered me. There seemed to be a disproportionate number of young boys coming in and out of room No. 2 – the *King Rat* cell – at all hours of the day and night. These were the skittish teenagers who mostly lived in cell No. 3. Some were as young as fifteen and all were desperately poor.

I'd never had any worries about being attacked sexually in Tawqeef because, as I understood it, the Afghan religion didn't allow for homosexuality, which was not only banned but punished severely. Because of the way the men behaved in not even showing their bodies, I felt safe. I thought I'd only be in trouble if a gang attacked me or one of the Taliban followed through on his threat to cut my throat. Talking to Habibullah, though, I was wrong to be complacent. I discovered that the Afghans believe that only the 'receiver' in a homosexual position is homosexual, not the 'giver'. So if the 'givers' in cell No. 2 wanted to amuse themselves with young boys they could – just as they got everything else they wanted. The idea of what might be going on in the adjacent room appalled and disgusted me. Is this what Rob had so feared about Pol-e-Charkhi?

I hoped not, because if I were to be convicted, that was where I was heading too.

Thirteen

I'd never forgotten the hunger strikes of convicted IRA members Frank Stagg and Bobby Sands in the late 70s and early 80s. There was such uproar about them at the time. When Stagg stopped eating, I'd just finished my first tour of Northern Ireland and was intrigued by what made the extremists tick. I'd read a great deal on the history of The Troubles in the hope of gaining greater insight into what might drive someone to set off a bomb in the middle of a busy high street. Although I believed there were good and bad on both sides, I still found it impossible to understand.

When Stagg and Sands became martyrs for the nationalist movement, it was difficult for people like me to understand the strength of feeling in support of men who'd been implicated in IRA plans to kill and maim. But the power of what they had done in refusing to eat – and the effect it had – never left me.

My decision to go on hunger strike if I was found guilty came to me out of the blue in those first few weeks in Tawqeef. It felt to me like the only thing I could do to make people sit up and take notice. I was increasingly worried about the time it was taking for Kim to arrange my first court appearance and although G4S was giving me support, I felt largely forgotten by the representatives of the country that I'd served.

The idea to do it first came to me after that initial visit

from British embassy staff. When others came with much the same message, I realised that their hands were tied. Wearily, I told them about the Sri Lankans in Tawqeef. 'If you can't do anything for me, can you at least see if you can help these poor buggers?' I asked. They confirmed that Britain looked after the interests of Sri Lankans in Afghanistan but had no idea they were there and promised to make sure they got proper representation from then on.

As I lay on Rob's wooden-slatted bed with its inch-thick mattress that was only marginally more comfortable than the floor, I mulled my situation over and over in my mind. I told myself that if my case was to go pear-shaped, then I'd stop eating until somebody listened to me. I was absolutely determined to go ahead with it; the only question was at what point I would start.

A few days later, Charlie Turnbull from G4S head office in London flew into Kabul to see me. He'd been speaking daily to Liz on the telephone and brought personal messages from family and friends. My mind was so focused on my situation, though, that all I could talk about was my case. 'I'm going to go on a hunger strike,' I told him suddenly. Charlie was visibly taken aback. 'It may be the only way to prove my innocence, or get somebody to intervene. I'm going to refuse all sustenance and go public if necessary. I can't think of what else I can do.'

Charlie did all he could to persuade me out of it but when he realised I was serious he asked, 'Promise me you'll take water and vitamins?'

'I'll only drink water and tea,' I replied, and decided to ask Mike the Medic how long I could survive without solid food.

Frank Stagg died after sixty-two days without food, and Sands after sixty-six. In Tawqeef, I worked it out in my head. Sixty-odd days from that point would take me to the middle of May, three weeks after my fifty-second birthday on 25 April. I wondered where I'd be then, and how I'd be celebrating my fifty-third birthday. If it was in Pol-e-Charkhi then I might as well starve myself to death.

So as not to upset the family, I decided that I wouldn't begin my hunger strike until after my trial and any subsequent appeal. Lisa's birthday was in June – the same day my sister Betty was due to get married, with me giving her away. The boys' birthdays were in September and January. Liz's birthday was at the end of September. We'd always made such a big deal out of family celebrations after the crap ones I'd had as a kid and I didn't want anything to ruin their special days. Then I realised that having me locked up for no reason in a prison three thousand miles away would probably spoil everything anyway.

My eldest son Craig sent me a letter via Charlie and was clearly struggling. In what was to become the first of a weekly missive to his 'Daddio', my twenty-seven-year-old son wrote, '*This whole situation seems so surreal I simply cannot believe it . . . The hardest thing is the waiting game, but try and stay strong . . . We are thinking of you every minute of every day and I am dreaming of the day the call comes to say you are finally on your way home . . . we are so proud of the sacrifices you have made to provide for us all. Love you millions and always xxxx*'

Charlie came back to see me two days later and was accompanied by David de Stacpoole, the G4S senior manager in London who deals directly with the FCO and knew the British Ambassador personally. I'd known David for many years and he was a quiet, proficient operator who told me he'd assure the ambassador of my innocence, integrity and unblemished service record. I was very glad he was on board. The two men told me that all Kim needed now was a letter from the NDS to endorse what Maiwand had said about Eidi Mohammad. 'If the man we paid the money to wasn't a government official, then no bribe could have taken place,' Charlie said. 'G4S was simply tricked out of $25,000 by a private individual and the case against you should be dropped.'

Kevin was my rock and came to see me as often as he could. Even though each visit lasted only fifteen minutes or so, he said, 'I told the Commandant I needed to come this frequently to check on your mental state.' We both laughed at that, but as the time went on I became more irrational and increasingly repetitive so there was some truth in what he'd said. Dear Kev definitely saw me at my lowest points – not that he ever told Liz.

'Tell her I'm doing great,' I made him promise each time. 'Tell her that I'm healthy, eating loads and sleeping well. Make sure she believes I'm in good spirits, OK?'

What I didn't know was that Kev was keeping as much from me as he was from Liz. It wasn't until much later that I found out she didn't even tell the children of my arrest for the first week for fear of worrying them unduly. When she realised I wasn't coming straight home, she arranged for friends in the military to inform each of them personally as she didn't want them to hear news like that over the telephone. She'd deliberately kept the rest of my family in the dark until she knew that it would be in the newspapers. It was so typical of my 'Lily' to worry about everyone else before herself.

Our daughter had definitely inherited her mother's fortitude and decided that her role was to keep my spirits up with jokey letters from home. She dubbed me '*Prisoner, Cell Block H*' and told me that if I went on hunger strike, she and Liz had decided to as well, to show solidarity. That really shocked me but then Bear added, '*Then so would every other bugger and we would resemble Ethiopians campaigning for food not freedom!*' which made me laugh. Maybe the hunger strike wasn't such a good idea after all.

The date of my hearing came through at last, almost three weeks after my arrest. Kim came to tell me that Maiwand and I would be attending court together on Monday, 22 March. She'd been to see the judge, a man named Abdul Farooqi, and she said he seemed sympathetic. Kev had also visited the judge to assure him of my innocence. 'Every time I go he offers me some *chai* and those sickly sweet Afghan cakes which I have to accept out of politeness. Kim's eaten her way through her fair share on your behalf as well!'

I was elated to finally have a date, and so soon. I knew from my fellow inmates that strings must have been pulled because few others had been seen so quickly. Buoyant, I hoped that this was a good omen. Liz sent me a letter as soon as she heard, calling me her 'beautiful man', which cut me to the quick. '*This has to be positive!!*' she wrote. '*At least it gets things moving. If it doesn't go your way, sweetheart, don't be too disheartened as that may happen first off but play the game and you will be home where you belong very soon . . . You are in my thoughts, dreams and every heartbeat so stay strong. Love always . . . and forever.*'

The weekend crawled by so slowly and my nights were

Betty and me in our new clothes for Whit Weekend, Salford, 1961

Young army cadet, Eccles detachment, aged fourteen (*front left*)

Our wedding day, Leeds, 21 May 1977

Keen as mustard in front of a truck in Lurgan, Northern Ireland, 1980

Armed and Proud

Royal Military Academy Sandhurst, with HESH the dog, April 1990

On patrol with a colleague in Armagh

In Hong Kong with my RMP colleagues, 1981

In the army combats I'd always wanted to wear

With my military police recruits in Malawi, 1996

Receiving my MBE from the Queen, 1996

Meeting then Prime Minister Tony Blair in Iraq in the Second Gulf War

With 1 Platoon at Safwan Police Station, Iraq, at the end of the Second Gulf War, June 2003

BritMil on the move in the desert

All in a day's work for private security contractors

A blown-up ArmorGroup 4x4 on Route Tampa, Iraq, 2006

free
Bill Shaw
MBE

22nd May 2010

Dear Queen Elizabeth,

I am writing a letter to you to ask you to try and free my Pop (Bill Shaw). My Pop has already been in prison in Afghanistan for 3 months. He will have to stay there for 2 years and that is too long. He is a very good man and is innocent.

We miss him so much. You once gave him a Medal (MBE) and he was so proud.

Yours sincerely,

Madeleine Luckyn-Malone

(Aged 7 years)

'Free Bill Shaw' campaign poster used on Facebook and across the UK

'Moo''s letter to the Queen

Facing trial, July 2010

In court with Maiwand

Drawing by Madeleine for the 'Free Bill Shaw' campaign

Tawqeef with Rob Langdon and some Afghan cellmates

'Lily' and 'Bear' on the sofa at *GMTV* with Andrew Castle and Emma Crosby

Back in Dover with my family: (*left to right*) Craig, Lisa, Caius, Madeleine, Liz and Lewis

'Pop' is finally reunited with 'Moo' and 'Chunky Monkey'

fitful. Long before the dawn on Monday I gave up on sleep altogether. Getting up, I made an extra effort with my ablutions, washed and combed my hair, and shaved my greying stubble as best I could without a mirror. Then I pulled on a prison uniform borrowed from a cellmate. As I waited to be called I was too anxious to face breakfast. I sipped some tea instead and momentarily regretted the fact that I'd never been a smoker. My parents had always smoked one after the other and I'd tried it when I was ten and hated it, but at least a cigarette might have calmed my nerves.

As the hours passed, I became increasingly agitated. Had the judge changed his mind? Was there a problem? Why didn't someone explain what was going on? Eventually, Maiwand came to tell me that the prison staff had forgotten to arrange our transportation to the court and our hearing had been rescheduled for the following day. I was gutted. Kim told me later that they'd all been waiting at the court, wondering where I was. The only good news – if it could be described as that – was that the Prosecutor had failed to appear also so even if I'd got there, I'd have been sent straight back to my cell. What an almighty Afghan cock-up!

The following morning, I went through the same rituals and pulled my prison uniform over my tracksuit. My cellmates made sure I had a clean one this time. When my name was called they came forward to pat me on the back and gesture good luck, their hands held in prayer. Outside in the corridor, I had to stand side by side with Maiwand as we were shackled together at the ankle. The cuffs were rusty and old and would have chafed if I hadn't been wearing socks. A three-metre long chain was then wrapped around my stomach and secured at the front. With final indignity, handcuffs were snapped onto my wrists and secured to a ring on my stomach chain. This meant I couldn't move my hands in any direction more than an inch. I couldn't scratch my nose or smooth down my hair; I couldn't do a bloody thing. The whole process felt unnecessarily cruel and medieval.

Taking several deep breaths I tried not to think how I must look. I had to stand stock still and look straight ahead just to get my head around it. In all my years as a military policeman, I'd only ever handcuffed one prisoner – a huge corporal from the Queen's Own Highlanders in Hong Kong who was so aggressive after a fight in a disco there was no other way to restrain him. Now, here I was – looking like some character from a Dickensian gaol – about to discover my fate.

In a kind of nightmarish three-legged race Maiwand and I hobbled painfully along the corridor and out through the main gate. It was almost impossible to walk because of the chains which rubbed and bruised with every step. Once we'd negotiated narrow passageways and restricted doorways we climbed sideways onto a rickety 14-seater minibus. The vehicle was old and decrepit with ripped seats. Its floor was filthy and littered with the usual unpleasantness. Its suspension shot, it lurched and jerked out through the gates of the prison compound and then into every pothole. I'd only ever driven around Kabul in 4x4s with wrap-around armour-plating before and it felt strange being in a soft-skinned vehicle without my body armour. I felt almost naked.

The weather was dry and cool but the traffic was dense. It was peculiar to see people, cars and animals. Even the once-familiar sight of rusting Russian tanks, stripped to the bone, seemed an oddity. Through grimy windows I watched 4x4s whizzing past on government business and diplomatic vehicles driving into secure compounds. Just a few weeks before, I'd been among their number, my freedom taken for granted. Now, I couldn't help but stare at the mountains or feast my eyes on the expanse of sky dotted with clouds. I watched planes taking off from the airport and military helicopters flying in low. Starved of visual input for weeks, I gorged on as much colour and vibrancy as I could. Looking up, I spotted an eagle with an enormous wingspan circling overhead. Or was it a vulture? Kabul had an abundance of both and from that distance I couldn't tell.

Having negotiated through the usual rivers of sewage and around potholes almost big enough to swallow our bus, we slowed in a street alongside a market. The officer in charge of our bus didn't seem to know where he was going and kept arguing with the driver. Pulling up at the entrance to a gated compound, we were ordered off. Getting out, we struggled once again to walk the hundred metres or so to a dilapidated government building. I found that if I leaned against Maiwand slightly and rocked from side to side, I could creep forward less cumbersomely. I was relieved that there were no waiting media, as I'd feared there might be. Kim had already fielded several requests for information and had warned me there'd be interest. The last thing I wanted was for my family to see me looking like this.

As we stepped into the building, we were greeted by a bemused janitor lazily sweeping an empty lobby. We were in the wrong place. As I watched the guards scratch their heads and make a phone call on an ancient mobile phone, I was overcome by frustration and anger. I was so keyed up that I thought I might vomit. Even when we got back onto the bus it was clear that no one had any idea where they should take us. Maiwand explained that we were going to a new court and no one knew the address. 'My father and cousin wait there. I call for way,' he said. The driver still got lost and had to keep doubling back as Maiwand remained on the guard's mobile phone being talked in. Fighting to hold myself together, I feared the worst. We hadn't turned up the previous day and now we were two hours late. What if the judge cancelled the hearing? I couldn't go through all this again.

After what seemed like hours more, we finally arrived at a walled villa close to the British embassy. It was part of the new anti-corruption court paid for, refurbished and furnished by the British taxpayer. To my horror, I spotted dozens of reporters and TV cameras along with many of my Afghan and Western colleagues and friends who'd come to give me moral support. I was embarrassed and overwhelmed by the turnout.

I have never been more humiliated in my life as when I had to stagger the thirty metres along that narrow pathway, running the gauntlet of lenses and microphones. Shackled hand and foot, lice-ridden and emaciated, I kept my head down and not just because the TV lights dazzled me. What would Liz think if she saw me like this? And my kids? What if my grandchildren saw their 'Pop' in chains? I wanted the red Afghan dirt to open up and swallow me whole.

I only relaxed a little once we were in the relative sanctuary of the court. In a small waiting room with Kim, Kevin and

Maiwand's lawyer, the guard unlocked our handcuffs but not our leg shackles. I rubbed my wrists and tried to shake some of the tension out of my arms as a cheerful Kim told me, 'I'm quietly confident that this will be sorted today because there really is no case to answer here.' I nodded my thanks but didn't want to say anything that might tempt Fate.

Maiwand and I were taken up a marble staircase to what was a former bedroom in the villa. We were led in first and a prison guard sat directly behind us in case we tried to escape. The media crowded in after us but, thankfully, no cameras were allowed. There were so many people in that small room that the judge – sitting with two others – opened by apologising for the lack of seats.

Our case was called – Number 79 – and Mr Ghafory stood up and read the indictment against us, which seemed to go on forever. Without my own interpreter I couldn't understand a word so I leaned over and listened to Kim's whenever I could, hoping that she'd tell me anything important that I'd missed. When the Prosecutor had finished, the judge invited Maiwand's lawyer to speak. Maiwand, too, spoke at length but he argued incessantly with the judge, which I didn't think would help his case. His father kept jumping up and down in the back of the court as well. All the while, Mr Ghafory took call after call on his mobile phone, even after the judge told him not to. It was a madhouse.

Finally, it was Kim's turn. 'The NDS has now confirmed that no money was paid to any official which means that there are no material elements for the crime of bribery under the rules of the Constitution of Afghanistan and your own Penal Code,' she told the court. 'The Prosecutor has failed to produce one material witness, and the evidence offered falls short morally, legally and materially.' To my surprise, the judge appeared to agree with her and concede that if no bribe had taken place then we had to be presumed innocent. I listened hopefully to the exchanges but was never invited to speak.

Mr Ghafory finally got off the phone and stood with a kind of world-weariness to be informed by the judge that Eidi Mohammad had run away. He claimed that we had produced no witnesses to confirm that we'd been cheated and concluded that as we were the only remaining defendants, the legal presumption had to be that we were guilty. Then he sat down and took another call.

There seemed to be much confusion then, with everyone speaking at once. Both Kim and I strained to hear the translation. As I sat in the middle of that madhouse, I felt the atmosphere shift. The judge stopped agreeing with Kim and then he asked for more evidence from the NDS. When she objected the judge was unexpectedly sharp with her and agreed to give the Prosecutor another week. I could feel my anger rising, not least because Mr Ghafory was taking telephone calls again. Everything seemed so unprofessional and haphazard. I wanted to jump up and activate some metaphorical kill switch so that I could freeze time for a few minutes to make them pay attention.

'Shut up, all of you!' I longed to yell. 'Sit quietly and pay very close attention here. This is my future you're deciding on!'

Sadly, there was no kill switch, and before I knew what was happening, the judge had refused Kim's application to grant me bail even though she offered herself as a guarantor.

The hearing would reconvene in a week. It was all over so suddenly. Dazed, I was ushered through the throng of journalists calling out, 'How do you feel, Mr Shaw?' as if they could have broadcast my answer.

Behind closed doors, Kim vented her frustration. 'This is absurd!' she cried. 'Don't worry. I'll push the Prosecutor daily to make sure he follows through on this latest evidence.' Seeing my expression, she added more softly, 'I know this isn't what we wanted but it shouldn't be much longer now, okay?'

I was going back to prison. That was all I could think of. 'How much longer?' I asked her, close to losing it. 'A week? A month? A year!?'

Kev placed a steadying hand on my shoulder. He had his telephone with him and the guards let me make a quick call home. Liz was sitting by the phone for news, and we were both emotional but I tried to sound positive. 'I'm fine, luv. Yes, really. The court's been adjourned for a week so that they can confirm some details, that's all.' I could tell she was expecting better news, but I reassured her that once the latest letter from the NDS was received, I'd be out. 'Just one more week, darling,' I said, trying to keep my voice steady. 'We can manage another week, eh?' We bid farewell with our usual '*Tschüss!*' before I handed the phone back to Kev and crumbled.

All the way across Kabul, still shackled to Maiwand, my head thumped painfully. It wasn't helped by the fact that he wouldn't shut up about the case and insisted that he'd get transferred to my cell so that he could persuade me to change my story to match his. I was so upset I could hardly speak but eventually I snapped, 'Shut up, Maiwand! I won't change my story. I *cannot* because I am telling the truth.'

Back in Tawqeef, everyone in my cell rushed forward, keen to know how I'd got on. When I told them they cried, 'William free next week! William go home!' I smiled at their optimism, but didn't dare believe it.

I was out into the courtyard trying to gather my thoughts when Sadiqi came rushing out. 'William on the TV!' he said, grinning. 'We saw you arrive at the court.' My spirits sank. If I was on the Kabul news then the chances were those images were beamed back to Europe. I was so ashamed that friends, family and military friends might have seen me. What about the men and women I'd commanded over the years, and my officer cadets at Sandhurst? What would my former commanding officers think? I felt weighed down by the shame I'd brought on them all and on the good name of the RMP. Sadiqi saw how upset I was but could say nothing to help. Despite having been held in such high esteem for so many years, I feared that people with no understanding of the corruption in Afghanistan might interpret my arrest the wrong way.

Wracked with guilt, I went to my new bed space, drew my 'curtain' and stayed there for the rest of that night. Switching on my iPod, I listened to Steve Harley's album *More Than Somewhat* in the hope of blocking out my worries about the day. The song that really got to me, though, had the line, '*The last time I saw you my eyes were red from constant crying. Blue moon was at my door. The leaping of my ransomed heart said trees can weep and stone can bleed. . .*'

I may have been a tough British soldier, but I have to admit that just about finished off this ransomed heart for good.

Fourteen

Wherever we lived – home or abroad – we tried to give our children as normal a life as possible within the military community whilst encouraging them to experience different cultures. They attended British schools and, once they were older, went to boarding schools in the UK to give them some continuity.

As a family it was probably hardest when we were in Germany from 1984–8 and again from 1990–3. While I was kept busy on military exercises and sorting everything from policing the troops to the death of a drunken soldier who fell from a window and the tragic suicide of a young army wife, Liz and the kids lived on the base. While they settled into life in a country where they didn't speak the language, I learned how to be a better soldier through the help and advice of my mentor there, the late Colonel David Wonson, CBE, who commanded me at 1BR Corps in Bielefeld Germany. Having originally told me he didn't want a 'drill-pig straight from depot', we became firm friends and he was the best officer I ever had the privilege of being commanded by.

We needed good commanders more than ever at that difficult time. The IRA were very active in Europe and we always felt we stuck out like sore thumbs whenever we went out anywhere in our BFG (British Forces Germany) plated right-hand drive vehicles. In May 1988, three British airmen were killed and three others injured in drive-by shootings near the German-Dutch border. On 9 July 1989, the IRA shot dead the German wife of a British soldier while she sat in a parked car in Dortmund. Then in October that year, a British airman and his baby daughter were killed by the IRA in Monchengladbach.

The shootings didn't stop. The following year, two Australian tourists driving in a UK-registered car were mistaken for off-duty British service personnel and shot dead in the centre of Roermond. Then five days later, Major Michael Dillon-Lee and his wife were ambushed as they arrived home from a party near their base at Dortmund. The 35-year-old Major was a battery commander of the Royal Artillery and had just got back to his quarters in the barracks when a gunman in a balaclava opened fire after shouting an Irish battle cry. He was buried in the Joint HQ at Rheindahlen where we were later based.

After that, the rules of engagement changed. The system of vehicle number-plates was changed to make them less obvious. We in the RMP were also allowed to carry pistols off base whilst on duty. I still felt so helpless with no means of protecting my loved ones. We were living inside the wire but the garrison was full of civilians (just as Lisburn had been) and we were open targets. A bomb planted in or under a car would kill whoever was in the driving seat, whether or not the kids were on board, so we always searched thoroughly as a matter of course.

'You're not to be frightened but there are some bad people sometimes who want to do bad things, so we have to be vigilant all the time,' I'd tell Lisa, the only one old enough to understand. I roped her in with games; giving her what I called a 'team task'. She'd take the ubiquitous mirror fixed to the end of a long pole which came with every Army house and check under the car after I'd already searched thoroughly. 'Remember, we're looking for anything that doesn't belong there – you know, like when one of the boys hides a toy car in one of your shoes,' I'd tell her, trying to keep it light. Even so, I noticed in the rear view mirror that she always held her breath every time the key was turned in the ignition – just in case she'd missed something.

It wasn't only the children who had to learn vigilance; many of my junior staff needed to be reminded too. Maybe it was because I'd begun my military career in the dangerous territory of Armagh but wherever I was posted, I always made a point of checking security awareness and orientating myself to the local area. In Rheindahlen, just a few miles from Roermond where the IRA had already been active, I went out on an armed patrol with one of my corporals one night.

'Drive as you would normally and perform your usual duties,' I told him. It was obvious to me as the journey progressed that he had become completely complacent and was a liability. He drove too fast, which meant that he could not take in any intelligence. His eyes were fixed on the road ahead and barely noticed what was happening on the streets. I waited to see what he'd do when he pulled up at traffic lights, and sure enough he stopped immediately behind a bus.

'Can you see a problem with this, Corporal?' I asked him but he just looked at me blankly. 'Situational awareness is everything. You now cannot see the road ahead and are blind both left and right. You have left our vehicle blocked in with no escape route. This is the exactly the scenario needed for a classic ambush used at least twice in Europe by the IRA – in Munster against two RMP NCOs and in Belgium when they killed an Infantry RSM at traffic lights.'

'Sorry, Sir,' came the reply.

'If you switch off mentally like this and leave yourself vulnerable you could not only end up a dead man but put your passengers at risk too.' Without raising my voice, I asked, 'Is there any particular reason you have such poor security drills?'

'I never really thought about it before, Sir,' he replied. 'It's not something I've been taught.'

'Well, from now on, you need to pay attention to everyone and everything and think of every eventuality. Now let's go around again and see how you do this time.' We spent the next two hours patrolling as I offered my guidance and the corporal couldn't believe how much he noticed when the journey had previously passed in a blur. 'Thank you, Sir!' he told me afterwards. He never forgot that night and mentioned it for a long time afterwards. Word quickly spread and I assessed every driver in the same way until I was sure they were up to the task.

It wasn't just Germany where we had to be careful. Liz and I were woken in the middle of the night at Sandhurst once by loud hammering on the front door. 'Staff Sergeant Shaw! Staff Sergeant Shaw, Sir! We need to evacuate the area,' one of my men was shouting. A suspicious package had been found and we had to carry the children in their nightwear to the garrison gym. They were scared at first as we waited for a security sweep to be done of some nearby garages, but they were soon distracted by the offer of biscuits and squash. This level of security became their way of life, but there were many sleepless nights when I worried what I was risking by having my precious family with me.

Now they were grown and should have been past all that and yet I had ended up in a place that brought new fears for us all. My guilt at what I was putting them through corkscrewed into my guts, robbing me of any mental peace. The day after my disastrous court hearing, Kev and Charlie came to see me and did all they could to boost my morale. 'A short adjournment isn't that unusual,' Kev told me cheerfully. 'It'll all be sorted next week, mate. You'll see.'

I wanted to believe them, but I wasn't so sure. In a letter they gave me from Lisa, the message was much the same. She wrote, '*It seems you have grown attached to that place and keep returning!*' Bear's letters to her 'Popsicle' always made me laugh, even at my darkest moments. She'd tell me to whistle the music from *The Great Escape* or she'd make out I was secretly lounging by the infinity pool at the Dubai Hilton and ask me how my 'holiday' was going. She might sign off by telling me she was off to bed shortly – '*you know, that big, squishy, comfy warm thing – not forgetting those fluffy pillows!*' She warned me I had to be out by April the first, so that we could continue with our 'Pinch, Punch' competition. If I wasn't free by then for any reason, she said she'd 'allow' me to be the winner for May 'out of sympathy', which made me laugh for the first time in days.

Her letter included a copy of an article about me in *The Times* and various comments people had added to the online version. Reading through them, I was gobsmacked. David Hurst was an RMP Instructor I'd served with in

Chichester in the early 80s. He wrote, '*I have the honour to have known Bill, although we last met many years ago. My thoughts are with you. You epitomised our motto, Exemplo Ducemus, to the full.*'

Liam Docherty, one of my recruits back then, wrote, '*Bill Shaw is one of the finest soldiers I have ever had the fortune to serve with. He was my Squad Sgt in '83 and there is not a corrupt bone in his body. He led by example then as now.*'

A former colleague and friend, Colonel Séan Harris, who was in one of my companies and with whom I later served in Cyprus and the Second Gulf War, wrote, '*I was taught at the Royal Military Academy Sandhurst by this officer and he was outstanding. I subsequently witnessed him serving in Iraq where he retained the highest standards expected of a British Army officer . . . The truth will out Bill – remain strong.*'

There were several more including one from a corporal I'd worked with in Germany called Les Wallwork who wrote, '*I worked for this outstanding man when I was also a Military Policeman. I only give credit where credit is due; Billy Shaw is one of the finest and most honourable men I ever knew in 22 years of serving with the military police. He rose from private to major, no easy feat.*'

I was deeply moved by all their comments and immensely grateful to Bear for sending them. It was amazing to me that people took the time to write or were even interested in what was happening to me. Their words of comfort made me feel far less isolated and I knew they would also have given the family encouragement and hope. I felt humbled.

A couple of days after my hearing, I was in the courtyard doing my exercises and trying to remain positive. Being in prison was beginning to wear me down, though, especially the filth, the vermin and the lack of a decent night's sleep. I wanted a piping hot shower and a home-cooked meal washed down with a pint of Spitfire beer or a glass of red wine. I longed to talk to someone in English in a quiet room and for more than fifteen minutes at a time. I wanted clean clothes and comfy shoes and a soft, warm bed at night.

The Commandant suddenly stood in my path, shaking me from my internal rant. He was clearly perturbed and summoned Maiwand over to translate. Through an interpreter, he said that he'd just learned that I was being transferred to another prison and added that he was very disappointed.

'What?' I cried. 'But I haven't asked for this and I don't want to go to another prison!'

I'm not sure he believed me. 'It is agreed,' Maiwand said. 'Your embassy arrange you a place better safe.' The Commandant sneered as he said something and Maiwand translated – 'Run by Americans.' I was to be transferred there in two days, on a Sunday.

The thought of leaving Tawqeef – stinky toilets and all – suddenly horrified me. It was a pit of a place but at least I was relatively safe with my cellmates and the mullahs. There were only a few days to go before my next court case and, hopefully, freedom. I had a routine and I'd rather stay with what I knew than begin again somewhere new.

The following morning, just before lunch, I was summoned to the Commandant's office. I hoped he might have some better news for me, but I was met instead by Jan Everleigh from the embassy. To my surprise, she was accompanied by Kim, Kevin, Charlie Turnbull and Mike the Medic, plus two of our company interpreters. The sight of all of them in that small room made me nervous. The Commandant glumly showed me my transfer slip as Jan told me that the embassy had written to the Minister of Justice himself to have me moved to a more secure location after reports of threats to my life.

'But I haven't complained about any threats,' I protested. It was true; I could take care of myself and I'd never wanted to appear a whingeing Westerner who expected special treatment. The 'complaint' had apparently come from the Afghan who'd been released and given me his pillow. He'd gone to G4S and told them that my life was in serious danger from the Taliban. It was this intelligence that had been relayed to the British embassy.

Turning to Kev, I asked, 'Did you know about this?'

'Not until a couple of hours ago mate.'

'It is for your own security, Bill,' Kim said, sensing my hostility. 'We've been asking the FCO to help you and they've made all the arrangements.'

'It should only be for a few days until your hearing anyway,' Kev added. 'And it's got to be better than this dump.' Fortunately, that wasn't translated for the Commandant.

'Well, where is this prison?' I asked. Jan said it was called the Counter-Narcotics Justice Centre (CNJC), a brand new American-built facility near Kabul International Airport.

'Have you been?' I asked.

She admitted she hadn't.

'Has *anyone* been to visit this place properly and checked on the conditions?' I asked. 'How do you know it's safer than here?'

Kim explained that as the CNJC had been open for less than a year few outsiders had yet been inside. She reassured me that it was an $11 million state-of the-art facility built by US Army engineers that would eventually house more than two hundred drugs traffickers, two to a cell. 'I know some of the American mentors who work there from the Justice Programme and they're good guys.'

I wasn't so sure, but with the deal done and the transfer slip issued I realised that I didn't have a say. Once again, events were running beyond my control.

'Two to a cell,' Kev said, trying to lift my mood. 'That'll be a luxury!'

That depended very much on my cellmate, I thought, but I didn't want to burst his bubble.

The guards allowed me to go to my cell and quickly grab a few of my most precious things to give to Kev for temporary safekeeping. I wasn't sure yet how much I'd be allowed to take into CNJC and I didn't want letters or photographs confiscated.

When I explained to my cellmates that I was leaving their distress was genuine. The mullahs even led a prayer for me. Afterwards, I sat in the meal circle with them and reflected how different things could have been if I'd been placed in another cell. Even though I'd been desperate to get out of Tawqeef that was only because I wanted to go home – not to another prison.

I fully expected that I'd have the rest of that day to pack up my belongings but two guards suddenly appeared to inform me that I was being transferred immediately. I was shocked but then realised that the Commandant had probably ordered it in a fit of pique. The way he saw things, my transfer implied the British embassy didn't believe he'd done a good enough job taking care of me.

With the guards standing over me, I stuffed the rest of my kit into a bag, gave away most of my food and bade a hasty farewell to Assam and Sadiqi, Abdul Wakil, Ali and the rest. In the unseemly rush there was no chance to nip out to say goodbye to my courtyard friends and I hoped they'd understand. Shackled hand and foot, I was led outside to shuffle down an empty corridor. Sitting in the back of the old minibus on my own, I didn't know what to expect at CNJC. I've always been a man of precision and planning. I am punctual to a fault. I like to recce a place before I visit it, and I don't enjoy surprises.

To my dismay, the first surprise was the sight of the deputy commandant, who suddenly appeared in the doorway of the bus, stepped on and sat down next to me. As soon as it lurched off, he became extremely intimidating in demanding money. 'Dollar!' he said, his open palm flapping under my nose. 'Dollar! Me! Give!' I shook my head firmly and told him I had none but he kept pointing to the pocket of my tracksuit. 'Dollar. Need. Pay my phone.'

After more than an hour of his relentless nudging, shouting, gestures and pointing, I finally reached into my pocket and gave him $6. 'Here's the bloody money!' I snapped. He was clearly insulted and demanded more but I ignored him until he finally shut up.

As before, I couldn't get over the amount of noise, dust, people and traffic thronging all around as the bus thumped into every pothole and the driver – one foot up on the dashboard – lent permanently on his horn. Our route via the back streets to avoid the worst of the traffic took over an hour and when we finally arrived at CNJC, I felt exhausted by events.

The Counter-Narcotic Justice Centre consisted of a series of brand new low-rise buildings which I later discovered also housed courtrooms and offices for the Criminal Justice Task Force. Looking around, I realised that I'd been there before, when G4S provided the guards whilst it was being built. 'Right then,' I told myself. 'Let's get on with it.' We pulled up in front of the compound and I had to shuffle about two hundred metres through a series of high gates topped with barbed wire and then across a courtyard to the Commandant's office. I waited in the corridor while the deputy commandant went in to meet him, and then I was invited inside. My new prison governor stood up, shook my hand, and gestured for me to sit. I sat in full chains for almost half an hour while the two men drank tea and chatted. All I wanted to do was get to my cell and face whatever new challenges lay ahead. Tapping my foot, I fought to remain calm.

Eventually the Commandant sifted through my paperwork but – even without an interpreter – I could tell something was wrong. There was no photograph of me attached to any of the documents. Without it, the Commandant announced gravely, I could not be accepted as an inmate. To my deep dismay, I was led back to the dreaded bus and returned to Tawqeef. The deputy commandant sat a few seats away, glaring at me in open enmity.

Everyone in my cell was so surprised to see me. Sadiqi was

lying on my bed, which El Gordo had already allocated him but he jumped up immediately and offered it back to me.

'No, I'll sleep on the floor!' I said, but he insisted I get it back for one night.

My short reprieve at least gave me time to say goodbye properly. Sifting through my kit, I grabbed some money and a few tins of corned beef and wandered out into the courtyard. Having said farewell to Habibullah and Sadir, I sought out the Sri Lankans, who were delighted to see me.

'Mr Bill! We thought you had left!' they cried. 'They said you go without goodbye.'

I explained what had happened, gave them $50 and some Afghan money, plus a few tins of food, my bobble hat, a fleecy top, a spare tracksuit and some clean underwear. It was March, cold and wet, and they wore only rags or thin clothing under their sleeping blankets which they draped permanently around their shoulders. I had them write down all their names, addresses and passport numbers so that I could give them to the British embassy staff the next time I saw them. I worried how they'd cope without me topping up their rations.

The following morning, Sunday, 28 March, the guards came for me again and demanded that I give them a photo-graph. 'I don't bloody have one!' I told them. After an hour of waiting around, the deputy commandant turned up with the prison camera to take a suitable picture. I resisted the urge to give him a cheesy grin. Nor was I smiling when he insisted I pay him 300 Afghanis for the privilege.

The bus driver took a different route this time, presumably for security reasons, and instead of the back roads we kept to the main highways. I was preoccupied with watching all the activity at first but then I began to recognise landmarks. There was a roundabout I was familiar with, and an embassy we guarded. We passed a Supreme supermarket that Azim sometimes used and I spotted the gates to an American depot.

Before I knew it, the bus had turned onto Route Violent – the Jalalabad Road – and was heading out towards the airport. I almost laughed. Dressed in prison garb and manacled, I was being driven past the very place where my troubles began all those months earlier when I was still a free man. Straining to see through the windows, I found just the spot. There, by a row of old sea containers. That was where an NDS commander out of his head on hashish had opened fire on us. This was the place and the moment that led me to become an innocent victim of a corrupt system. I couldn't have made it up if I'd tried.

At CNJC, I knew the score and lumbered out of the bus and across the courtyard to the Commandant's office. This time, though, I was formally admitted and escorted down a series of long corridors to the cells. My first impression was how incredibly clean everything was after Tawqeef. Even the air smelt clean – a novelty for my nostrils. But it was also completely sterile; equipped with nothing but the basics. The deeper into the building I was taken, the more overheated and airless it became. The walls were battleship grey and the floors squeaked as you walked on them. The whole place had the feeling of a hospital or some sort of mental institution. Maybe that wasn't so far from the truth.

I was led to a prison wing which comprised a central corridor with fourteen cells, seven down each side. There was a floor to ceiling grille at the front of every cell clad in heavy mesh, which gave them the appearance of animal cages. Each of these was approximately three by two metres with two bunk-beds screwed to the walls, one above the other. At the back below two high 'arrow-slit' windows with thick double glazing were a toilet and a sink. As I walked past all the other cages I could see that two men occupied each but I deliberately kept my head down and didn't peer in.

Accompanied by an officer I dubbed 'The Quartermaster', I was taken to the last cell on the right – No. 7 – in which a young bearded Afghan was lying on the lower bunk in a brown prison *shalwar kameez*. On the guards' instruction, he stood up, lifted the striped mattress off the top bunk and threw it onto the floor. Looking up, I realised that no one could sleep in the top bunk because it was too close to the ceiling and the two 150-watt fluorescent lights covered in a metal grate.

The guards handed me a blanket, a sheet and a flat pillow before nudging me into the cell. Then they slammed the door shut behind me. Surprised, I spun round and asked for my bag. No one understood so I pointed and made gestures but they refused to let me have it, much to my distress.

'No!' I cried. 'Mr William needs bag!'

They ignored me and bundled my bag into a cupboard next to my cell, which they then locked. All my toiletries were in there along with a change of clothes, my underwear and writing materials. There was also $400 hidden in the lining, under a Velcro strap. To add insult to injury, the guards then ordered me to strip to my underwear. I had to hand everything to them through a kind of hatch at the front of the cage. Everything was taken from me, including my shoes and my lip salve. As before, I fought to keep my precious comb, which was only plastic. The Quartermaster then picked through my clothes with the precision of a forensic scientist and quickly pocketed the $13 I had, never to be seen again. I was given the heavy brown khaki prison uniform to wear, along with a pair of cheap plastic sandals. They issued me with a tiny bar of soap, a towel, a small tube of toothpaste and a plastic toothbrush. These were not quality items, but 'jingly' ones with no durability or substance. The only other thing I was allowed to keep was the old pillow I'd brought with me from Tawqeef.

The prison guards then disappeared, leaving me standing in the middle of the cell with virtually nothing. Fighting to control my anger, I laid what I had on my mattress which was filthy. I straightened out the creases in my scratchy, over-sized uniform and looked around to get my bearings. It didn't take long. All there was to see were three grey walls and the bars of the cage. The cell opposite had two young men in it but the mesh was so thick that we could hardly see each other. There were no photographs or pictures and not a glimmer of colour anywhere. I was in a monochrome hell – and a hot and smoky one at that. I was sweating already from the heating system built into that unventilated corridor with its thick walls and twenty-eight bodies lying in close proximity to each other.

Across from my cell and slightly to one side was a shower cubicle in white ceramic with a grey steel door, which locked from the outside. The sink in a corner of my cell was similarly moulded. The toilet – the usual open trap with footholds either side – was at least plumbed in and relatively clean compared to Tawqeef. There were a few sheets of thin loo paper but no privacy. I'd have to do my business and wash myself in full view of my cellmate who lay on the bed chewing green tobacco that stained his teeth. On the wall, in an arc around his bed space, was the familiar flecking of spit and sneeze that accompanied all Afghans, it seemed. His dirty underwear lay in a heap under his bed.

I nodded to 'Green Teeth' out of courtesy but he ignored me. I noted that he was smaller than me and thinner; if he tried anything I could handle him. I was too tired to engage him in conversation, so I sat on the mattress and contemplated my fate. All I could hear around me was silence. No one was talking or moving about. There was no music, no announcements, and no TV blaring in the corner. I never thought I'd miss the Koran Channel, but I did.

Trying to get comfortable I could tell that although the mattress was thicker than that in Tawqeef, it still wouldn't be easy on my back. I'd lost my sleeping bag and my spare blanket along with all my creature comforts. Without anything to do and no diary, writing paper, books or my iPod, I'd be climbing the walls if I had to stay here for any length of time. The thought was too terrible to contemplate.

'This won't be for long,' I told myself. 'Stick it until the next court hearing in a few days' time. You can do this. Think about Liz and the kids.'

I thought of my last letter home when I told her all about my military routine and I knew how worried she'd be that I'd been moved. I should have been on home leave by now, enjoying some long-anticipated downtime with her and the boys. There'd have been noisy barbecues round the pool each night with music and dancing and the boys larking about as much as me.

The silence in our wing pressed in on me. My ears ached to hear a snore, a movement, a whisper, but there was hardly anything. I couldn't even hear sounds from outside – no traffic or aircraft, not even distant explosions or gunfire. Why weren't these prisoners talking to each other? Was it forbidden? As far as I could tell there wasn't a guard in with us, and I hadn't spotted any CCTV cameras. What had been done to them in this place that they couldn't even speak? My thoughts were like horses galloping through my imagination.

At that moment, I heard a sound further down the wing that was so sudden and so surprising that I thought my ears were deceiving me. Jumping up, I tried to see along the corridor but my view was too limited. Pressing my head against the mesh, I listened intently until I finally figured out what it was.

For some reason in this clinical environment without a single embellishment, there was a musical clock marking the hours. I couldn't see it, but I could hear it all right. Having chimed twelve times to inform us that it was noon, its cheap electrical circuit began to transmit a tinny tune. I could hardly believe it, but the song it was playing was 'Home! Sweet Home!' with its line, *'Be it ever so humble, there's no place like home . . .'*

Fifteen

When I was three years old, my mam moved in with her parents for a while, taking me and my sisters Elsie and Betty with her. I didn't know it at the time, but Dad was in prison and we were temporarily homeless.

Nana and Grandad were the nicest people I knew and they spoiled us rotten. Their council house in Enbridge Street, Salford, was clean and warm. I remember sitting by the open range listening to records on their gramophone. One of the songs was 'Home! Sweet Home!' and their house truly was a home – unlike anything I'd ever known. The table was well stocked and they had proper wooden furniture and carpets. One of my happiest childhood memories is of waking up there in a big, soft bed.

From a little scullery with a small gas cooker and a cold water sink, my nana produced real food, prepared and cooked from scratch, not just tipped cold out of a tin. I can remember filling my belly with her delicious hot meat pies, apple crumble and fresh-baked bread until I was fuller than I'd ever felt in my life. Nana used to give me money to go to the corner shop so I could buy my favourite Merry Maids chocolate caramels. One day, she took us to Cross Lane Market and bought us new clothes – the first I'd ever owned. It was coming up to Whitsuntide and she wanted us to look our best for the famous 'Whit Walks' – an annual tradition in the North

West in which everyone put on their Sunday best and marched in procession through the streets. Betty and I even had a photograph taken of us all suited and booted outside the Salvation Army Hall, which I have to this day. In the background, people are hanging up bunting for the parade. When I look at that little boy squinting into the sun in his oversized blazer, cap and shorts, wearing spanking new shoes and socks, I can hardly equate him with the soppy lad I remember being at that age, crying all the time.

My father had been a general labourer before he was sent to prison. Then his accident stopped him working for good. His mother died when he was a kid and he was estranged from the rest of his family. I don't think he'd ever known love or physical affection, and he always kept his distance. My mother worked part-time as an auxiliary nurse in the Salford Royal Hospital but when one baby started coming after the other, she had to give it up. They both came from great poverty but it is amazing to me that my mam must have grown up with the love of Nana and Grandad but seemed to have given up hope by the time she became a mother herself. Maybe she was just too exhausted to try.

She was certainly very old-fashioned and shied away from any physical contact or talk of emotional matters. When she was heavily pregnant again with one of my brothers, I remember asking her, 'Where do babies come from, Mam?'

Clipping me round the ear, she snapped, 'Don't talk dirty!'

Despite their constant fighting, my mam and dad stayed together until the end; although it was more of an existence than a case of growing old happily side by side. Liz's parents, Maureen and Leslie, couldn't have been more different. They treated me like a son from the moment I first met them, and asked me to call them 'Mum' and 'Dad', which I was honoured to do. Maureen worked as a waitress at the famous Harry Ramsden's fish and chip restaurant at Guiseley and Leslie was a regional manager in canned foods. When Liz first took me home I had no idea what to do with all the plates and cutlery lying in wait for me on the dinner table, but she whispered, 'Just follow my lead.' Her parents would have made me feel welcome no matter how I behaved, and when we had children they treated them just the same.

By contrast, whenever Liz and I took the kids to visit my parents at the Ladywell Flats we'd only stay for fifteen minutes at a time. My mam and dad smoked hundreds of cigarettes a day between them with never a window open. Everything was stained yellow, including their fingers, and the fireplace was piled high with cigarette butts. We couldn't sit down anywhere because it was so dirty, so we'd stand and chat in the living room, our shoes sticking to the carpet.

'Go on, Billy, take a seat,' my mother would say, puffing on her cigarette right down to the dimp – a Manchester expression for the very end. The telly was never turned off.

'No, it's fine, Mam,' I'd tell her. 'We've been in the car a long time. It's good to stand.'

All my father would ask is, 'Where's my baccy?'

When it was time to go, my mother would call the children over and give them what came to be known as a 'Nana kiss' – almost a lick on the cheek, stinking of cigarette smoke. Just a mention of a Nana kiss can still make my children (and now my grandchildren) recoil. Even after just fifteen minutes in my parents' company, their cigarette smoke would cling to our hair and clothes so badly that we'd have to roll the car windows down all the way home to get rid of the stink.

That same smell clung to me in CNJC, where within a few hours of my arrival, the guards returned to our wing. I could hear their footsteps echoing down the corridor and then the gate opening. There was the tell-tale sound of chains and murmured responses to orders. It was difficult to tell what was happening but it sounded like my fellow prisoners were being taken out, cell by cell. Was it visiting time? Would Kev be waiting? But why chains? We were in the heart of the most secure compound in Afghanistan, surrounded by impenetrable rings of steel, concrete and barbed wire. Where were we going to go?

When the guards reached my cell, they gestured for me to stand back and beckoned Green Teeth forward. He put his hands through the hatch to get them cuffed and then they let him out, shackled his feet and led him away. I stepped forward, expecting the same, but they shut the gate on me. For the next two hours I was left alone, the only prisoner in our wing. Without a watch I had no idea of the time apart from the 'jingly' clock, which played a different tune on the hour. First of all 'Yankee Doodle Dandy', of all things, and then – even more incongruously – the chimes of Big Ben. Confused and disorientated, I'd been stripped of my belongings and access to anyone who spoke English. I was alone in a sterile space, silent apart from some mad machine that played songs that only reminded me of the world beyond my walls. If this was some kind of mental torture, then it was working.

Struggling to keep my sanity, I busied myself rearranging

my mattress and pillows. I did one hundred press-ups followed by fifty sit-ups. I ran on the spot to keep my body from seizing up, but there wasn't enough room so I kept banging into the bed or the wall. I washed myself with the soap they'd given me (which barely produced any lather). I brushed my teeth with the disgusting chalky toothpaste and a brush which felt like it would snap at the slightest pressure. I couldn't shave and with no mirror I had no idea how I looked.

After an hour, the gate opened and I felt a blast of cool air which I hoped might clear the smell of cigarettes, BO and smelly feet. I called out 'Salaam!' but no one answered. It took me a while but I finally figured out that a cleaner was moving along the wing, mopping the floors and spraying each cell with disinfectant. When he reached my cell I could see he was an ancient Afghan with a stooped back. Ignoring me and my cell, he looked straight through me as if I didn't exist – and by then I was beginning to wonder myself.

It was over an hour later before the prisoners returned. Sniffing the air like a dog, I smelt rain. They must have been allowed out for exercise; a privilege I'd been denied. Green Teeth shuffled in last of all, his clothes and hair damp. The first thing he did was wash himself and then he fished out his prayer mat from under his bed to kneel on. I heard shuffling in the neighbouring cells and imagined they were doing the same. Then a mullah further down the wing began the adhaan and his voice filled the air. Green Teeth repeatedly gestured for me to kneel too but I shook my head. 'William, no Islam,' I said. For the next hour, I had no choice but to stand in the corner watching him pray. There was nowhere else for me to go.

When it came time to recite the Koran, the wing was filled with voices and the human contact was a comfort to me. My cellmate tried another tack, saying a line and gesturing for me to repeat it. I did as he asked at first just to be friendly and his laugh surprised me. Then he shouted to his fellow prisoners to tell them what he was making me do and their laughter rippled along the wing.

At around 20:00 hrs, the evening meal was brought in. It was served to us on metal trays passed through the hatch in the mesh by an elderly prison guard called 'Ba Ba', which means old man. It consisted of greasy rice, a small pile of beans, a banana, a triangle of Red Cow processed cheese and some flat bread. We were also given half-litre bottles of water and some orange juice. Silence descended again as everyone ate. I settled down to do the same and thought wistfully of my friends in Tawqeef sitting in their noisy meal circle.

After dinner, Green Teeth put a fresh wad of tobacco in his mouth and began to chew. Like all Afghans, he did this repeatedly until he retched. Then he'd try to cough up as much phlegm as possible. As before, I found myself having to constantly avoid it as he spat. The time came when I had to use the toilet so I went over and faced the trap, undid myself, and began to urinate. Green Teeth said something sharply to me and I turned to see him gesturing that I should squat instead of stand.

'No thanks, pal,' I told him. 'I'll go the way I want to.' He shook his head and frowned so I shook my head and frowned right back at him. 'I'll start squatting when you stop spitting!' I told him but it was a culture divide we were never able to bridge.

Trapped in my cell with no diversion, I lay down on my mattress and tried to get some shut-eye. The fluorescent lights directly above me and in the corridor were never dimmed so the brightness was overwhelming – even under my blanket. Green Teeth coughed, snored and farted while I tossed and turned. Alone with my mind, I became increasingly angry. Someone from the embassy should have checked CNJC before they arranged my transfer. If I'd known that I'd lose the chance to exercise, buy food, or have deliveries, I'd never have agreed to it, no matter how much the FCO pressed for it.

Of all the memories that bubbled to the surface that first night in CNJC, it was my time in the mountains of northern Spain and the noble *cazadores* of the 66th Mountain Regiment, with whom I spent six months in 2002. Having taught me to ski, rock-climb and abseil, they took me with them on a gruelling three-week exercise to the high Pyrenees, where we lived together in snow holes or tents when we weren't carrying out ski patrols across a vast frozen terrain. I was the only Englishman among them and we lived on meagre rations with limited water. I still stripped off each morning and washed myself with snow, just to be clean, although they called me the *'extranjero loco'* or crazy foreigner. I could do nothing about my facial hair, though, and by the end of the three weeks I'd grown my first beard.

Despite dreaming of the intense cold we'd had to endure in the snowy landscape of northern Spain I awoke sticky with sweat, my body unaccustomed to the heat. Looking around me, dazed and blinking, I couldn't think where I was. Then I remembered. Slumping back onto my mattress, I retreated under my blanket. The next time I woke was a few hours later but with no watch, I couldn't tell what time it was. The narrow windows were so high I'd have had to climb on the top bunk to see if it was light yet. Rubbing my chin and feeling several days' growth, I realised that unless I shaved soon, I'd start to look like a mountain *cazadore* again.

Green Teeth was at the sink, washing. I could hear running water in the adjacent cells so the other prisoners must have been doing likewise. The guards came in to light cigarettes through the mesh and a couple of prisoners were individually taken to the shower opposite my cell. Once in the cubicle, their handcuffs were released and they were locked in behind a metal door for a few minutes at a time. I longed for a shower to wash away the night so I called to get the guards' attention, using the word Idris had taught me – '*Zorbed! Zorbed!*' I pointed to the shower and then my soap and towel and mimicked washing myself. It took a while, but eventually one of the guards locked me into that claustrophobic cubicle for my first hot shower in a month.

When everyone was ready, the mullah began the *adhaan* in his haunting alto voice. It must have been just before dawn. There was some shouting further down the wing, which I finally figured out was the older men yelling at the younger ones to observe their prayers.

Breakfast was brought at around 06:30 hrs by Ba Ba pushing a trolley. I soon learned to recognise the distinctive rattling of its wheels. We were handed some stale flatbread and a hard-boiled egg. Bizarrely, we also received a small Madeleine sponge cake each, wrapped in cellophane. I kept mine for later. We were allowed one polystyrene cup of black *chai* each but I asked Ba Ba to pour some extra tea into one of my empty water bottles. He agreed only after gesturing that this would cost me my egg. I wasn't bothered as long as I had sufficient tea, even if he did scald my fingers as he poured it shakily into my bottle.

Time lost all meaning and it took a while for me to realise that the jingly clock had stopped. I didn't miss its irritating tunes but at least it had marked the hours. I couldn't even remember what day it was at first and then I worked it backwards and realised it must have been Monday, 29 March – my twenty-seventh day in captivity. I paced the cell like a caged animal. I didn't want to lie still like Green Teeth all day. But the more I paced – reaching the end wall and turning, reaching the mesh and turning again – the more frustrated I became.

About three hours after breakfast, I heard the guards coming back. Standing up against the mesh I listened closely as they released prisoners two by two. This time I was determined I wouldn't be left behind. The wait for my turn was killing and by the time they appeared in front of me, I was like a jack-in-the-box. Mercifully, they handcuffed and chained me before leading me out. Halfway down the wing, I spotted the chiming clock for the first time. It had a gaudy face with so much gold paint that I could barely make out the numbers. For some reason, it had been screwed into the ceiling with its wires and battery dangling. No wonder it didn't always work.

I was led through a gate and then right past the office of the Quartermaster and out into a small courtyard, twenty metres by sixteen. My first impression was of wall after wall of razor wire. Taking up the majority of the space were four caged exercise areas, side by side, like dog runs in a kennel. Wire mesh and barbed wire formed the roof as well as the walls. At one end of each was a covered area for when it rained, but without any drainage the ground was a quagmire.

There were seven prisoners locked into each cage and I was the only Westerner. Some began jeering and a 'long beard' gestured my throat being cut, but then I was used to that. The guards led me to the farthest run, which was empty, and placed me there on my own. My cuffs were released so I could at last move freely again – well, as far as the kennel fence. Lifting my face to the sky, I breathed in deeply and relished the cool air against my skin. Through the razor wire I could see that it was a clear day, with a few puffy grey clouds. I could hear planes taking off for the first time, and saw a C130 flying off into the distance. I'd forgotten that we were close to the airport. There was no greenery of any kind – not a tree, plant, a blade of grass or a flower – and I longed for that suddenly, missing my Spanish garden with its lawn, olive grove, and orange trees.

Shaking out my legs and arms, I did a quick recce of my surroundings. The cage was twenty paces long by three paces wide so I began to march briskly up and down, as my fellow prisoners watched bemused. The turns at the end came so quickly, though, and I longed to really stretch my legs and run somewhere open and free. It was also difficult to walk in cheap flip-flops and I wasn't sure how long they'd last. Hopefully, I wouldn't be in there long enough to find out.

At the far end of the courtyard behind a large plastic screen was a large, official-looking building that I later learned was a *mahkama* or courthouse. Beyond the barbed wire fence I could see prisoners in chains walking back and forth. At the opposite end of the courtyard was a food preparation area from which I could smell meat cooking. There was also a small sick bay where some of the prisoners were waiting to see the doctor who was probably as poorly equipped as the previous one.

Determined to make the most of my exercise time, I continued marching back and forth, pumping my arms to give me an extra cardiovascular workout. To my dismay, though, the guards came back for me after just half an hour. Having been trussed up like Houdini, I was led through a door in the corner of the courtyard into a small room with a chair in the middle. A burly Afghan stood waiting. At first I thought I might be getting a shave. I hadn't had one in a while and the bristle was starting to itch. Then I saw that the floor was covered in hair. Struggling to get back out of the room, I resisted the guards' attempts to push me towards him.

'No!' I cried, shaking my head vehemently. 'No! Please! I don't want a haircut!'

The guards laughed in my face. No wonder they'd chuckled when they'd allowed me to keep my comb. No one spoke any English and I demanded an interpreter. '*Sedakuo tarjomaan!*' I cried. '*Sedakuo tarjomaan!*'

This just made them laugh more and two guards moved in to force me into the chair. Panicking, I protested loudly and struggled some more. I have always taken great pride in my hair as both a soldier and a civilian. The lads at work used to take the mick about me never having a hair out of place, even when I was in the gym. I was damned if I was going to let some prison barber hack at it. But as the guards laughingly prepared to pin me down, I realised there was nothing I could do anyway. My wrists were chained to my stomach, my ankles were shackled and I had four guards bearing down on me. If I'd resisted further, it could have ended in serious injury. I had no choice but to sit down, hang my head and allow them to do their worst. I gritted my teeth until they hurt as the scissors snipped away and I watched my hair fall at my feet. Then the barber produced an electric razor and shaved off the rest, giving me the shortest haircut I'd ever had in my life, even when I'd had nits as a kid.

I was taken back to the dog run, utterly degraded and shaking with anger. The other prisoners pointed and laughed and it took all my resilience not to shout back at them. Then I realised that most of them had shaved heads too. Slumping to the ground, I brought my hands to my head and tentatively felt what little stubble was left. There was virtually nothing.

Just a few days earlier I'd believed I was about to be freed to fly home to my loved ones. Now I was in the Afghan equivalent of Guantanamo Bay. Traumatised and depressed, I returned to my cell where Green Teeth never let up on his spitting and the clock chimed intermittently. There was nothing else to distract me from this living nightmare. It was only Monday afternoon. How on earth would I make it through the next few days?

When the guards came for me later that afternoon, I thought, 'What next?' Reluctantly, I was taken through a door which led into a small visiting room, divided into three sections, each with a concrete stool bolted to the floor. Cutting the room in half was a wall topped with bulletproof glass and a small mesh grille to speak through. Waiting on the other side were Kev and Charlie.

'Look what they've bloody done to me!' I shouted the

minute I saw them. My fury finally erupting, I almost tripped over my shackles as I stumbled closer to yell, 'I want the FCO here now and I want to be moved back to Tawqeef immediately!'

Both men were visibly shocked at the sight of me. 'They bloody held me down and did all this against my will!' I carried on, unable to rein myself in. 'You've got to get me out of here!' I stood right up against the glass to rant and rave until the guards made me sit on the stool. I tried to hold myself together but it was impossible then – the events of the previous few hours overwhelmed me.

Kev was brilliant. He perched on the narrow concrete ledge beneath the glass and pressed himself right up against the grille. 'All right, mate,' he said softly. 'Let it all out. We're here for you now. Don't worry. We'll make a complaint and see if we can get you moved.'

Deep down, I didn't hold out much hope. The embassy had gone to a lot of trouble to get me in to CNJC and I doubted the Commandant at Tawqeef would have me back. Before I could even discuss that though, the visit was over and the guards led me back to my cell, a broken man.

Something must have been said because within a few hours the Commandant appeared at my cell with two American prison mentors. They politely called me 'Mr Shaw' and asked me how I was settling in.

'I'm not settling in at all!' I told them. 'I hate it here and I want to see my lawyer and an FCO official immediately.'

The Americans briefed me as if they were reading from a script. They told me that the prison was run on US lines and no one would get special treatment, regardless of nationality or status. 'Visits are allowed once a week on a Thursday, for 15 minutes at a time. Attorneys can come any day except Friday. There is to be no physical contact, and no gifts or food can be received from the outside.' Just like some prison guards I'd met in Britain, these men were extremely black and white, and showed no emotion or humour. 'If you need anything we will pass your request to the Commandant who will make the ultimate decision,' one told me.

The other added, 'You can also request one book at a time from the Quartermaster's small library of donated books. These can be swapped any day except Thursday or Friday.' Having done their duty, they left me to my fate.

That night marked probably my lowest point since my arrest. The passing of each hour was agony. As I ground my teeth smoother still, I kept trying to remind myself that once the judge had what he wanted then Kim could work on getting me freed. If that didn't happen soon, or if there was another adjournment, then I'd think again about a hunger strike. As ever, it was Liz and the kids my thoughts focused on. Without news of me daily via Azim, Kev or Charlie, they'd be anxious. I only hoped Kev spared them details of my true mental state and didn't mention my haircut. My family had a running joke about how I couldn't manage without my comb in my back pocket. They, of all people, would feel my pain. Running my hands over my naked skull, I prayed that my hair would grow back – and fast.

Sixteen

Unlike a lot of civilians who hate their jobs and cannot wait until the end of each working day, we in the military were volunteers, loved our work and were always there for each other. Whenever we were out on operations, we knew we could depend on the man or woman next to us if we were injured or in any kind of difficulty, and it worked both ways. All for one and one for all – that was how we lived.

In February 1999, I was sent to Bosnia as a Captain and Operations Officer in the British HQ as part of the NATO Stabilisation Force. The war was over by then but there was still a lot of tension between the various factions and then the conflict in neighbouring Kosovo kicked off as well. This brought a new threat from the Serb elements that tried to mount an operation in Kosovo but were penned in by our Czech contingent. Nevertheless, we were placed on high alert.

One cold wet afternoon, I was escorting a bus full of soldiers into Bosnia from Croatia, where they were about to begin their tour. I could tell these youngsters were nervous about being in a strange country, and I felt for them. Suddenly, there was a loud bang and the bus was filled with acrid smoke. The driver stopped the bus, jumped out and ran away, which is never a good sign. Almost everybody else dived for the door too and jumped into ditches at the side of the road. I didn't move from my seat as I tried to assess the situation. Once I'd figured it out, I walked calmly to the steps of the bus and peered down at the lads and lasses crouching together, ready to protect each other's backs. 'Come back, you silly buggers!' I shouted. 'It wasn't a bomb. The air conditioning unit just blew up.'

As in all conflicts, undercover forces were working behind the scenes to gain intelligence on the ground and try to prevent further flare-ups. They were also hunting those on The Hague's extensive wanted list for some of the most heinous war crimes since the Nazis. One night I was summoned to the Banja Luka divisional HQ, which was set up in an old metal factory. From there, I was despatched to the Police HQ at Prijedor, the town that had seen some of the worst mass rape and genocide of Bosniaks and Croats by the Serbs. More than 14,000 people had been listed as killed or missing during the war, many of them victims of Prijedor's notorious concentration camps where prisoners were treated with sickening violence.

My task that late night in the summer of 1999 was to retrieve an undercover soldier who'd been caught at a snap VCP checkpoint as he tried to reverse away in an old saloon car. The police detained him and claimed the car was stolen (it was). Having informed them that he was a British soldier, he locked his vehicle and refused to let them see inside the boot which was full of weapons and top-secret listening devices. Fortunately for him, a team from the International Police Task Force (IPTF) was monitoring the Prijedor police at the time and was able to alert us of his arrest.

My orders were clear. 'I don't care how you do it, Captain, but get this man back, at all costs. And whatever you do, don't let the police get their hands on that vehicle or the equipment.'

It was pitch black when I left Banja Luka in a three-vehicle convoy on the dodgy Bosnian roads. Almost an hour later we arrived at the police station, a former hotel. The soldier was locked in one of the bedrooms and refused to hand over the keys to his car. There was no sign of the IPTF team who'd reported his arrest so I had to face the Prijedor criminal police on my own. Lounging around the hotel foyer dressed in long black leather trench coats smoking cigarettes, these so-called officers of the law looked more like the Mafia than the Mafia ever did.

With the help of my young male interpreter, I found out who the commander was and introduced myself. After some small talk, while I clocked how many armed men he had around him (too many to take on), I politely asked what the problem was.

'We have arrested a suspect driving a stolen Bosnian-registered car who refused to stop for my men,' he told me. 'He is refusing to cooperate so we shall keep him until we find out exactly who he is.'

'I'm afraid that's not possible, Sir,' I told him. 'This character belongs to the British military and we know him well. I can assure you that his only crime is that he is an ill-disciplined soldier. The car he is driving isn't stolen; it belongs to us and is registered to the British military through Sarajevo vehicle records.'

The commander arched one eyebrow and drew deeply

on an untipped cigarette. I don't think he believed a word I said.

'What needs to happen here, Sir,' I persisted, 'is that I speak to our man on my own. He'll have to answer my questions because I am his senior officer. Then I will arrest him for failing to stop at your checkpoint. I'm going to handcuff him and take him back to the military jail where I can assure you that he will be dealt with most severely. One of my men will drive his vehicle back with us and then we'll all be out of your way.'

He eyed me suspiciously. I was sure he'd seen straight through my bluff but I held my nerve. 'First thing in the morning I'll arrange for the documentation to be sent to you to confirm that this vehicle is ours,' I reiterated.

Prior to the Bosnian War, I would probably have been arrested too at that point by this man and his team of hoodlums, maybe never to be seen again. But the involvement of NATO forces and the attention of the world had made them more cautious. Dropping his cigarette to the floor and grinding it in with his heel, he reluctantly agreed to let me interview the soldier alone. One of his men took me up to the locked room where I found our man sitting on the bed.

'I'm Captain Shaw from British HQ,' I told him. 'I've come to take you back but first, I need to see some form of ID.'

'You don't need to know who I am,' he replied. He was dressed in civilian clothes and eyed me coolly.

'Okay then, let me put it this way. Unless I confirm exactly who you are and that I have the right man, I'll be leaving here with my men in five minutes and you'll remain in this hotel as a long-term guest of the Prijedor police.' He thought about that for a moment before pulling out the ID he'd secreted on his person.

'Right then, this is the deal,' I told him. I explained the cock-and-bull story I'd concocted for the police commander. 'To make it look authentic I'm going to cuff you, take you downstairs and put you in the back of my vehicle with an armed guard. One of my lads will drive your car back towards Banja Luka. When we get thirty kilometres or so outside Prijedor, I'll stop the convoy so you can get into your car. We'll escort you as far as you want us to, until you can peel off and do whatever you need to do.'

Our plan set, I returned to the lobby where I made my 'prisoner' publicly apologise before I handcuffed him. I then thanked the commander profusely for his help and promised once again to send him the relevant paperwork. He and his men followed us closely as we made our way outside and watched suspiciously as we bundled our man into the back of my vehicle. Taking the keys to the saloon car, I unlocked it and ordered one of my men to follow our convoy. As we drove away, I gave the commander a cheery wave. Somehow, we managed to get out of there in one piece. As arranged, a few miles outside Banja Luka, our man got out, started up his vehicle and melted away into the night.

In those first few horrible days stuck in CNJC, I only wished some RMP Captain would come and get me out of there with a similarly clever ruse. I knew I'd never have such luck, though, so all I could do was harden myself to my circumstances and get into a new routine. My time in the exercise yard was the only highlight of my day. We were either allowed out between 09:00–11:00 hrs or 13:00–15:00 hrs, alternating with another wing.

On my fourth day, though, the guards didn't come for us. No one came to explain and there was no one I could ask. Fidgety, I jumped up at every sound. When nothing happened by mid-afternoon, I began to worry. What if exercise had been suspended? If there wasn't even that to keep me occupied, I knew I'd go under. Then I remembered that it was a Thursday – visiting day. I so longed to see a friendly face. Sure enough, Kim and Kev were waiting for me and I was quite overcome to see them. It was so frustrating not to be able to reach out and touch them. I couldn't even hear them properly unless I leaned right up against the grille.

If Kim was shocked by the sight of me, she was careful not to show it. She assured me that she was pressing the Attorney General's office and the judge to rule on whether I could be bailed and was still pushing the NDS daily for the letter. I couldn't imagine why a straightforward statement of a simple fact was taking so long.

'We're getting fat on the judge's bloody cakes,' Kev told me. 'I don't think I can stomach much more so you'd better get out of here soon!' He promised he'd try to get Mike the Medic in to see me and would push for me to have some essentials I'd asked for like anti-perspirant, proper toothpaste and disinfectant. Best of all, Kev told he had some letters from home which he'd been obliged to hand to the mentors to censor. Annoyingly, I didn't get them for two days as the mentors took Fridays off, but when I did I held them as if they were made of glass. I read Liz's first:

'*Hi sweet cheeks, I hear you are now in your new digs and*

even have a bed this time lol. I knew the move would upset you as you had established a routine. Keep strong though, babe, as not much longer and you will be home where you belong . . . You have so much support from all areas, so don't wobble just yet . . . that's my job he he.' She went on to tell me all sorts of chatty news from home although I could tell her cheerfulness was forced. She said she was going ahead with the decorating we'd planned and had organised the pool man and renewed the car insurance. Lewis was on a parachute course and Lisa had got the teaching job she wanted in Dover. She said 'Bear' wore one of the bracelets I'd made in Tawqeef for good luck and reckoned that was what swung it for her.

'Well as you can see darling we are coping quite well so don't rush back from your holiday too soon as would prefer to get all finished first he he . . . Love you gorgeous so stay positive. Missing you with every heartbeat.'

I couldn't have put it better myself.

There were other letters, too, from Craig and Lisa. My youngest son Lewis phoned Liz for updates every day but he'd never been a letter writer and only ever sent me one note. When it came, I wrote straight back joking that someone had written to me claiming to be my son. Craig, who was more prolific, wrote, *'Hi, Dad . . . I am sure you are getting more and more frustrated by the day as we all are but please just keep the faith as surely the court hearing cannot be too far off now . . . you are the first person I think about when I wake up and the last one I think about before drifting off to sleep. Love you so much as always.'*

Lisa cheered me up no end with her letter and assured me that Liz was holding up well. She suggested I plan some orienteering adventures in Spain for when I got home. She told me to sketch out a map for a treasure hunt with refreshment stops along the way – gin and tonics for the grown-ups and ice lollies for the kids. '*Keep going Dad,*' she wrote. '*I can only imagine how depressing it must be and how painfully slow this process must be for you. Relax as best you can, enjoy the peace because my goodness you will be nagged once you get back into a routine at home!*'

What was especially cruel about CNJC was that I was only allowed to keep one or two letters with me at a time. They feared I might start a fire with more than a few sheets of paper even though I didn't even smoke. This meant that once I'd pored over my precious letters for a day and a night, I had to choose which to keep with me and which to hand in, maybe never to be seen again. It was a tortuous decision to have to make because I wanted to keep them all.

On the Friday, I was allowed two pieces of flimsy paper and a pen so that I could write back to the family at last. The US mentors informed me that this was to be a weekly allowance and that I'd have to hand both paper and pen back when I was done. It was difficult balancing the paper on my knee, writing tiny words so as not to fill up the space too quickly. I tried to sound cheerful but I hated that the mentors would be reading my innermost thoughts and warned the family to use code so as not to cause any offence. Prison became '*Karzai's guesthouse*', my cell was my '*room*'; I was a '*guest*' not a prisoner, and the chains I had to wear were '*jewellery*' or '*silverware*'.

In my first letter home from CNJC, I wrote, '*Hi, darling and the kids . . . After being uprooted I was bitterly disappointed but now settled again into a routine and am fine . . . Brand-new centre, very well controlled and strict – All very fair indeed and although limited personal stuff allowed, I now have my own room . . . so content for now . . . I am getting plenty of sleep (too much) . . . the food is very edible so no complaints at all . . . Kim and Kevin have been outstanding in all of this . . . Kim is my safety blanket in the country. Out of the country you will always be my safety blanket – always there to catch me and look after me on many occasions. . . . Well, darling, just about out of page. I blow a kiss every night and whisper in your ear . . . I love you. It is only the distance that keeps us apart. Our hearts are joined as one . . . as always . . . Love you all, xxxx.'*

I had to calculate the passing of the days in my mind, based on Thursday visits and Friday holidays. Letters with dates helped but I didn't always get them immediately so that would throw me out. I told the mentors that I needed my watch. 'I want to know what time to go to bed and when to be ready to go outside,' I said. As usual, they deferred to the Commandant who wouldn't do a thing without the Americans' say-so which left me in a catch-22 situation. Eventually, the Quartermaster caved and I finally got my watch, which was absolutely fantastic. Now I at least had a proper sense of time – not that it made it go any faster.

The Quartermaster also brought me a book from the library which I devoured greedily. It was a battered paperback called *The Seventh Scroll* by Wilbur Smith and its epic tale of an Egyptian pharaoh's tomb provided a welcome escape. I'd never read anything so quickly in my life. As soon as I'd finished it, I asked for a new one but not being able to read English he brought me back the same book. 'No, I've already read that one,' I told him. 'I need something different.' I didn't always succeed, but Wilbur Smith saved my life and I read his *The Leopard Hunts in Darkness, When The Lion Feeds* and *River God*. I devoured Nelson Demille's *Cathedral* which was about the IRA in New York. I also enjoyed a terrific thriller called *Rat Run* by Gerald Seymour about a former military intelligence officer who battles drug lords and I loved Oscar Hijuelos' *The 14 Sisters of Emilio Montez O'Brien*, which was full of sex scenes which made a change from police or prison stories.

Through the US mentors, I also pleaded to be allowed my Spanish study book, *501 Spanish Verbs*. After much debate, that too was allowed. Although I had the concentration span of a gnat in there I made myself study for at least an hour every day. I felt sorry for the poor Afghans who couldn't read as there was zero else to do.

My life improved considerably when the Commandant came to see me with his interpreter. 'Is this prisoner annoying you?' he enquired, glaring at my cellmate gobbing noisily on the floor.

Green Teeth irritated me intensely but for fear of retribution I said, 'No, you're alright.' Later that day, however, he was relocated three cells down and then transferred to Pol-e-Charkhi. I had the 'luxury' of a cage to myself. I was over the moon.

Humming, I spent the rest of that day washing the place down with soap and water. I used anything I had – my hands, the sleeve of my uniform, even my socks. While scrubbing the corners, I came across a small spider and airlifted him to the sanctuary of the window ledge. Then I washed my clothes with the latherless soap and hung them out to dry on the rail of the top bunk or the mesh of the cage, poking my socks and underwear through the holes with my toothbrush.

I shifted Green Teeth's heavily stained mattress from the bottom to the top bunk and put mine on the bottom. In an attempt to dim the overhead lights, I stuffed some damp socks into the metal grate that surrounded them but the guards made me take them out. Even without the soft lighting I'd hoped for, the place felt much more like home.

Liz would have been proud of me. No matter how rubbish our Army accommodation was when we first arrived at a new posting, she'd soon make it homely. She regarded it as a personal challenge. Whenever we arrived at a new house, we'd be greeted by a tower of brown removal boxes. First things first, the kettle came out as did some plates, then we'd all have tea and cake from the NAAFI. For the next week or so, she'd spend every day unpacking and deciding where everything would go. The phone line often wasn't connected at first, and once Liz had to send Lewis out on his bike to collect or deliver messages. When she'd got everything unpacked, she'd change the lighting, hang pictures, light a few candles and fill a vase with flowers. Within days what had looked like a complete dump was cosy and welcoming. Even when she was pregnant or secretly dying inside as the kids went off on the 'lollipop plane' back to boarding school, she remained cheerful and strong.

Our worst Christmas as a family was undoubtedly crammed into a one-bedroom flat in Selsey in Sussex in the late 1980s. We had no money for presents, or anything else for that matter. We'd bought it as an investment just before the interest rates went through the roof so we ended up paying double the mortgage on top of the rent for my single Army quarters. I worked nights as a truck driver while Liz somehow scratched around with the little we had and managed to give us all a merry Christmas. Bless her loving heart.

My cell might not have been quite up to Liz's mark but being on my own was so much better and meant that I could focus on my routine. I kept myself and my cage clean, and stayed fit. The trouble was that walking around on a concrete floor in open sandals made my heels crack. I'd had problems with my feet since I was a nipper but now they opened up and bled. Reluctant to visit the prison doctor, I eventually capitulated. All he could offer me was Algipan, a red hot liniment for aches and pains – not something I wanted to rub into an open wound. I had no choice but to suffer in silence but my once military march became much more of a civilian limp.

The luxury of my privacy in the exercise yard came to an end when the other prisoners complained that they were squashed into their runs because of me. The Commandant decided that I was only at risk from the older hard-line Taliban, who were kept in the one farthest from me. With six cage-mates, I now had to navigate around their recumbent bodies as they played chess or draughts on sets donated by the Red Cross. Some wanted me to play with them even if they were in the next run, inviting me to poke my fingers through the mesh. To mollify them, I did play a couple of games and let them beat me, which they always found amusing. Mainly though I walked, gradually wearing out my flip-flops.

By this time, a young Afghan had been admitted to our wing who was distinctive for his long black dreadlocks. His name was Yama and he approached me on his second day. 'Good afternoon,' he said with a smile.

'You can speak English!' I cried, stupidly happy to hear my own language. Then, realising that he might be a ringer sent in to catch me out, I became more cautious. Yama didn't notice and chatted away to me anyway. The twenty-four-year-old son of two doctors, he and his uncle had set themselves up as loan sharks. One man they'd lent $5,000 to so he could buy some opium had bubbled them to the authorities. Pending their trial, they were both sent to CNJC where they shared a cell. Although he had moments of panic about facing a drugs court where the sentences averaged twelve years, Yama fully expected his wealthy father to arrange his release.

When he asked me what I was in for, I said, 'I'm an engineer. I had a problem with my passport.'

Out of the blue, he told me he'd applied for a passport and visa to Pakistan and then one for England. 'I have a sister who lives in Britain, near a city called Manchester,' he said. 'Do you know the Salford precincts?'

I was extremely wary then and said nothing. He carried on blithely; telling me that he'd applied to Salford University and hoped to start in September. In spite of my initial coldness, Yama always made sure we were in the same exercise run. Even when I was pacing, he'd walk alongside me, keen to practise his English. The only time he'd give up was when it was raining. Determined not to interrupt my routine, I used my bed sheet draped around my shoulders while my fellow inmates huddled miserably under the shelter. They thought I was deranged – even more so when I began singing out loud to give myself a beat.

Mostly I sang songs from the musicals of Andrew Lloyd Webber – especially *Evita* and *Jesus Christ Superstar.* I'd first seen the latter at Eccles Cinema in 1973. In Cyprus in 1998, I'd played Judas Iscariot in a charity production at the barracks. I saw *Evita* at Bradford's Alhambra Theatre in the late 1970s and loved the film version with Madonna which Liz and I watched often. Even though I can't sing for toffee, I'd patrol that kennel belting out the words to 'Another Suitcase in Another Hall' or 'Don't Cry for me Argentina' at the top of my voice.

Yama was the only one who didn't think I was crazy, but then he'd had a rarefied upbringing. Clean shaven and with spotless fingernails, he liked scented soap and was furious when the guards confiscated it. He was extremely proud of his dreadlocks, which had been specially styled at great expense. He claimed they'd taken him a year to perfect. Perversely, I began to trust him a little more the day he was dragged off kicking and screaming to the barber's.

Randomly, the guards singled people out for a haircut whether they liked it or not. Whenever they came looking for victims we'd bunch in a corner with our hands over our heads so as not to be picked again. There was one old man who was humble, gentle and devout and he grew his hair long as part of his religion. The guards shaved it off anyway – a lifetime's growth. He never recovered. When it was Yama's turn, I heard the electric razor hum to life. A few minutes later he emerged almost bald. I knew how humiliating the experience was and felt sorry for my vain young friend. The new Yama became my only ally in that prison. As I used to tell him, 'I like you – I think I'll kill you last!'

He was with me one day in the dog runs when we spotted a group of prisoners walking from the court at the end of the exercise yard. I suddenly recognised Abdul Wakil, 'El Gordo', and cried out, '*Salaam alaikum!*' He was delighted to see me and tried to wave back but couldn't because of his handcuffs. Through Yama, I learned that he'd been sentenced to eight years in Pol-e-Charkhi so I called out, '*Moafagh bashed!*' Good luck.

If I hadn't appreciated it before, I soon learned that the Afghans hated the United States more than any other country in the world. They loathed the mentors and the fact that CNJC had been built and funded by the US. They vowed revenge on all its nationals once they were released. Yama felt just the same but he made me laugh out loud one day when he stopped in his tracks and shouted, 'Bloody bastards!' at the fury of it all. It seemed so funny to hear him say that very English expression and it became a catchphrase of ours whenever we saw the mentors coming. 'Bloody bastards!' we'd mutter and then fall about laughing.

When a couple of inmates confused me with being American, Yama pulled them up sharply. 'No, no! William British!' he cried. 'William okay. William no bloody bastard!'

Each time a military helicopter or plane flew in low overhead preparing to land at the nearby airport, he'd join the others in jumping up and shaking their fists whilst shouting, 'Bloody bastards! Down with the USA!'

Seeing those planes coming and going was hard for me. I'd used that airport unthinkingly for years, never once imagining that I might be prevented from doing so. Most of those aircraft were headed for Dubai and then back to

Europe and I longed to be a passenger on one of them, flying home.

Thanks to Yama, though, life in CNJC became slightly more tolerable. He was in cell No. 11, three down and across the corridor from mine and became incredibly useful. Through him, I was able to have a shower almost every day and get some extra undies and a T-shirt from my bag so I could wash the sweat-stained ones I'd been living in. Once a week or so he'd persuade them to lend me a (blunt) razor which tore my skin but at least made me feel more like a British soldier and less like a scruffy Afghan.

Best of all, Yama cajoled the Quartermaster into letting me sort out the books in his 'library'. I made two piles – those I wasn't interested in (mostly prison stories), and those I wanted to read. My new obsession became to make sure I'd finished the book I was reading by Wednesday because on Thursdays and Fridays I wouldn't be able to get hold of a replacement and I couldn't bear to be without one.

Yama was fearless and the other prisoners looked up to him. He was a natural leader. He wasn't afraid of the guards and complained whenever our belongings were stolen while we were in the exercise yards. We didn't have much but the buggers would take anything – any leftover food or water, and the little cakes I saved for my afternoon cup of *chai*. I started to put my most precious items in my pocket.

No one from the embassy bothered to come and see me and it seemed that my whole future rested on Kim's slender shoulders. The elusive Eidi Mohammad haunted my dreams, smiling slyly at me in his mirrored glasses and brown leather jacket. He reminded me of the spivs I'd known in Salford with the flashy cars and the cheap-smelling girlfriends who were always on the make.

The spider I'd rescued from the corner spun a majestic web on the ceiling as I watched, fascinated. He was like a diligent little Sapper engineering the perfect span between two points. One of his lesser brethren had weaved another web across the mesh on the cage door, but his work was far less precise. He reminded me of a rookie I'd known in the cadets who'd always tried to cut corners and had to be pulled up short. I dubbed them 'Sapper Spider' and 'Rookie Spider' and treated them as equals. Watching them go about their business helped relieve the monotony.

After another week and no progress, Kim and Kev came to see me with more family letters but Kim also had some distressing news. 'I'm going on leave back to the US to see my family,' she said. 'It's been arranged for months – long before I took on your case.'

My stomach flipped and I felt physically sick. 'No, Kim! You can't leave me.'

'Don't worry, Bill,' she said, smiling through the glass. 'I'll be away for six weeks but I'll be available night and day on email, and the phone. My legal team is still working on your case and as soon as the letter arrives from the NDS, I'll come straight back.' Kev assured me then that although he was also due some leave he had no intention of taking it until I was released.

The palpitations I'd first experienced in Tawqeef came back with a vengeance that night and continued on and off for some time. I'd be breathless and hotter than usual, with a dull ache deep in my chest. What if I had a heart attack and never set eyes on Liz and the kids again? The Commandant had refused permission for Mike the Medic to examine me and I didn't trust the prison doctor. Despite all his bravado, Yama had experienced similar anxiety attacks and the doctor gave him an injection which only made him worse. He was very poorly after that and lay on his bunk for days.

My palpitations came mostly when I was thinking about the family coping without me. What were they thinking? How was Liz handling all this? The tone in some of her latest letters had shifted as the waiting was getting her down. She'd written things like, '*Hi gorgeous, well, yet another letter . . . I keep thinking each one is the last!! . . . Each day they seem to do so much but it just doesn't end. I wait for Kev's call daily with the update and can't settle to anything just in case I miss a call. One day it will be what we are all waiting to hear.*' In another, she said, '*I miss you so very much and long for this nightmare to end for you. You have done no wrong and been very patient.*' In a third, she wrote, '*I don't think I will get much sleep tonight and will be anxious for some news tomorrow but as long as I know you are safe and well, I can cope. I just dream of you being here and us doing all our jobs together . . . I never ask for much in life, as long as you are sharing it with me. Love you, want you, need you so come home soon babe.*'

Wednesday afternoons were the worst – when I knew there'd be no exercise for two days and I'd be locked in until the Friday afternoon apart from a 15-minute visit. Everything started to build up and my mind began to play silly tricks on me. I had the odd nightmare and there were times when I secretly wondered if I was going mad, as everything kept playing in a loop in my head.

Kev always did his best to distract me and to gently remind me when I started repeating myself, but he sometimes forgot I had no access to world news. One day, he chatted away about how some of the lads who were due to go home on leave were frustrated they couldn't get a flight out. 'It's all because of this bloody ash cloud,' he said.

'What ash cloud?'

Kev looked at me for a moment and then he laughed. 'Sorry, mate,' he said, shaking his head. 'You don't know, do you? A giant volcano's erupted in Iceland and the cloud of ash its making is too dangerous for planes to fly through. The whole of Europe and beyond is pretty much shut down. It's nuts out there. People are having to buy or hire cars to drive halfway across continents just to get back from their holidays. No one this far away can get anywhere near the UK.'

'You're joking!'

My immediate thought was of Liz in Spain and whether this would affect her getting home to the kids. I hoped she wasn't stranded without support. And what if anything happened to her or the kids while I was stuck in CNJC? My chest tightened at the thought. Desperate to get out of there, I became obsessed about why everything was taking so long. Weeks had passed – I didn't even know how many anymore. I felt as if I was losing all sense of time and reason. Kev was my conduit and although I couldn't have been in better hands, he also became the target of all my frustration, distress and resentment. He must have been exhausted from having to hold me and Liz up every day, as well as working flat out in his full-time job (made all the harder by Mark having to leave the country). It was also his duty to make sure that Maiwand was receiving food and visits from the company as well. No matter what our interpreter may or may not have done, he was still an employee of G4S after all.

Poor Kev. I broke down on him often, but he never cracked and continuously assured me he'd tell Liz I was fine and happy.

We both knew I wasn't, though.

Far from it.

Seventeen

Whenever I began to feel sorry for myself, I made myself think of those far less fortunate than me. There was poor Rob Langdon languishing in Pol-e-Charkhi, along with those I'd got to know at Tawqeef. Not to mention the ordinary Afghans struggling to exist in a country ravaged by war, corruption and privation.

The last time I'd witnessed such poverty was in Africa in 1996 when I was sent there by the Ministry of Defence to build Malawi a military police force. President Hastings Banda had recently been defeated after more than thirty years in charge of one of the most repressive regimes in Africa and his people were finally moving forward. As a former British colony, they'd requested our assistance and I was selected to lead a military police course along with two fellow SNCOs. My mission was, 'Find fifty Malawi soldiers and turn them into policemen.'

I spent the next month studying everything about Malawi, especially its legal system. Fortunately, their military law was based on an abridged version of our old 'Judges Rules', much of which mirrored the British version. It just hadn't been updated since 1964. With Staff Sergeant 'Pop' Larkin, I prepared all the lesson plans and devised a six-week programme with on-the-job training afterwards.

From the moment we arrived in Lilongwe, we were

immediately struck by how poor the country was. We were based at the Livingstonia Beach Hotel on Lake Malawi because the army barracks were virtually uninhabitable. We still managed to contract gastroenteritis, though. The young Malawi soldiers who had been selected for the course for their grasp of English were a pleasure to teach but they all suffered from malaria, which would frequently wipe them out for days. AIDS was the biggest killer and many of the local villagers died of what they called the 'mysterious illness'.

I spent any free time in the local village of Salima, and was often invited into mud hut homes for the staple diet of *nsima* or maize dough balls. I wrote home and asked my family to send parcels from home so that I could distribute clothes and sweets. One package full of fridge magnets caused much amusement as there was no electricity and no fridges, so the children used the magnets as toys. Liaising with Eileen Considine, a relative of Liz's, and the head teacher of Rothwell Infant and Junior School, West Yorkshire, I set up a twinning system in which the children wrote to each other and swapped stories.

One Sunday, I visited a local leper colony with Ralph Arundel, a fellow Captain from the Light Infantry, who was in the country training up its soldiers. In the mud hut village with a few brick buildings scores of badly disfigured men, women and children lived side by side, with even less to live on than ordinary folk. Still, they greeted us warmly. Many had limbs missing, some were blind, and most were disabled in some way. As we were being shown around, we suddenly heard the most beautiful singing coming from inside a dilap-idated building in the shade of a large acacia tree. The voices were so angelic that we felt compelled to go in.

Inside a makeshift chapel we found the space packed with lepers singing their hearts out under an old tin roof. The sound and sight was so humbling that it moved us both to tears. Even those without proper mouths were joining in. Stumbling outside afterwards in a daze, I was approached by a pretty young woman who held out hands that had been turned into stumps by that cruel disease. I reached into my pocket for any spare *kwachas* and gave them all to her. To my horror, she dropped to her knees in thanks.

'Please. No, get up!' I told her, feeling that it was me who should have been kneeling before her. It was so humbling that a pound in loose change could mean so much.

Back at the barracks, the training continued and I was delighted when we managed to get all fifty Malawi soldiers through the course. We gave them a grand parade with the military band in attendance. My final mission then was to set them up with their own HQ in Lilongwe but the building the General allocated them had been stripped completely bare, including all the light switches and wiring. I went out and bought everything they needed to get it shipshape with my own money and set my new recruits to work. 'Whitewash all the walls and anything that needs freshening,' I told them as I went off to source some more equipment. When I came back, I found that they'd taken me at my word. Even the trees had been whitewashed.

I took my leave of Malawi with a heavy heart. I would never forget those kind people or their amazing fortitude in the face of adversity. From the ordinary soldiers to the maimed singers in the leper colony, their spirit humbled me. It was precisely that kind of spirit I tried to cling to for inspiration in CNJC.

On Tuesday, 20 April – my forty-ninth day in captivity – Kev came to see me with the momentous news that the Prosecutor had finally received the requested letter from the NDS. The simple one-page exhibit that he'd originally been promised within a few days had taken exactly a month to rustle up. Now that it had been received, my next court hearing was set for just under a week, Monday, 26 April. Kim was flying back to Afghanistan for it and would go straight to see the judge to collect the new indictment. Conveniently, my hearing was to be held at the courthouse within the CNJC compound, at the far end of my exercise yard. The date set was the day after my fifty-second birthday. I hoped that was a good omen.

As if this news wasn't birthday present enough, I received personal letters from all the family as well as letters from Nick Buckles, the CEO of G4S, and Nigel Billingham, the managing director of G4S Risk Management. Nick said that he and the company believed the charges against me were 'totally misconceived' and spoke of the high regard with which I was held in the company and the industry. Nigel said that securing my release was the company's highest priority and he spoke of my personal integrity and courage. Both were a source of great comfort to me and when the Quartermaster came to take any extraneous mail away from me that week, it was those I chose to hang onto.

When I told Yama that I had my new court date at last he was genuinely happy for me. He told all the men on my wing and the mullah held a prayer for me that night. The days dragged as I waited for the Monday but I tried to stay positive and focus on how lucky I was compared to many of my fellow inmates, most of whom hadn't even seen a lawyer yet. Besides, failure was not an option.

Needless to say, I didn't sleep well all weekend as the possible outcomes of my imminent hearing raced through my mind. I tried reading but had one eye and half a brain on the book and the other half on my case. Every waking minute, I went over the facts time and again and always came to the same conclusion – how could this have gone so wrong?

On the Sunday morning, Yama presented me with his small breakfast cake in the dog run. 'For your birthday and for your good luck,' he announced with a grin. I thought back wistfully to previous birthdays. My childhood ones had hardly been marked, of course, but Liz and the kids always made a fuss of me. This year they were baking a cake back home and were going to let Madeleine and Caius blow out the candles for me. I'd have given anything to have seen that. They promised me my own cake when I got home.

In her latest letter, Liz had written, '*Sweet cheeks . . . my heart has been lonely without yours. Stay strong this weekend, enjoy your birthday as best you can and remember we will all be thinking of you and dreaming of an end to this come Monday. Love, hugs and a million tender kisses . . . everywhere. xxxx*'

She reminded me that she'd be driving from Spain to Dover with Lisa a few days before my hearing, which worried me because it was such a long way, but the ash cloud was still grounding all flights and they had no other choice. At least she'd be with Lisa when news came through of whatever the court ruled. She and the children had decided that if it went against me then they were going to end their media silence and tell the world what was happening.

I was determined to look my best for the court so I requested a shave for Sunday night or Monday morning. When it didn't happen on the Sunday, I began to panic and asked Yama to make the request again. He finally secured a promise that I'd be allowed one early Monday. I didn't sleep that night and got up at 04:00 hrs. My stomach was in knots and I couldn't face any breakfast but I drank some tea. I said good morning to Sapper Spider and Rookie Spider telling them, 'Big day, lads.'

Five hours later the guards came to get me for my ablutions. It wasn't easy shaving a week's worth of growth with a cheap razor and soap that never lathered. Having to see my reflection in the mirror was even more difficult. I looked more like a career criminal than a proud former member of Her Majesty's armed forces. As I waited to be taken to the nearby courtroom, I thought about Liz and Bear waiting in Dover for the outcome. I thought of my two wonderful sons Craig and Lewis, increasingly angry and frustrated at home. Both of them such handsome young men who were making new lives for themselves in their respective jobs; both unable to concentrate because of what was happening to their dad thousands of miles away. And then I thought of little Caius and Madeleine who couldn't understand why we hadn't spoken lately and kept asking their mum and grandma when 'Pop' was coming home.

I thought too about Kim and Kev, who'd become so important to me. I'd never have got through the previous eight weeks without them. Eight weeks? When I was first arrested, I'd thought I'd be out within eight hours. And even if it ended that day, it wouldn't be over yet. Kim had warned me that under Afghan law, regardless of the verdict, I'd have to go back to prison until the Prosecutor decided if he wanted to appeal. That was the system, however cruel it might seem. 'If we do have to appeal,' she added, almost in passing, 'there's a small risk that your sentence could be increased but don't worry, it'll never come to that.'

And then it was time. Chained up, I was led to the courthouse to be met by a sullen Maiwand. On a nod from the guards, I took a deep breath, and shuffled a few noisy steps. My co-defendant and I clanked into court together flanked by three guards armed with Glock pistols; one stood at the door and two accompanied us as we were led in and directed to a bench near the front.

Just like the prison, the courtroom at CNJC was built by the US as a replica of one of its own and had a very American feel to it. Waist-high wooden panels divided off different areas. At the back on wooden bench seats were the public, press and embassy officials. There must have been thirty people but it was far less chaotic than the previous court. I spotted Jan Everleigh and then I saw Kev among the crowd and we gave each other a nod. Kim sat at the front. She looked as calm and organised as ever and had her flip charts pre-positioned in order to present her well-rehearsed defence. 'I have all the paperwork ready for when the judge acquits you so that we can get a quick release,' she said. 'It won't be long now!'

The three judges entered the courtroom and I was surprised to see them dressed formally in official dark green robes which they hadn't worn before. Judge Farooqi declared the court open and confirmed that Maiwand and I were fit to stand trial.

Mr Ghafory stood and read out the indictment which again seemed to take forever. When he'd finished, the case began. By leaning forward and listening to Kim's translator, I learned that the NDS's letter stated that Eidi Mohammad was not in their employment but had acted as a guarantor for the release of our vehicles because he had a cousin in the NDS.

The judge spoke then and Kim objected because he kept referring to me as the 'criminal' or 'guilty person'. 'My client has not been found guilty of anything and the crimes against him are only alleged Your Honour,' she reminded him. All of a sudden, he turned on her. He said that I'd been given plenty of time to find witnesses to back up my story, but Kim reminded him that I'd been locked up since 3 March and the only witnesses were me, Maiwand and Eidi Mohammad anyway.

The Prosecutor continued with his argument that we had still paid the NDS, albeit indirectly, and were therefore guilty of bribery. Whenever Kim objected that I couldn't speak Dari and had merely delivered what I believed to be an official release fee, the judge continually interrupted or cut her short. His body language was hostile and he often looked at the ceiling whenever she responded. I wondered if it was because she was a woman in what the Afghans perceive as a man's world, or whether it was because she was American. Maybe it was because she was black. I'd seen some of the racism towards the Sri Lankans and Nepalese in Tawqeef and knew the Afghans didn't always take kindly to people of a different colour. Kim had already received threats for daring to criticise the Afghan legal system and had been warned to increase her personal protection. Whatever the reason, the judge's sudden hostility seemed strange when he'd been so friendly with her up until now.

This was a completely different atmosphere to before. Just as when I'd gone to see the Prosecutor in his basement office the day I was arrested, I picked up on the vibe immediately. Warily, I shifted in my seat, inadvertently rattling my chains. From that moment on, I can remember watching the drama unfolding as if it was happening to someone else. Everything seemed to go into slow-motion. Like a fascinated observer, I studied the way the judge grimaced, rolled his eyes, or smirked. I watched as Kim jabbed her beautifully manicured hands into the air whenever she wanted to press home a point. I saw Maiwand and his father jumping up and down like nervous meerkats. I listened to the laconic Mr Ghafory, who behaved as if the verdict was a foregone conclusion. Strangely, I felt numb about it all. The more I watched the day unravel, the more it seemed to me that no matter what Kim said, the judge's mind was made up.

In a momentary lull, the judge turned to me for the first time that morning and asked me what I wanted from the case. I stood more steadily than I felt, and was grateful to be weighed down by my ankle chains. I could imagine seeing myself from the judge's perspective, with hair less than an inch long, nicks on my face from my morning shave, my baggy brown uniform hanging off me like a sack. I looked like a thug; just the kind of untrustworthy Westerner who'd bribe an official.

I'd gone over my speech a hundred times in my head and said it by rote. 'I am an innocent man, Your Honour,' I told him. 'I came back to Afghanistan willingly and did not run away from pursuing this matter because I want justice. It was me who reported this incident in the first place. Now I just want to see my family and get back to my Afghan friends.'

As soon as I had finished, he adjourned for lunch, stating that the court would reconvene at 14:00 hrs. I was whisked out and taken back to my cell. My lunch of rice and beans with a rubbery slice of chicken was cold and I couldn't eat anyway. I drank the Capri-Sun orange juice through a straw and left the rest.

Sitting on the edge of my bed, I rewound the hearing in my mind and came to the remarkably calm conclusion that the judge was going to find me guilty. If that was the case then I just wanted to get it over with so I could hear my sentence and start to deal with what was to come. I counted out every second of that interminable lunch adjournment as they ticked away in my head like the timer on a bomb.

Back in court, I was resigned to my fate. Kim tried to reassure me but I told her gently, 'Thank you for all you've done and I'm sorry, but this is going to go wrong.'

'No!' she insisted. 'You must remain positive!' She stubbornly showed me the letters she'd written so that the judge could release me within days. We both looked at them hopefully, willing them to be required but we both knew they wouldn't be needed.

Kev looked like a rabbit caught in the headlights so I leaned across the crowd to reassure him. 'Please tell Liz I'll be fine and that she shouldn't worry for me either,' I added.

The judges came back into the room with a flourish of their robes and sat down. Judge Farooqi reached for a scrap of paper and read out the verdicts. Kim's interpreter was moved between me and her.

'You have been found guilty,' the young man said, above the murmurs and gasps.

I nodded.

'The judges have imposed a two-year prison sentence, William.'

Two years.

'Maiwand, son of Limar, is sentenced to two years.'

Maiwand went ballistic and the Afghans in the court erupted too. I sat there trying to take it all in as the world went mad around me.

Two years.

Go to Jail and do not pass Go. We never had toys when I was a kid and I only learned to play Monopoly as an adult. Always picking the little silver dog as my playing piece I'd become unreasonably upset if I picked up a Chance card that sent me to jail. Well, I was out of chances now.

Kev sat staring at me, his mouth open, shaking his head. I looked across at Jan Everleigh, who also appeared shaken but she quickly left the courtroom.

When Kim had composed herself enough, she stood to inform the judge that she planned to appeal. He told her coldly, 'Think yourself lucky that I have only given William the minimum sentence.'

The interpreter then translated something else the judge had added for good measure, 'You must pay a fine of $25,000.'

$25,000? It was probably the shock but I almost laughed

out loud then. I felt like asking the judge, 'Do you want that in cash? Hundred dollar bills OK? Oh, and don't worry about a receipt.'

My sense of humour failed me then as I began to calculate how long I might actually have to serve. I'd been inside for almost two months, so that meant twenty-two months to go. I might get time off for good behaviour (if they allowed for that), but the worst case scenario was that I'd be released in February 2012.

It was April 2010.

Two years.

Before that realisation could sink in, I was beckoned by the court clerk to place my thumb onto an ink pad and then roll it onto the verdict sheet. The guards had to remove one of my cuffs. Everything was written in Dari so I didn't have a clue what I was 'signing' anyway. This was madness.

The press pushed forward then for my reaction and the guards muscled in around me. Through the crowd, I could see that Kim was upset as well as angry, but I wasn't allowed to comfort her before I was pulled away. I learned later that she and Kev had sat together weeping outside the court.

I don't remember the walk back from the court to my cell at CNJC but before I knew it I was back on my wing. Once the guards had left, Yama shouted, 'What happened, Bill?'

'I got two years,' I said. The words sounded impossible in my mouth.

As Yama relayed the information along the corridor there were cries of delight and much banging on the cell doors. The noise jerked me from my shock. They were *pleased*. The Afghans were genuinely pleased for me. For them, two years was no time at all. They were all expecting to be jailed for between ten to fifteen years, after all. Although that humbled me, I still slumped back onto my bed my mind and body suddenly weak.

Two years.

All I could think about was the moment Kev broke the news to Liz. She'd be devastated.

Two years.

I'd have to wait until my next visit now to find out how she and the children were coping, and that might not be until Thursday. That was three days away and it seemed like a lifetime. How would I feel in three weeks, or three months even?

Two years.

I, Billy Shaw, was a convicted criminal – just like my father and all those bad lads I'd grown up with. Where had it got me? All that exemplary conduct in the military, and all our hard work? Two years in a Kabul jail, that's where.

This meant the end of my career. No one would take me on in the security sector after I'd been convicted of corruption, no matter how much I pleaded my innocence. And what about my MBE? Did the Queen ever demand them back?

Two years.

This was it, then. This was how it was going to be. Locked up. With no one to talk to and minimal communication with the outside world.

Two years.

How the hell was I going to survive?

Eighteen

When I was a kid in Tootal Drive Primary School, there was a young teacher I liked called Mrs Blackburn. She was my main form tutor but she also taught us geography – country by country, letter by letter. The first was Afghanistan, the faraway country conquered by Genghis Khan. I loved learning all about the Silk Route and the dramatic landscapes of its mountain range.

This land with its exotic-looking people was where Afghan hounds came from, one of the oldest breeds of dogs in the world, bred to hunt gazelle and deer. I'd wanted my own Afghan from the day I first set eyes on one and when Liz and I married, we had two named Jason and Jasper but she became allergic and sadly we had to give them up.

Without a dog to make a fuss of at home, I had to make do with those I came across at work. The first was an enormous Rottweiler at Sandhurst who was called HESH for High Explosive Squash Head, a type of armour-piercing anti-tank shell. His owner was a captain in the Royal Horse Artillery. I taught that big brute of a hound to balance biscuits on his nose and to take one from me, mouth to mouth. Then there was an aggressive stray in Iraq who'd been mistreated by the Fijian guards and attacked every bugger except me. We named him Neville, after a former member of staff who was bald. Finally, I adopted a fearful stray puppy in Afghanistan I called Van Gogh because he only had one ear, but sadly he was knocked down and killed. Now we had our eight-year-old beagle, Trotsky; sold to us with the villa in Spain and, despite always living outside as he has done all his life, is a much-loved family pet.

Random thoughts of all the dogs I'd known filled the empty corridors of my mind in those first numb days after my sentencing. I guess it was a kind of defence mechanism to live in the past rather than face the present or the future. Unfortunately, my future kept tapping away on the inside of my skull. Amongst my many concerns was my eldest son's wedding, which Craig and his fiancée Rachel (known by me as 'Scraggle Head') had set for Morpeth, Northumberland in August 2011. Even with time off for good behaviour, I doubted I'd be out. I feared Craig wouldn't go ahead without me but I didn't want them to change their long-prepared plans on my behalf.

The day after the hearing Kim came to see me in ebullient mood. 'We have ample grounds to appeal,' she told me, 'both on the basis of the evidence presented and the way the trial was run.'

'No, leave it,' I said. My response shocked her. 'I don't want to get off on a technicality. I want a clear acquittal and I think it's too late for that. You said if we appeal there's a chance the judge will increase my sentence. I just can't risk that.'

Kim was returning to the US to finish her leave and asked me to think seriously about what I was suggesting while she was away. 'We have twenty days in which to lodge the appeal. You have until then to decide. Once we do, the court will have to organise a new hearing within two months, which will take us to the end of June. Think about it, Bill. If we do this you could be back with your family by July.'

She had other news, too. 'The Commandant has requested that you be transferred to Pol-e-Charkhi now that you've been sentenced. This is quite normal and he needs your cell.'

I was torn about leaving. I hated CNJC for so many reasons but, as in Tawqeef, I'd got into a routine and made a friend in Yama. I was also afraid that Pol-e-Charkhi could be worse. Kim assured me that I'd have more freedom and be sharing a wing with two other Westerners. She then informed me softly, 'Besides, Bill, you don't have a choice.'

Lying on my bunk later that night, my mind was all over the place. I could barely sleep and couldn't face food. I requested a pen and some paper and began a letter to the family to reassure them. Inwardly, though, I was dying. I thought again about my hunger strike. Maybe I should just try to get my head around the two years, do my time, and get the hell out.

Kev came to see me on the Wednesday – the first time he'd seen me since my conviction – and was still very distressed. 'I've made a few bad phone calls in my lifetime, Bill,' he said, 'but calling Liz after your hearing rates as one of the worst things I've ever had to do. And to think of all those bloody cakes I had to eat and the bugger still sent you down!'

Like me, the whole experience had left him feeling sick and disillusioned, as well as questioning what we were trying to achieve in Afghanistan. 'I know we're here for work but most of us are really trying to help them get back on their feet and yet this is how they treat us!'

When I quizzed him, he admitted that my family had been absolutely shattered by my conviction. Liz had almost fainted and had to take to her bed, which was completely unlike her. In emotional turmoil, she'd been unable to speak to anyone for the rest of that day. Kev promised me that she'd rallied a little since and was now focusing on launching a massive media campaign to gather support. 'The company has sent people to see them and they've appointed a PR agency to get the ball rolling,' Kev said. 'Don't worry, Bill, this isn't over yet.'

In the privacy of my cell, I pored over the letters he'd brought me. I could see that my wonderful little family was trying to be strong and I knew I had to do the same. Lisa wrote: *'Dearest Pop, What a shocker! We really weren't expecting that . . . I was right beside Mum when the call came through from Kev . . . I was able to take the phone and finish the call . . . You would be amazed at what is happening back here. You are a celebrity. I am so pleased you were never a nasty man – you have had thousands of comments and all so amazingly positive. Lots of 'regards to Uncle Billy' from your old soldiers . . . We set up a family Facebook group called Free Bill Shaw (thought of the name Free Billy!) and also learnt to 'tweet' on Twitter . . . G4S have arranged to have flyers handed out at the Army and Navy (rugby) game at Twickenham . . . And, the worst one yet to come . . . GMTV! Oh my god, you so owe me when you return!!'*

Bear said that Marcus was about to be deployed to Helmand with his regiment, which must have been hard for her – having her husband and her father both in Afghanistan at the same time. She brushed it aside in typical style, though, to tell me that the new MP for Dover, Charlie Elphicke, had promised to bring my case up in his maiden speech in the House of Commons. Then she revealed that she'd finally told Madeleine and Caius where I was and why. '*They have both taken it very well . . . and it is a relief they know . . . Loads of love and big hugs, Bear xx P.S: Pinch, Punch, first of the month again!! I win! xx*'

My dearest wife 'Lily' was equally encouraging and said that although she was gobsmacked at first, she'd woken up the day after the news determined to crack on and fight my corner. '*You would not believe the support, love, and everywhere I look there are petitions etc. This afternoon somebody started a support group on Facebook and a few hours later there were 600-plus people signed up.*' She asked me to reconsider my decision not to appeal which she said would be 'throwing in the towel'. Maybe she was right.

Craig's letter was in the same vein. He wrote: '*Hi Dad, I was devastated on Monday as we all were and have felt sick and empty all week but I am going to try and pick myself up and make sure that I do all that is possible to get this over-turned as soon as possible . . . Who would have thought you would have to go to such lengths to get some bloody attention? ha-ha.*'

I was relieved that G4S had sent their HR director Tina Easton, who soon became Liz's lifeline. She was accompanied by Paddy Toyne-Sewell, its director of communications, to offer family support. They say what goes around comes around and that's true because Paddy was in my platoon as an officer cadet at Sandhurst in 1989. The spitting image of Hugh Laurie's character in *Blackadder*, I nicknamed him 'George'. We'd never lost touch and I always called him 'George, my boy!' whenever I saw him. Fortunately he had a healthy sense of humour.

One day during an inspection on the parade ground, I examined his uniform closely before giving him the order, 'Show parade tonight, Mister Toyne-Sewell!' He looked confused. 'Show yourself free from bringing pets on parade.' Paddy looked even more puzzled until I said, 'Take off your beret.' He did as I asked and then I pointed out a greenfly clinging to the black felt. I think Paddy thought I was joking but at 22:00 hrs he was on parade as instructed telling the duty officer, 'Second-Lieutenant Toyne-Sewell, showing myself free from bringing pets on parade, Sir!' It was all good fun.

The next few days in my cell and the dog runs, I replayed the family's words of encouragement in my head, determined not to let them down. I convinced myself that the move to Pol-e-Charkhi would be a welcome break from the clinical routine of CNJC. Rob Langdon was there and some friends from Tawqeef. Best of all, I knew that this would be my last move – one step closer to the door and eventual freedom. The sooner I got there, the sooner the time would pass. The days trailed so slowly, though, and then they turned to weeks. Desperate to move, I began to be irritated by everything about CNJC from the squeak of Ba Ba's trolley to the tinny tunes of the jingly clock. I recognised every noise on the wing, including the rattling of chains, the murmuring of prayers, the constant spitting, the sound of someone using the toilet or crying out in their sleep.

With nothing to do but think, I began to go quietly bananas. Without any music, I hummed to myself constantly, trying to remember the lyrics of our favourite tunes. Lisa had told me to see how many titles of Queen songs I could recall but with nothing to write them down on, I could only add them up in my already overcrowded head. I felt increasingly paranoid and depressed and began to imagine all kinds of conspiracy scenarios. My dreams were filled with dark thoughts.

On one visit from Kev I was so worked up that I leaned forward, looked right and left, and asked him through the grille, 'Kev, do you think I'm guilty?'

'What do you mean? Guilty of what?'

'Corruption.'

'Don't be stupid!'

'Well, maybe I am. Maybe I did something wrong. Maybe that's why they gave me two years.'

Kev came right up to the glass. 'Do you think I'd be here if I thought that?' he said, his eyes blazing. 'Come on, Bill! This isn't like you. Stop it!'

The trouble was that I had nothing else to think about and each dawn brought a fresh mental battle. Trying to boost my morale, I forced myself to write breezy letters home, letting them know that I was okay. '*Two years is actually the minimum set. It could have been worse . . . Do not worry at all. I am very strong and can handle this. I just feel sorry for all of you. Please crack on and be assured I am fine . . . we just have to treat this as our bad year as a family.'*

My tone seemed to have the desired effect because they wrote straight back to say how much my letter had lifted them. Liz reminded me to think of the move to Pol-e-Charkhi as a new posting to new quarters. *'We have had a few of them in our lives. The difference this time is I won't be there to titivate. I wish I was there with you darling – well, I would prefer you here with me but if we were together then I wouldn't care where . . . I can't tell you how much I miss you, even your annoying habits he he . . .'* With such little variation in the routine and so few highlights, anything out of the ordinary was a big deal. So much so that when the prison received an unexpected visit from the Red Cross, Yama and I were like excited little kids. They came to visit us first in the exercise runs and to hand out some gifts. Scrambling for the best position at the fence, we each received a small carrier bag of goodies including some proper toothpaste and a toothbrush, a thin towel, a bar of perfumed soap and one of carbolic soap. The team of four men and four women made it clear that they could do nothing about our cases; they just wanted to know if we were being looked after. I assured them that I was and then asked, 'Have any of you ever been to Pol-e-Charkhi?'

'I have,' said one.

'What's it like?'

'Crowded. The prisoners I saw were living forty-eight to a room.'

Another said he found seven to a room. 'They're only allowed out once a day for an hour. Visits are every two weeks but they can have personal effects and parcels from outside.'

'Are they allowed music?' I asked, hooking my fingers through the mesh in hope. The disappointing answer was that they didn't know.

Later that day, two volunteers came to each cell to hand out thin notebooks and flimsy refills from a ballpoint pen. Once we had them, the guards refused to issue any further paper or pens. As it was almost impossible to write with the refill, I unwrapped a label from a bottle of water to wrap around it and give it more stability. The front of each notebook featured a photograph but it was pot luck which one you got. Some had the Taj Mahal or the Coliseum, I saw. Mine was of downtown Belfast; a place I knew well. It was the only image I'd had to look at in weeks and I studied it minutely through my broken specs; childishly excited when I recognised the Ulster Bank, a British road sign, or a public house. The thought of a cold pint of Guinness made me salivate.

A few days after the Red Cross visit, I was called from the exercise yard because Kev had come to see me with Kim's assistant, Mustafa. As I was being led past our wing I spotted the guards throwing belongings out of the cells and went mad, shuffling to my cell and yelling, 'Hey! Leave my stuff alone!' They'd thrown my new toothbrush onto the floor, and I managed to drop to my knees in my chains and retrieve it. But they confiscated my carbolic soap, claiming that a mobile phone was found inside one bar in the other wing.

When you have nothing, everything is precious. Losing

that small bar of soap upset me beyond all reason. It had been such a treat to be able to wash my clothes properly in a place where I was constantly sweating. The guards had also disturbed the latest web spun by Sapper Spider, who was nowhere to be found. That really did it for me with CNJC. I couldn't bear to stay there another day and begged Kev to hurry my transfer through. To compound my misery, I developed a raging toothache and had nothing but some useless tablets from the prison doctor to numb the pain.

To make the time pass more quickly, I went to bed earlier and earlier. Like Rob in Tawqeef, I spent much of my day in bed, reading or dozing. At least when I was asleep I could dream of being home and free – maybe walking Trotsky the dog up through the orange groves behind our villa or taking the grandchildren on a tour of Dover Castle. Anywhere but prison. My fellow inmates tried to rally me by repeatedly inviting me to play chess with them in the dog runs. On the wing, they'd devised all kinds of games, including who could spit the highest or leave the most sneeze particles on the ceilings. Lovely. The best they came up with was a method of swapping food. Putting their hands through the hatch, they'd throw eggs, cakes, pieces of fruit, or bottles of water to the opposite cage. The recipient would catch whatever it was in a makeshift cradle fashioned out of a towel.

Once caught, it could be kept or swapped by slinging it diagonally across to another cell on the other side of the corridor and passing it down the wing. If it was dropped, many an hour would be spent trying to retrieve it with a comb, toothbrush, or even a flip-flop while others cheered.

If it was out of reach then it could be retrieved at exercise time, unless the guards grabbed it first. The only thing I ever had to give away were my morning eggs, which I never ate. If I didn't give them to Ba Ba in return for more tea I'd keep one for a game of swapsies.

I kept track of UK time on my watch and tried to imagine what the family were up to. They were four-and-a-half hours behind Kabul so I'd picture them getting up, having breakfast, and then starting another day without me. At least they had the campaign to keep them busy. I thought about my sister Betty's wedding too – I was meant to be giving her away on 19 June in Salford. She was the sibling I was probably closest to and I would be gutted not to lead her in to the registry office to marry her lovely Jim, who'd made her so happy late in life, but I'd insisted in my last few letters home that she should go ahead without me.

One afternoon when I was especially low, I heard the guards come in and then the voices of the US mentors. They eventually stopped at my cell and I was surprised to see a Western woman with them. She was dressed in civilian clothes, her head covered in a scarf, and she smiled and told me that she was checking the facilities. Leaning forward, she asked quietly, 'Do you recognise me?'

I had to admit that I didn't, but then I was in such a daze by then I don't think I'd have recognised my own sister.

Out of earshot of the mentors she told me that she was Lt Col Debbie Poneskis, a member of the RMP and the ISAF Provost Marshal, who'd come to visit me on behalf of the military police family. Apparently, we'd served alongside each other in the Gulf War when I was OC and she was 2IC of a sister company. When she began to tell me of all the support I had from the military, I cracked. She reached through the hatch to shake my hand and covertly slipped me a rubber wristband, which I quickly secreted.

'Thank you,' I told her, 'and please forgive me for being so emotional. I am truly grateful for your visit.'

Once she'd gone, I sat on my bed and examined the wristband, which was in support of all our fellow military policemen lost in Afghanistan and Iraq. The inscription, '*They led by example. Gone but not forgotten. Exemplo Ducemus*'. I turned it inside out so that no one could see the red RMP flash on it and managed to hide it under my watchstrap. Inhaling, I quickly realised that it was highly perfumed from Debbie's scent, which smelt like heaven to me in that clinical, unfragranced place. The memory of it will stay with me for a very long time. My fragrant 'angel' came back to see me a couple of weeks later with a copy of the RMP corps journal, which I read from cover to cover, devouring news of friends and colleagues serving around the world.

The journal reminded me of happier days, when being in uniform meant something. If I'd been suspected of a crime as a soldier not as a civilian in Kabul, the Afghan authorities would have alerted the British military, who'd have investigated. In the unlikely event that I'd have been prosecuted, I'd at least have been tried in a court where I understood all the proceedings and would have been able to plead my own case and then appeal without fear. If convicted, I'd have served my time in British military detention before being discharged from the service. Without the protection of that uniform or the red beret I'd been proud to wear for almost thirty years, I was left to rot.

A few days later, I had another visit – from the British military chaplain, the Reverend Michael Meachin, who was with the Royal Navy. A good and kind man, he offered up some prayers and brought me a box of sweets and toiletries, promising to send me a New Testament Bible in a day or two. It arrived but the guards wouldn't let me keep anything until my transfer. Sensing that I might be leaving soon, the Quartermaster came to see me in the dog run. Through Yama, he said he wanted me to buy him and one of his guards a digital camera each for 'looking after' me. I wasn't allowed a single personal possession but they'd bend the rules to suit them. The answer was 'No chance, pal!' but I politely said I'd see what I could do.

I was in the exercise run a few days later when several prisoners from Pol-e-Charkhi limped past the razor wire on their way to the courthouse. One was a former inmate of CNJC whom some of my cellmates recognised.

'Please ask him what Pol-e-Charkhi is like,' I asked Yama.

The response was encouraging. Yama told me, 'He says Pol-e-Charkhi is a hundred per cent better. He says to tell you he'd rather have four years in Pol-e than forty-four nights here.'

That was good to hear. Now all I wanted was to get transferred there as soon as possible.

Nineteen

'Conduct After Capture' was a training technique I'd first been briefed on ten years earlier in Argentina. Previously known as Resistance to Interrogation, it was designed to train soldiers on how to deal with the stresses and strains of captivity.

In Buenos Aires in November 2000, as part of a United Nations Military Observer's Course, I learned how to behave with any possible captors in order to avoid further violence or confrontation. The key lessons were to remain subservient, never argue or antagonise, and to carefully take in as much as you can about your surroundings. If it is possible to escape, then the advice is to do it early and not leave it a year down the line.

During one of our regular briefings in a building on the UN base, a group of heavily armed 'insurgents' suddenly broke in and took us all prisoner. They prodded and poked us and screamed that we were '*Cerdos extranjeros!*' (foreign pigs). With alarming speed, we were trussed up, hooded, and thrown into the back of a truck. To keep us disorientated, we were driven what seemed like miles, making sharp right and left turns which rolled us painfully around the back of the vehicle. We had no idea how far we were going or where we were being taken. For a moment, the thought occurred to me that this could be for real.

The truck stopped suddenly, and with much shouting of '*Madre putas!*' (mother f***ers) we were manhandled off and rolled onto the ground, where we suddenly felt cold liquid being poured all over our clothes and hoods. There was an overwhelming smell of petrol. Even though I kept telling myself this was an exercise, it certainly activated the adrenalin as I lay there fearing a lighted match. My heart was still pumping long after they'd pulled our hoods off and laughingly patted us on the backs.

Two years later, I found myself teaching exactly the same techniques to ex-special forces and former police personnel in another South American country. I'd been nearing the end of my attachment with the Spanish Infantry in Pamplona when I received a phone call from our RMP Close Protection (CP) wing in Longmoor, Hampshire. 'We're sending a small team to Colombia,' I was told. 'The mission is to train up fifty bodyguards to protect embassy staff and their families. The Revolutionary Armed Forces of Colombia, known as FARC, have made some serious threats against British personnel there, and we need to make an urgent response.'

I'd heard of the FARC guerrillas and knew how feared they were, not least because they controlled over a third of the country, much of it jungle. They funded their campaign to the tune of hundreds of millions of dollars a year by kidnapping wealthy businessmen and foreigners, as well as bank robberies, extortion rackets and taxation of drugs cartels. In 2001, the CIA reported a longstanding connection between FARC and the IRA, and later that year three IRA explosives experts were arrested in Bogotá and charged with teaching FARC bomb-making methods. It was following those arrests that new threats had been made to anyone with a connection to America or the UK.

The British Ambassador and his team had their own special security advisor, who was ex-SAS, but their protection largely involved a few local bodyguards and frequent 'lockdown' procedures. They lived in various houses in the diplomatic quarter and their embassy was in a building shared with a private business. Colombia had plenty of former Special Forces officers and policemen willing to take on the FCO protection role but they needed to be trained in defensive not offensive action. I was picked for the specially named Overseas Advisory Protection Team not only because of my language skills but because I was a weapons instructor, qualified in training, field tactics and self-defence techniques. Needless to say, our younger colleagues quickly dubbed us the 'OAPs'.

Colombia's sprawling capital Bogotá teemed with traffic and people. The air was choked with exhaust fumes and its streets with armed police and soldiers. Almost as soon as we arrived we were presented with our potential CP candidates, and we hand-picked the ones we wanted, rejecting several we thought weren't up to the job. They all knew about firearms and dealing with nasty individuals and had seen more than their fair share of violence. A few had worked in undercover killing squads where they'd be sent into mountain villages to break into a suspect's home and cart them off, never to be seen again. It had been felt that this was the only way to deal with criminals at that time. The trouble was that we needed to retrain them not to kill unnecessarily.

'Protect, use suppressive fire, and withdraw with no loss of life to those in your care,' was our repeated message. 'It's all very well to go in spraying bullets, but you must think about the safety of who you are protecting first.' Teamwork was not always easy to teach to trigger-happy mavericks, but they were enthusiastic and we hoped that with enough practice to instil muscle memory, we'd be able to teach them how to maintain the required protective bubble.

Because our arrival in the country made us immediate targets ourselves, we were armed and deployed to the remote and heavily protected '*Caribineros*' College at Facatativá an hour from the capital. At 2,500 metres above sea level, it was often hard to breathe while training in the forested hills. Over the next eight weeks, we embarked on an intensive regime. We spent hours on the firing range, and did environmental testing and ambush drills. Every eventuality was rehearsed and then teams were sent off on long drives with us acting as personnel in their care.

Armed vehicle checkpoints were commonplace in Colombia and you never knew if they were legitimate. Many a kidnap took place at these VCPs with frightening speed and accuracy. Our trainees used to laughingly tell us it was easy to spot a FARC checkpoint because they always wore the same baby blue rubber Wellington boots. They must have nicked a truck-load.

We were on constant alert and on the odd weekend we got back to Bogatá, we'd keep a very low profile and only go to certain bars in the heavily patrolled '*zona rosada*' (pink zone). We only ever went out in pairs and carried 9mm Sig Saur pistols. There were 'No Weapons' signs at the entrance to every bar and searches were frequent. Shots and explosions would fill the night air as FARC or some other criminal element had a pop at someone. On one of our last weekends, four of us flew to Cartegena on the northern coast for some

R&R. It was a beautiful town and we visited the local fortress and port. We ended by sipping coffee and taking in the views at a café opposite a government building. We'd only just left and walked about fifty yards away when there was an almighty explosion. Smoke billowed out of the windows of the government building and there was glass and debris everywhere. We withdrew to a safe distance as the police arrived in strength and found out later that a FARC guerrilla had planted a suitcase bomb in one of the offices. Another lucky escape and a bitter taste of what the men we'd just trained would be up against almost daily.

In CNJC, I couldn't help but think back to all that we'd taught those men about conduct after capture and how to escape if they could. There was no possible escape for me and, from what I'd heard there'd be none in Pol-e-Charkhi either. I'd just have to continue to adopt the other techniques of keeping my head down and coping instead. I only hoped I'd be able to practise what I'd preached.

When Kev came in to see me to tell me that he had a surprise, I couldn't dare allow myself to think that it might be my transfer. His news stunned me – I was to have a visitor from the UK. My son-in-law Marcus was coming. He was stationed in Helmand Province with 2 Scots but was making the dangerous journey north. I was thrilled and anxious all at once.

Lisa and Marcus had first met when we were based in what we called the 'sunshine posting' of Cyprus in 1997. She came to visit us one summer from Durham University and quickly fell for the handsome ADC to the commander of British forces. I don't blame her – he's a smashing lad. Five years later, he and I were both posted to Rheindahlen where he was a Captain, Staff Officer at the Allied Rapid Reaction Force Headquarters, and I was the OC of the Military Police Company. His previous tour of duty in Helmand was in 2008 and when he'd come to Kabul for a conference, he and a colleague stayed with me at Anjuman for a couple of nights and we'd had a good time. This would be very different.

It was something of a military operation in itself for Marcus to get into CNJC. The company laid on an armed CP escort and advised him to dress in civilian clothes to keep a low profile. I could tell he was shocked to see his normally pristine father-in-law led into the visiting room handcuffed, chained and in prison uniform. It wasn't easy for me to greet him looking the way I did either, but I fought to keep a grip and yelled a cheery 'Welcome to Guantanamo Bay'.

It all seemed so surreal and humiliating. Thankfully, Marcus was extremely sensitive to how I felt and played it down, joking about the difficulties I faced. We swapped some squaddie humour and he told me about the amazing campaign Liz and Lisa had started in the UK. Although I found it hard to hear news from home, I soaked up everything he told me. I thanked him for having Liz to stay for so long and made a few 'mother-in-law' jokes but he brushed it off. Marcus is a bit like me – whenever there are too many women in the room he just buggers off. I told him I'd arranged for a bouquet of roses and freesias to be delivered to Liz the following day, 21 May, our thirty-third wedding anniversary. The flowers were provided by the company to mimic her wedding bouquet. 'Please make sure she's home to receive them?' I asked.

Marcus said the new British ambassador, Sir William Patey,

was very interested in my case which gave me some hope that he might be persuaded to ask President Karzai for a possible pardon further down the line. He also had an appointment with the Deputy Ambassador and had dinner with the Defence Attaché Colonel Simon Diggins, who was totally on side.

'I know you have to be careful what you say, Marcus,' I told him, 'but please tell them that if this goes even more wrong then I really need the embassy to kick in.'

Frustratingly, he was only allowed thirty minutes with me – longer than usual but no time at all after the palaver he'd gone through to get there. 'You know the girls want to fly out to see you,' he told me, as the guards indicated it was time for him to go.

'No!' I replied, a little too sharply. 'Thank you, but please pass the message on that I'm fine but I couldn't bear any other family visits.'

The guards made me stand then and as I was led shuffling away, I looked back over my shoulder to see Marcus watching my every painful step. It was such a wrench to go, especially when I knew he was going back to the base to call the family. 'Please don't tell them about the conditions here or that my head's been shaved,' I'd pleaded. 'You know how much they tease me about my hair.' He promised to be economical with the truth.

My next visitor a few days later was almost as much of a surprise. Mark Spandler had flown back into Afghanistan now that he was no longer considered at risk from arrest. He was glad to be back but it was clear from the outset that he felt somewhat responsible for my situation and was very distressed to see me in prison garb. 'Neither of us did anything wrong,

Mark,' I reminded him. We shared some tears and he vowed to keep chasing the judicial system and the British embassy and I really appreciated his visit.

By this time, I'd been in CNJC for nearly nine weeks. It had been over a month since I'd been sentenced and Kim had given verbal notice of our intent to appeal, but my promised transfer to Pol-e-Charkhi still hadn't happened. My sense of utter helplessness was now complete. A pawn in a political game over which I had no control, my spirit felt all but crushed. I didn't even have the strength to follow through on my hunger strike. What was the point? Who'd even notice in there? Apart from Kev, perhaps. He never failed to come and see me as often as he could and even cancelled his own leave back to the UK so as not to abandon me. He was always his cheery self, trying to keep me buoyant and updating me on what was happening with world news and tales of the lads back in Anjuman.

'Kim'll be back in a few days, Bill,' he told me. 'You know she's going to need you to follow through on the appeal process before the new deadline.'

I was delighted that she was coming back but was still very worried about rocking the boat. My so-called 'crime' carried a sentence of two to ten years and they'd given me the minimum. What if the prosecution decided to stick the boot in and give me the maximum sentence because I'd dared appeal? That wasn't a risk worth taking.

Kim came to see me on Saturday, 29 May. She was furious that I hadn't been transferred to Pol-e-Charkhi yet and could tell what effect this was having on my mental health. When one of the guards came to tell her that visiting time was up, she went mad. 'I'm his attorney and can stay as long as I need to!' she countered. When we'd finished, she went straight to see the Ministry of Justice and the British embassy and secured a promise that I'd be transferred the following week.

Kim wasn't the only one who was adamant that we should appeal. In letters from home my family said I had nothing to lose. The clincher for me came when the appeal court judge gave Kim a guarantee that he would not increase my sentence beyond the two years. 'All right then. Let's do it,' I told her finally. 'I only hope it's the right decision.'

Then came the news that Liz and Lisa were flying out to see me the following week, no matter what. 'No, they mustn't!' I told Kev. 'It's far too dangerous!' The honest truth was that I was too embarrassed to be seen in chains. Kev told me that no matter what he or I said, they'd made their decision and were on their way. 'You know what women are like,' he added with a shrug.

Inwardly, I was elated at the thought of seeing their beautiful, smiling faces, but I was equally scared for their safety. Kev promised me they'd be in the care of the best CP team he had and that everything had been set up for their arrival, including transport, security and accommodation. He went over all the details with me until I was satisfied. The Commandant initially agreed that we could have a private room for the family reunion, which was fantastic news, but then came the sting in the tail. He said that if the US mentors found out they'd almost certainly disallow this and would insist on no physical contact. Unfortunately, of course, the humourless mentors did find out and refused to grant me any special privileges.

On the morning of Monday, 31 May, I awoke to the knowledge that I'd be seeing my wife and daughter that day. It hardly seemed possible. I'd last set eyes on Lisa in Dover in December and I'd kissed Liz goodbye in Spain in early January. So much had happened since then – for us all.

I paced my cell all day, waiting for visiting time. Thanks to Kev, I knew their timetable intimately and kept checking my watch to figure out where they'd be and when. They'd flown into Dubai on the Sunday and been met there by Kev who sorted out their visas. Then they'd flown into Kabul airport early Monday. If I'd been in the exercise yard then I might have seen their plane overhead. They'd been met by the CP team and issued with body armour before being briefed on what to do in case of an insurgent attack or IED. God forbid. Taken on that bumpy, uncomfortable ride to Anjuman they'd been given a full tour of the base. Kev was going to show them all the things he and I'd set up there, including the bar, gym, BBQ, and a 'beach' complete with deck chairs and sand.

After lunch, they'd be re-equipped with body armour and then separated so as to minimise risk. The lead vehicle was always the one most likely to drive over an IED first and I wondered which of them would have been placed in that one. Then they'd be taken out of the compound in a convoy of armoured Land Cruisers. With four heavily armed bodyguards each along with Mark, Kim, and Kev, they'd head out onto the Jalalabad Road – Route Violent. Dear God. My girls were going to be on one of the most dangerous roads in the world. How could I ever have allowed them to come?

I knew that once they arrived at the prison there'd almost

certainly be a long wait as their papers were checked and sorted. They'd also be searched. I knew they'd be nervous and I hoped someone warned them that there weren't any public loos. By the time I heard the gate to my wing open, I had plotted their route every step of the way and knew that they had to be in the building already. I was full of such trepidation that my stomach was churning. Adorned with my usual 'jewellery', I was led outside.

As I walked out into the tunnel of barbed wire that formed one corner of the courtyard, I suddenly spotted my lovely Liz and Lisa entering the compound on the other side of the wire. Fortunately I saw them before they saw me. They looked small, vulnerable and utterly panic-stricken. To break the ice, I shouted, 'Pinch, Punch! First of the month for tomorrow. I've won this time!'

They spun round and saw me for the first time and I shall never forget their shocked expressions. I was two stone lighter, pale from a lack of sun, and draped in chains. Liz ran across to the fence to try to kiss me as I limped towards her to do the same. The guards rushed forward and tried to stop her before she could reach me but she pushed on anyway. All I could manage was, 'I'm sorry, Lily, I am so, so sorry.' I couldn't even wipe away my tears with my hands.

The guards intervened then and insisted Kev take them inside. In that horrid airless room we sat separated by plate glass after almost six months apart. We did our best to communicate as the guards leered openly at my wife and daughter. We tried to be brave for each other but it was hard to have them so close and yet so far. Knowing that we didn't have long, we talked as quickly as possible as they filled me in on news of the family and the campaign. 'The petition to Downing Street has more than 5,000 names on it already!' Liz said, repeatedly wiping her eyes. 'Lisa and I are going to take it there ourselves. Someone suggested we chain ourselves naked to the railings but then we'd only end up in jail too!'

Bear added that although she and Liz had tried to take the safety talks and security seriously when they'd arrived in Kabul, their nerves got them giggling. 'The CP team told us that if we're forced to stop, we should exit the car as quickly as possible and crawl along the ground to get away. Mum and I couldn't stop laughing because the body armour's so heavy if she dropped out of the car she'd hit the floor like an upturned turtle and never be able to move!'

They couldn't believe how thin and tired I was and had never seen me so weak and vulnerable. I was always the tough guy – the husband, the soldier, the father, the policeman – unbreakable. Or so we'd all thought. My letters had done a good job of tricking them into thinking I was in better shape than I really was. They, too, looked exhausted after so many months of worrying and their long journey to see me.

'Madeleine has written to the Queen and David Cameron to ask for their help in freeing her Pop,' Lisa said, struggling to keep the conversation upbeat. 'And both children have done you some lovely new drawings. Madeleine has even done one of Lady GaGa because she knows how much you love her songs. It won't be long now before we get you out of there, Dad, and don't forget what an amazing team you have behind you. Kev especially is being an absolute trouper.'

'Yes,' I agreed. 'He's been a rock for us all.'

The guards were unusually lax and allowed us to have longer

than usual together – probably because they were enjoying the leering. After twenty minutes of this emotional spectacle, though, they'd had enough and told us the time was up. My girls promised to come back and see me the following day and we pressed the palms of our hands to the glass. Outside, Liz and Lisa waited until I emerged so that they could run to the fence as I passed. Both managed to peck me through the wire. They then poked their fingers through the fence to stroke my face and wipe away my tears.

Just then, one of the mentors came around the corner and went absolutely mad and demanded to know what was going on. The guards pulled me away unceremoniously as the girls watched in anguish as I was led back to my cell.

Lisa had brought a copy of the *Daily Mail* for me to read; the first British newspaper I'd seen in months. The guards checked it and then brought me the front and back pages only. 'No!' I cried, 'I need it all.' I lost it then and asked Yama to explain. Eventually, they relented and brought me the rest. Agog at the unfamiliar photographs and news stories, I read about the General Election and wondered if the campaign to free me might be affected if the hung parliament was slow to start up. I was amazed by how much disruption the volcanic ash cloud had caused. Then I spotted a small mark in biro under one of the pictures and realised it was a message from Lisa. '*Luv U*' it said in tiny writing. I started to look very closely then and discovered lots of similar messages throughout – a few funny one-liners and lots of good wishes and hugs. She'd scattered them all over the place so that the guards wouldn't notice. It was like a game trying to find them all and the whole time that I spent doing it, my funny 'Bear' was in that cell with me. Talk about a pick-me-up!

The guards came back later that night and I worried they were going to take my precious newspaper away. Instead, they stood the other side of the mesh and made a series of gestures. I didn't need a translator as they pointed to my things and said, 'Pol-e-Charkhi!' At last! I thought. The final jail.

'Tomorrow. You go tomorrow,' Yama explained. I could tell from his voice that the news saddened him. Without me, there'd be no one else to talk to in English or to call the Americans 'Bloody bastards!'

I didn't sleep at all well that night, mulling the events of the day over and over in my head and wondering what the next would bring. I was also worried what the transfer might mean for Lisa and Liz. Would they still be able to come? I was up well before dawn and went through my routine for the last time in CNJC. I listened to the prayers at 04:00 hrs and waited for my breakfast. I read Lisa's newspaper again, delighted to spot a couple of new messages that I'd missed, including a smiley face and one which just said, *'Pop, xx'* Then I waited.

Just before 10:00 hrs, the guards appeared, opened the cell door and made me pass out all my bedding. They then retrieved my bag from the storage locker, rummaged around inside and passed me some clothes. Without a moment's hesitation, I stripped off my prison uniform and pulled on my tracksuit bottoms and polo shirt. It was fantastic to wear personal clothes again. I'd forgotten what it felt like to have the freedom to move and cloth that was comfortable against my skin. I kept asking for the bag so that I could put on some deodorant but they refused, placed the 'silverware' on me and led me away.

'Good luck, William!' Yama cried. Apart from a Taliban commander, every prisoner in the wing banged on the mesh or waved through their hatches, pushing out their hands to shake mine. If I hadn't hated the place so much, I'd have been sorry to leave but then the jingly clock chimed ten and, as if on cue, played a few tinny chords of 'Auld Lang Syne'.

The guards took me to a holding cell where two Afghan prisoners from the opposite wing were also waiting for transfer. I nodded hello but one spat on the floor and refused to acknowledge my presence. We were taken outside and helped onto a minibus with metal grilles over the windows. There was no air conditioning of course and the heat was stifling – probably thirty-three degrees. Two armed guards joined us and we set off for Pol-e-Charkhi an hour away on the outskirts of the city.

Looking through the rear window at that place where I'd spent the most dispiriting nine weeks of my life – time I could never get back – the words of 'Auld Lang Syne' repeated themselves in my head as I thought of the poor buggers locked up within its walls. '*Should old acquaintance be forgot and never brought to mind?*'

Facing forward, I tried to think ahead. Once again, I had no idea what I was going to or how long I'd be there, but I needed to believe that the next prison would be better.

It had to be.

Twenty

Not only hadn't I seen one glimpse of the world beyond CNJC's walls for nine weeks, I hadn't been in any kind of moving vehicle for all that time either. The strange rocking and bumping sensation as the minibus moved along the busy roads gave me motion sickness.

I'd almost forgotten about Kabul's potholes, traffic and dust until my throat, nose and eyes quickly clogged with the stuff. All I'd seen of the sky in over two months was the small square patch above the dog run and that was usually cluttered with the sight, sound and smell of military aircraft and aviation fuel. Out in the open again, my eyes couldn't begin to take in all the fast-moving images, bright colours and familiar landmarks that I recognised as gladly as old friends. When we drove past the end of the road leading to the Anjuman base, I spotted some of our vehicles driven by my lads and almost cried out in pain.

I knew we'd reached Pol-e-Charkhi when we came to a series of outer checkpoints that formed a ring of steel around the complex's medieval-looking mud-plastered walls. So this was it; the prison known as Afghanistan's Alcatraz. It was built in the middle of desert scrub where escape was virtually impossible. After passing through a large metal gate we drove into the car park of what seemed to be a massive building site. The high walls of the prison looked extremely daunting and I could see the various blocks which I knew represented the shape of a cartwheel from the air. We pulled up outside one building and a guard alighted to find out where to take us.

Melting in the full glare of the sun, I squinted and did a quick recce of the car park and was surprised to see two of our G4S vehicles from the British embassy contract. Three of the lads I knew were standing next to them armed and ready; completely unaware of my presence. I gestured to the remaining guard that I wanted to say hello but he refused. I banged on the windows to try to attract the lads' attention through the scratched glass but, frustratingly, they couldn't hear or see me. Elsewhere, I could see queues of wilting Afghans carrying bags of what looked like food and clothing. It must have been visiting time.

The first guard returned and helped me off the bus in my chains. With my awkward gait, I was led to a ramshackle building near the car park and towards a flight of stairs. Lenny, on the embassy contract, was waiting at the bottom. When he saw me he literally threw himself at me, crying, 'Bill! Oh, Bill!' It felt so incredible to be hugged – my first physical contact with anyone for over two months. Unable to hug him back, I just leaned my body against his in silent gratitude.

'Don't worry, mate!' he told me, his eyes glinting. 'Everyone's behind you. This bloody nonsense has to be over soon.'

Outside the Commandant's office, my leg chains and hand-cuffs were removed and I was allowed to sit. The guard then ushered me into the office to meet a man about the same age as me with a ready smile and curly grey hair. He shook my hand and welcomed me through an interpreter. I found out later that the Commandant spoke perfect English, but wouldn't use it. We weren't alone. Also in the room was a British lieutenant-colonel from the embassy with a female colleague, neither of whom I'd met before. They were accompanied by a member of the RMP. I didn't know him either but he shook my hand enthusiastically, covertly slipping a few dollars into my palm. 'Good luck, mate,' he whispered.

I thought these people must have been there to check on me but it soon became apparent that they were simply there to discuss British support to the prison. We stood chatting for a bit, which felt so unreal – as if we were standing around with schooners of sherry in the officer's mess. Then the Commandant explained that I was to be placed into Block 10. 'It is maximum security and the cell has been selected specially,' he announced proudly. 'Your wing has recently been redecorated.' I think he was showing off for the visitors.

'Is that where Robert Langdon is?' I asked. 'He was with me in Tawqeef. It would be good to see him again.'

'No. The Australian is in a separate unit. It is impossible for you to see him.'

I wondered if I'd also be prevented from seeing Abdul Wakil, Marbat or some of the other men I'd come to know in the early days. It was frustrating to think I had friends there I might never be able to meet again.

The niceties over, I was re-shackled and led back outside. As I shuffled towards the bus, I spotted the embassy lads waiting for me. Lenny must have told them I was there. They all waved and shouted their encouragement, which really cheered me up.

The driver drove us to the inner gates of the giant wheel

and stopped at one of the forbidding-looking blocks where the two Afghans were taken off. The bus lurched forward again and stopped further along at a different block. I was helped out by one guard and the second followed with my belongings. As we entered the corridor, I was shocked to see how rundown and filthy the place was. Stuffy and airless, it was buzzing with flies and mosquitoes. This was almost back to Tawqeef standards and yet this was meant to be a new, high-tech prison. My heart thumped with anxiety and I kept thinking, 'No . . . not again . . . Please . . . don't leave me here!'

To my enormous relief, the guards exchanged words with a man in sweat-stained khaki who indicated that we weren't in the right place so it was back to the bus. Our driver was directed instead along a dusty track to a separate square compound. There were manned guard towers on every corner and razor wire more than a metre deep on all the ramparts. Guards armed with automatic rifles kept me in their sights as I passed through a series of impregnable metal gates. This place was reserved for the most dangerous members of Al-Qaeda as well as senior Taliban commanders. Maximum security or not, I was about to be thrown in among them.

The interior was all concrete and metal; far cleaner and newer than the previous wing but with no air conditioning. I waited at a reception area whilst my bag was searched. My CNJC guards removed my chains and left me without even a backwards glance, swinging the much-hated shackles as they walked away. Having been thoroughly searched, I watched my belongings being tipped onto the concrete floor. To my dismay, one of the guards found my $400 but not another $30 hidden in a tube of calcium tablets. They confiscated the cash and handed me everything except my iPod and charging unit. I was desperate to hear some music again but at least I had my cherished toiletries and medicines as well as some books to get stuck into.

I couldn't get over the freedom of being able to walk without chains as the guards led me deep into the building. This was the furthest I'd walked in a straight line for months. The whole place smelled of wet cement and paint. Kev had warned me that there were several thousand prisoners in Pol-e, hundreds of whom were foreigners: mainly Africans, Iranians, Russians and Chinese on drugs or trafficking charges. At the next gate I was taken aback to be greeted by a young Westerner with a shaved head and a long straggly beard. He was in Afghan clothing but his accent was British. He told me his name was Anthony Malone as he smiled warmly and said, 'Welcome to Pol-e. The guards say you're to be moved to a holding cell. Don't worry, Bevan and I will make sure they move you to your proper cell soon.'

'Bevan?'

'Bevan Campbell. South African. Good bloke. He and I share a cell on your wing. You must be hungry. I'll get the guards to bring you some lunch.'

After he left I was ushered through the gate and into a long corridor with seven cells along the right-hand side. I was placed in cell No. 3 and allowed my belongings. The guards also passed me a blanket, a metal plate, a plastic cup and a spoon. I was even handed the sleeping bag I'd had in Tawqeef along with my original pillow. Luxury.

My new quarters consisted of two metal bunks screwed to

the wall below a small window with bars but no glass. Large blowflies buzzed freely in and out. The mattress was nothing more than a thin piece of foam with the lattice frame showing through. It didn't look very comfortable but it was better than the floor. The two by three metre space was divided by a wall, behind which lay the toilet and an open shower with a button to activate a single cold water tap.

I measured out the cell in paces and discovered it was four by seven. It had recently been decorated in creamy yellow gloss and stank of paint. Whoever had been wielding the brush had been very sloppy and paint was dripped all over the old brown carpet, the metal bedsteads, and splashed over the toilet and shower. I didn't care because I was so happy to have shampoo, soap, deodorant and a decent towel. My God! I could wash and shave whenever I wanted.

After a short while, a second Westerner appeared at the door of my cell, accompanied by two guards. My first impression was of a long-haired chap with a beard, dressed in jeans and a T-shirt. 'I'm Bevan,' he said in a broad South African accent. 'Don't worry. Me and Anthony'll look after you.'

He passed me a mop, some disinfectant and a broom. Although the cell was quite clean, I was eager to get it ship-shape before I unpacked. Bevan spoke very good Dari and the guards seemed to do everything he asked. In front of them he confirmed that I'd safely received all my belongings. 'All except my iPod and my money, which were confiscated,' I replied.

'Leave that to me,' he said, returning soon afterwards with a senior officer who produced my folded wad of dollars and counted it out in front of Bevan to confirm that none had been stolen. I didn't yet know if I'd need money in Pol-e-Charkhi but I was grateful to have it just in case. The officer seemed reluctant to hand over my iPod and Bevan explained that he'd never seen one before and needed to check it wasn't a telephone. Fortunately, it had some juice in the battery so when I placed it on the docking station music burst from it suddenly, filling the wing. The song was 'Make Me Smile' by Steve Harley and the words were, *'There's nothing left, all gone and run away. Maybe you'll tarry for a while. It's just a test, a game for us to play. Win or lose, it's hard to smile . . .'*

Bevan's face cracked into a grin. 'I've hardly heard any music in three f***king years!' he cried.

Three years? My God.

I spent the next two hours cleaning and sorting my kit. Even though I knew I could be facing two years in that small, sterile space, I had all my stuff and people to talk to in English. I even had music again. Life was sweet.

After a while a prison 'trusty' brought me some lunch served from two plastic buckets on a trolley, one which contained rice and the other beans and potatoes. Made in a kitchen that catered for thousands of prisoners and staff, I didn't expect much and I wasn't disappointed.

At about 14:00 hrs, Bevan turned up once again. 'Would you like to join us for tea and biscuits?' he asked. I couldn't bloody believe it as a guard unlocked my door and let me go with him. The three of us sat in cell No. 1 talking and laughing. Having proper tea and biscuits was brilliant – the traditions of the military continued. The lads filled me in on the prison and said everyone on the wing knew exactly who

I was and what I was in for. 'There's already a bounty on your head,' Bevan told me.

'Oh,' was all I could say in response. 'How much?'

'$10,000.'

I didn't know whether to be frightened or disappointed. I'd half expected more.

'Our fellow "guests" are in for life so they might as well slot you; they've nothing to lose,' said Anthony. 'Keep a low profile and don't go anywhere on your own.'

Bevan nibbled on a Rich Tea and added, 'The guards are another worry. They are very low paid and the price on your head is about three years' salary to them. It'd be easy to let someone slip into your cell at night.' Suddenly, life didn't seem so sweet.

'Could be worse,' Bevan added. 'If it wasn't for the bounty and the death threats you'd be in one of the barrack blocks where they live fifty to a cell.'

Those two men looked after me so well from Day One. They shared the food they paid the guards to buy for them from the prison shop, and the rations sent into them by well-wishers. When Anthony discovered I could get supplies brought in from G4S, he gave me a list of items to ask for that might make us all more comfortable. It included peanut butter, Pot Noodles, cheese and crackers. 'We could also do with some soap powder, disinfectant, antiseptic wipes, coffee, tea, bins, plastic crockery and flasks,' he said. I added sheets and a duvet to my list.

Our cells were locked during the day but many Afghans were allowed to walk freely up and down the corridor of our wing. Bevan and Anthony were also allowed out to cook meals or make tea at a small food preparation area of sorts. It had a jingly electric hob and bare wires hanging from the wall they could splice the cable from a kettle into. Because of my high security status, I wouldn't be allowed out but Bevan and Anthony could cook me food and make me hot drinks. 'Don't worry. We'll work on the guards to let you into our cell now and again,' Bevan said. 'And when it's time for exercise, I'll make sure you always go with me.'

Keen to learn everything about Pol-e-Charkhi and my new friends, I bombarded them with questions. Anthony, a thirty-seven-year-old former British paratrooper from Teesside, explained that he'd converted to Islam and was renamed 'Al Hudein', adding, 'Please call me that if ever the Afghans are around.' He spent a lot of time in prayer in the Taliban corridor. Handing me some Afghan clothes, he added, 'You'd better put these on so that you don't stick out so much.' So much for the joy of wearing my tracksuit.

Although Bev hadn't cut his hair or beard for two years, he was even more pernickety about cleanliness than I was, and freely admitted he suffered from Obsessive Compulsive Disorder. I nicknamed him the 'OCD DCH' (Drug-Crazed Hippy), a moniker he loved and used ever after. Looking at his Western clothes, though, I countered, 'But you wear what you like!'

A devout Christian who'd refused to convert, Bevan explained, 'It's taken me three years to get accepted, mate. The Afghans respect my faith even if they don't agree with it. You should really grow a beard and convert like Anthony, Bill. It'll make your life in here a lot easier.' I didn't mind the first so much, but I'd have to think seriously about the second.

Gently, I asked them why they were there. Anthony said he'd come to Kabul to set up his own security and logistics business. He'd been charged with non-payment of a $60,000 debt and was imprisoned for ten months. Unfortunately, the money he owed belonged to a senior Afghan politician who'd lent it to him as the deposit for an armoured vehicle. Anthony claimed he suspected the politician of being involved in the opium trade, had a disagreement with him, and was then arrested. He successfully appealed against his conviction but was hauled back before the courts on ten fresh charges of fraud and sentenced to two years. Even though he'd served his time, the authorities refused to release him until he paid his debt, so he was trapped. He'd gone on a hunger strike but no one had taken any notice and he'd almost died, so that put paid to my idea then.

Bevan was a forty-five-year-old former security contractor who'd been sentenced to sixteen years for drugs trafficking. He was caught at Kabul airport carrying crystal meth but insisted he'd been set up. His wife had paid $50,000 to secure his release but when he still wasn't freed she left him, taking their two children with her. When Bev took his case to appeal he not only lost, but the court ordered him to pay a $100,000 fine. Using loans and savings, his elderly parents managed to stump up the cash. Sadly, they were tricked out of it by one of Bevan's former inmates who'd offered to help. He still had another thirteen years to serve and wasn't sure if he'd ever see his parents alive again.

Saddened by their stories, I returned to my cell and changed into the white 'dish-dash' they'd given me. It swamped me but was cool and airy at least. Then I put on the plastic flip-flops, reluctantly swapping them for the shoes and socks which I'd hoped would protect my heels from further cracking.

At 15:00 hrs the guards unlocked the cell and gestured that I was to be allowed out for some exercise. Bevan and I followed them along a corridor, moving freely, and then out through a gate to what I'd been led to believe was the courtyard. The sight that greeted me snatched my breath and robbed me of the power of speech. This wasn't a courtyard as I'd expected it to be – with limited space surrounded by mesh. It was a garden, at least thirty metres by seventy metres. Pol-e-Charkhi had a garden! I couldn't believe my eyes. With Bev's bemused encouragement, I took a few tentative steps deeper into it. Although the grass was scruffy and uncut and the entire walled space fringed with coil upon coil of barbed wire, I thought that it was the most beautiful thing I'd ever seen. I disregarded the rats scurrying between heaps of rotten food. I overlooked the piles of rubbish the other prisoners had left. I didn't even smell the whiff of drains. In fact, I didn't notice anything bad at all.

This was the first time in months that I'd set eyes on greenery or been able to look up at the sky for any length of time unimpeded by razor wire. I could hear birds and see some flying around. I spotted a butterfly and thought of the film *Papillon* in which a man is wrongly convicted for murder and sent to Devil's Island. There was one scene where, after years in solitary confinement, he was allowed out to squint into the sunlight. That's exactly how I felt.

The freedom and the beauty dazzled me at first. I could walk around with ease. I could take off my sandals and feel the grass between my toes. I carried no chains and had no guard standing over me. Testing my limits, I allowed myself to walk further than twenty paces in one direction without bumping into anything. I could breathe fresh air and feel the sun on my face. There were ferns so green they hurt my eyes and other overgrown plants I didn't recognise that hadn't been tended to in a while. Then I spotted something that made me gasp.

Roses. Someone had planted roses. Untended, they'd gone wild, sending out whippy bracts covered with thorns and straggly flowers, but they were roses nonetheless. I approached them cautiously, as if they were a mirage that would melt in the shimmering haze as soon as I reached them, but they didn't. Burying my nose in a rose as red as any of those in Liz's bridal bouquet, I closed my eyes and deeply inhaled its scent.

Twenty-one

My wonderment at the Pol-e-Charkhi garden took me straight back to the day we invited my mother to come and have a meal with us one Christmas. It was December 2000, and I'd only just returned from my tour in Bosnia and settled back into life in Catterick when my sister Betty rang me to tell me that Mam wasn't well.

I hadn't spoken to my mother for a long time chiefly because she'd had her telephone cut off for not paying her bills. 'She's in hospital with angina and pleurisy,' my big sister told me. 'You should maybe go and see her, Bill – before it's too late.'

On Christmas Eve, Liz and I drove to the hospital in Bolton from our home in Oxenhope, West Yorkshire, and found my sixty-seven-year-old mother about to be discharged. She looked twenty years older and seemed incredibly frail. She looked even shorter than her five feet and had withered away. Despite all the money and gifts we'd sent her over the years, her life involved drinking cans of beer in front of the telly and not eating. There was no meat on her bones at all. She had no warm clothes and a kind old lady on the ward gave her a coat to put on before she went out into the cold. We drove her back to her bedsit in Little Hulton, Salford, where I noticed she'd never even used the walk-in shower that had been fitted for her. The squalor and the cigarette smoke was worse than it had ever been, only this time she was on her own and not at all well. It was time to make my peace.

'Come and have a meal with us over Christmas, Mam,' I said. 'We'd love to have you.'

Betty drove her across to ours on 28 December and when she got her out of the car outside the Victorian house we'd bought, my mother's eyes virtually came out on stalks. Wandering into the living room with its big stone fireplace, she touched everything and stood in front of the Christmas tree Liz and the kids had decorated, staring up at it in wonder.

'Oh, Billy, this is lovely!' she cried, lighting a cigarette. 'It's so much nicer than where I live, and you have plenty of room, don't you?'

We offered her a pre-dinner drink and she asked for Baileys. 'That's an after dinner drink, Mam,' I corrected her. 'How about a sherry?' We laid all the food out on the dining table ready to eat and she started on it straight away, as if she'd not eaten in weeks. She probably hadn't. We all fell about laughing because it was like watching a chimpanzee's tea party.

'Oh, I could really enjoy living here,' she said, stuffing another roast potato into her mouth and taking a swig from her glass. She ate us out of house and home that day and probably filled her pockets full of food to take home as well. It didn't matter; we had plenty and she had a truly fantastic day, exploring every room and continually hinting that she could move in. When it was time to go, she gave the children a dreaded 'Nana kiss', and then turned to me.

'Can I have a word, cock?' she asked. I melted for a moment, thinking she was finally going to thank me for such a lovely day, but instead she said, 'Could you lend me a fiver?'

I sighed. 'You can have as much as you want, Mam, as long as you don't use it to buy cigarettes.' I peeled off some cash and gave her a bottle of sherry and a large box of liqueur chocolates along with all sorts of other goodies, including the leftover chicken. She sat in the front seat of Betty's car laden with booty, looking up at us all with a big grin on her face.

Three days later, when my brother David couldn't raise her at the flat, he called the police and they broke in. It was 09:00 hrs on New Year's Eve. They found Mam dead in bed with her crossword book and dictionary at her side and her glasses perched on her nose. On top of her bed lay our empty bottle of sherry and she was surrounded by chocolate liqueur wrappers.

One of the detectives called to the scene looked at some of the photos my mam had lying around and asked David, 'Do you have a brother in the Army? Is his name Bill Shaw?' He'd been one of my corporals in Germany seven years earlier, who'd left to join Manchester police. He was a lovely lad and as honest as the day was long, with an affectionate nickname, 'Fingers'. When my brother rang me to tell me of Mam's death, he handed the phone over to Fingers who offered me his condolences.

I was able to thank him for what he'd done and then, with the awkward embarrassment about my parents that I'd known all my life, I added, 'Listen, lad. I know how my mother's flat looks. You need to know that I don't live that way.'

'Yes, Sir. Don't worry, Sir. Completely understood.'

When I rang Betty in Manchester to tell her what had happened, her immediate reaction was, 'Bloody hell! We must have poisoned her! You'd better get rid of the rest of that leftover chicken!' We laughed but the truth was we'd given Mam a lovely day before she'd had a massive heart attack at home in bed doing what she most enjoyed. I only hoped when my turn came it would be just as peaceful.

Still, things were looking up for me and Pol-e-Charkhi had been such a surprise I could hardly credit how my luck had changed. I had new friends and a cell to myself. Then the day got better when Bev came to tell me, 'The Commandant wants to see you.'

Two guards appeared and I reluctantly slipped back into my jewellery although I could at least walk freely and the cuffs came off once we reached the Commandant's office. Expecting a general debriefing, I walked in to find Liz and Lisa sitting there waiting for me. Crying and laughing all at once, I waved my arms around and said, 'Look, no chains!' before running to my girls. Over their shoulders, I pointed at my mate and said, 'I can't believe it! Big Kev's crying! Brilliant!'

'We only have half an hour, Bill,' Liz told me then.

'What?'

'We've got to get them back to Anjuman before dark,' Kev explained.

They promised that they'd come back the next day when the Commandant assured us we could spend three hours together. I didn't dare hope so. When the time came to go, we headed off together hand in hand to the main gate until it was my turn to peel off. As they watched me start the long walk back to my cell I did a little skip and sang, 'See you tomorrow!'

Although it had been fantastic to see them I was worried

about them getting back to the base safely. They had to pass through a hostile village where the families of the Taliban prisoners lived. At that time of night, there'd be a lot of activity and the drivers and bodyguards would be nervous as hell stuck in traffic. If anything happened to them, I'd never forgive myself. I didn't sleep at all well that night on my wafer-thin mattress with my fears cantering through my head.

I was up very early on Tuesday, 2 June and took a cold shower without having to ask anyone. I dressed and waited to see if Liz and Bear would come, painfully aware that they only had two more days in Kabul. Bev and Anthony served me coffee and hatched a plan. 'We'll get the guards to let us out too,' Bev said, 'so we can finally meet these women you never stop bloody talking about.'

At 11:00 hrs, I was taken to a guard's room in the old court house. I opened the door to see the girls, along with Kim and a couple of lads from work. After a few minutes, I asked the guard, 'Can Bevan bring us some tea?' Sure enough, my friends walked in with big smiles on their faces for their first social interaction with Westerners in a long time.

Even better than promised, we were allowed three-and-a-half hours together. The girls brought me newspapers, puzzle books, *Top Gear* magazines, sweets, liquorice, and Merry Maids chocolate caramels – my childhood favourites. Liz brought some of what people had written on the petition to Downing Street and from the Facebook pages. She also brought me a chicken salad sandwich which I fell upon the same way Mam devoured her last Christmas dinner. Bear joked, 'It's like visiting someone in hospital!' I found out later that she wasn't feeling well that day but she never let on. Neither did Liz confess to her breathing problems due to the dust-laden air. And they completely forgot to mention that there'd been an attack on a hotel in Kabul and that they'd nearly had to turn back. The following day President Karzai was hosting an international peace *jirga* and they'd been warned that there'd be a security lockdown which might mean they wouldn't be able to come again.

'Everyone's been so kind,' Liz said, 'and I've never seen so many emotional people. Your assistant Jamshed told us his wife wept every time your story appeared on the news and the Gurkhas apparently cried for three days after your arrest! It's so nice to know that other people see in you what we do.'

There was too much for me to take in as the girls told me of their efforts to get my case publicised and how they'd even handed out flyers at the England v Mexico International Friendly at Wembley Stadium, where fans signed their petition. I felt humbled by all the support. Someone discreetly recorded a message for me to send home to the rest of my family so, grinning, I told them: 'I'm in good hands and everyone's looking after me.'

Liz and I never stopped holding hands throughout and when we had to say goodbye it was hard to let go of her fingers. But night would fall soon and they were due to meet the Ambassador early the following morning so they left and I walked in a daze back to my cell. Bevan and Anthony were genuinely happy for me and we shared the first pizza any of us had eaten for a long time. I went to bed thinking how lovely Liz and Bear had looked. Whatever happened next, I'd have that memory to cling to.

I watched the gate hopefully all the next day, but as I'd feared they weren't able to come. Although gutted, I was also relieved as it would have been hard to say goodbye all over again. There was nothing for it. I just had to wait my time out until the appeal. With that in mind, the next few weeks were taken up with getting into a new routine. My days rarely varied – I had breakfast, showered, did my exercises, read, wrote letters or slept until my time in the garden with Bev, then I showered again and took afternoon tea and stickies with the lads. At night, I spent hours poring over crossword puzzles, just like my mam. As often as I could, I washed my dish-dash in the shower tray with soap powder and then stamped all over it to simulate the action of a washing machine. It was a bit like treading grapes only far less rewarding.

With no air conditioning at Pol-e it was beginning to get seriously warm. Despite the heat, I covered my entire body with my sheet at night to keep the mosquitoes at bay. I sprayed insect repellent everywhere but the lights attracted them and I was covered in bites. I blocked the bottom of my door with books to stop mice getting in. To keep myself from getting muscle wastage, I devised a punishing regime of cardiovascular exercise, including upside down pedalling with my legs in the air followed by press-ups. At one point, I lost my balance and bashed the side of my face on the bare metal bunk, giving myself an impressive black eye. With no mirror I couldn't see how bad it was so I touched it but that only opened it up and made it much worse.

Bevan and Anthony continued to take care of me and our banter reminded me of the sergeant's mess. At my request, they discovered that Rob Langdon shared a cell with seven

Nigerians on drugs charges and only had visits occasionally from the Red Cross. Just as in Tawqeef, he lay in his pit all day and didn't integrate, which he probably would have done had he been in with us. It was frustrating that I couldn't even pay him a visit.

Kev had gone out of the country for a while and Tim Ward was my new point of contact. He'd been one of my Staff Sergeants in Rheindahlen in 2002 and came to work for G4S once he learned I was there. Azim, whom I hadn't seen since Tawqeef, turned up a couple of times too with some provisions. All I had to say was, 'How you diddling?' and he'd throw his arms around me and burst into tears. It had been over three months since my last visit from any British consular official. So much for, 'Britons never, ever, ever shall be slaves!'

Kim came to see me as often as she could but she didn't have much to report apart from trying to get me onto CNN. She brought some new letters from home, though, which were great – even if the girls' meeting at the British embassy hadn't gone quite to plan. Lisa wrote, '*It was a total farce as they were not really prepared for us . . . We felt more anger than anything else and completely let down by the one area we had expected absolute support from.*'

The guards charged up my iPod which allowed me to escape from my worries about what might happen when my case went to appeal. One album I particularly enjoyed was *SAHB Stories* by the Sensational Alex Harvey Band, which I'd first heard in the 1970s when I was working as a butcher. One song had the line Liz and I always liked which went: '*This here's a story about Lilly and Billy; how they got married and lived happy ever after.*' I took the iPod to the lads' cell and we'd sit with a brew listening to the playlists I'd put together as a free man. Fortunately, Bev liked exactly the same songs as me and Anthony's favourite was 'Streets of Fire' by Bruce Springsteen. Part of the lyrics went, *'When the night's quiet and you don't care anymore, and . . . the weak lies and the cold walls . . . eat at your insides . . .'*

The Taliban (whom we codenamed 'Tangos') were constantly active and the guards were always shunting them from cell to cell to separate troublemakers and those suspected of organising insurgent attacks on the outside. I'd heard that some prisoners had been murdered in Pol-e-Charkhi when they didn't do what the Taliban wanted so I remained fully on guard. Bevan pointed out one inmate who'd been given a good hiding by those loyal to Al-Qaeda. Another man was so badly beaten that they'd had to wash his blood off the ceiling.

A couple of senior Tangos came to see me on a regular basis to try to persuade me to convert to Islam. One who was especially persistent was Wais Hudein – at twenty-eight years old, already an extreme fundamentalist. I'd listen to what he had to say but then I'd tell him politely, *'Kam-kam'* (slowly, slowly). Religion wasn't something to make rash decisions about and I knew I'd only be doing it to appease the Afghans, which would have been dishonest. When word got out that I was resisting, a few who passed me gave me the old 'finger across the throat' routine or spat into my cell, but I ignored them.

Mobile phones were forbidden in Pol-e but most of the Talib had them quite openly and used them often. Anthony had one too, hidden in his cell. I was too afraid to keep one because if it was found you could get six months added to your sentence. Instead, the G4S lads brought me a SIM card loaded with credit so every few days, I'd use Anthony's phone and text home. Occasionally, I'd make a quick call in the rose garden while someone kept lookout.

When the guards confiscated all the Taliban phones, the mood turned nasty. There were a few fights and some rumours of escape plans. Seven senior Tangos had escaped in March after bribing guards for the keys. 'Wait a minute,' I said to Anthony and Bevan, when they told me. 'If the Tangos can bribe the guards for the keys, what's to stop them bribing one to get into my cell and have a pop at me?'

'Nothing at all,' Anthony replied. He looked at Bevan who shrugged his shoulders in agreement.

Great.

I wondered how many of the prisoners in Pol-e-Charkhi were innocent, like me. I, too, had longed to escape but I was a realist and knew that it just wouldn't be possible in such a place. But for the first time in my life I felt some of the desperation I'd first seen in Hong Kong in the 1980s when I'd volunteered to work on the Chinese border with the Gurkhas. Our job was to lie in wait and catch the hundreds of illegal immigrants who scaled the razor wire fences hoping for a better life in Hong Kong. When word got out that any immigrants who reported to the Immigration Centre by a certain date would be registered and could stay, we were deluged. Although it only applied to those already on the island, hundreds of Chinese immigrants either tried to cross the fences or swim across the marshes between China and the peninsula. They were poor, tired and desperate. Escape from a repressive regime meant everything to them – it was even worth risking their lives for, poor buggers.

Entire families often sat watching the fences for up to six weeks, learning the patrol patterns and waiting for their chance to cross. Wrapping their hands and feet in rags, they'd scramble up over the brutal fence, often cutting themselves badly. Little did they know we were watching from the bushes and would appear the minute they touched down on the Hong Kong side. I felt so sorry for the many we caught near the border at Sek Kong, especially the women. I always made sure to carry plenty of sweets with me to give to them and we treated them well. But from the moment we handed them over to the Chinese military at the border, the beatings began. They'd hit them with rifles and sticks before throwing them in vans to be carted off to prison.

'No! There's no need for that!' I'd remonstrate. Through interpreters or using my own limited Cantonese, I'd plead with them not to hurt the immigrants but they'd laugh at me and carry on. Helpless to intervene, all we could do was walk away. It was terrible to witness and really began to get to me. So much so that one day not long after I'd finished that particular part of my tour, I spotted two Royal Hong Kong Policemen beating an immigrant on a boat and I went mad.

The young lad had been fished out of the Mai Po marshes along with many others, including children, who used carrier bags or inflatable pillows as buoyancy aids on the long journey across. Some had been in the water so long that their skin was pale and wrinkled. Pulled onto the boat, their hands cuffed behind their back, they looked like drowned rats. When I saw the RHKP officers laying into one of them with their truncheons as they were pulling him onto the dock, I jumped on them. 'Stop that right now!' I yelled and pulled them off. Furious, I took down the numbers of the officers involved and reported them to their superiors, thinking of all those others immigrants I'd seen snagged on the border fences, bleeding and exhausted, all hope gone.

Imprisoned behind my own razor wire in Pol-e-Charkhi, my hope was bolstered by the hour I was allowed in the garden every day with Bev. We found some dumb-bells made of two paint cans filled with cement connected by a rusty metal bar, and took turns to do some weight lifting. I also helped Bev water the roses. We found some hosepipe and made extensions. There were no secateurs allowed so we couldn't do any pruning, but we did deadhead them. I snapped off a few of the blooms and took them back to my cell, putting them in a vase made from an old Coffeemate container. They were almost as good as the pretty crayon vase of flowers Madeleine had drawn for me with the message 'To Someone I Care About'. I stuck that up along with about two dozen other paintings, photographs and letters, on what I called my Happy Wall.

There was a friendly parakeet in the garden that flew around our heads squawking. There were also a few sparrows. There was no dog, but I named the garden rat 'Mr Jingles' after the pet mouse in Stephen King's prison story *The Green Mile* and we didn't mind him at all because he cleared up the leftovers other inmates threw away.

One day, when we were allowed out a little later than usual, the light was fading fast so we had to work quickly or the roses wouldn't get watered that day. Suddenly, I noticed that

Bev was standing stock still, the hose leaking water all over his feet.

'Look!' he gasped.

Getting up from where I'd been kneeling, I walked to where he was standing like a statue and followed his gaze. There was the most glorious sunset settling behind the purple mountains, filling the entire valley with an almost magical iridescence. It was the first sunset I'd seen in over three months because I'd always been back in my cell by then. God knows how long it had been since Bevan had seen one.

He and I stood side by side in stunned silence and watched through the barbed wire as the sun sank lower and lower until it dipped behind the peaks of the Hindu Kush. Neither of us said it but I know we were both wondering when we'd be free to see another sunset.

Twenty-two

When I got home from Iraq and the Second Gulf War after six months away, I took Liz and the kids on a two-week holiday to Spain. During what was known as my 'post-operational leave', I rented a pretty white villa by the sea in the unspoilt town of Moraira on the Costa Blanca. Our granddaughter Madeleine, who was only a year old, came too but sadly Marcus couldn't join us as he was deployed to Northern Ireland at the time.

We swam and sunbathed, had picnics on the beach, and enjoyed being back in each other's company. I took the kids out water-skiing for the first time since Cyprus which brought back many happy memories. It was the best therapy after what had been a long and arduous posting, made all the more difficult by the tragic loss of so many of our own towards the end. I was painfully aware how lucky I was to have come home to my loved ones and felt keenly for those families having to go on alone.

There was no general psychological debriefing when we got back from Iraq, as there is now after any period of time spent in a theatre of war. We were just handed a few leaflets and told, 'Things change. Your partners have been running every-thing back home. Make sure you don't go barging in back home.' Feeling that my company needed more than that, I debriefed them myself. 'If any of you feel the need to talk about what you went through once we're back in Germany then you can come and see me, the RSM, the Families Officer or ask to see the padre or the doctor. No one will think any less of you and all information would be strictly confidential.'

These days there are far more structured debriefings on how to cope with 'survivor guilt', and the reliving of horrible experiences. 'The slightest thing can trigger a memory when you least expect it,' the psychologists warn. 'It might be a song, or a smell, or a particular date. The flashbacks can last for seconds or hours and it is often hard to remain focused when even the smallest task can seem daunting, or if you are finding it difficult to sleep.' The advice is to keep busy and surround yourself with friends and family who can love and support you. Well, I was certainly doing that in Moraira and what was distracting me most successfully from thoughts of dead comrades or headless corpses was my choice about what I was going to do next.

Sitting at a beach bar at sunset on one of our last nights, we chatted about our plans for the future. Given the choice, I'd have stayed in the RMP forever but we realised that wasn't possible and would have to make a decision soon. 'Whatever happens, your mum and I are going to start looking for a holiday home in Spain,' I told the kids. 'We've always had such good times here and I speak the lingo so it makes sense.'

'Great!' was the response. 'Free holidays!'

The Spanish dream became a reality four years later when we found the place we'll eventually retire to. We knew it was 'the one' the minute we saw it, nestling on the side of a hill just up from a road lined with olive trees and fragrant pine groves. Throughout my time in prison, I thought of that road a hundred times and longed to drive back down it again, turn left, and climb the hill to our little *caseta*. But that family holiday in Moraira also became a talisman because it truly marked the beginning of what was to be a whole new phase for us all.

In Pol-e-Charkhi, Bev was a tower of strength for me too, and would often read me passages from the Bible or talk to me about his faith. He even gave me a letter to take back to my cell for when I felt low. He wrote: '*I know there are times when you get down, think you are losing it, are angry, sad, despondent and miss your loved ones etc but I want you to know that you are never, ever alone! . . . You have a wonderful family/friends and know that you are loved . . . You are in the hearts of many people . . . Bevan.*' The wheels of the Afghan legal system ground slowly on, despite Kim's best efforts. Frustration was wearing her down too but having just marked my hundredth day in captivity, I was powerless to help. What was a welcome distraction was the football World Cup, which started on 12 June. It might not have been as momentous as Man United beating Liverpool on my wedding day, but listening to the matches on the radio might waste a few hours a day. With the shortwave radio G4S brought me I was able to tune into the BBC World Service for highlights of the first game – England v USA – even if the one-all result was disappointing.

A couple of days later Miles Amoore, a journalist from the *Sunday Times*, arrived to interview me. I was allowed to spend an hour-and-a-half in the courtyard with him and gave him the full story from the seizure of our Land Cruisers on the Jalalabad Road. I was careful not to complain about anyone and to praise the way I was being treated in prison.

The following day I had my first visit from Jan Everleigh of the British embassy since Tawqeef. After admitting that she'd been shocked with the court's verdict in April she said they still couldn't intervene, so – same old, same old. An hour after she left, though, I was finally moved to the cell that had first been earmarked for me. This was much improved with a sink and an electric socket as well as a kettle so I could make myself a proper mug of Yorkshire tea, because like every good soldier I had my own brew kit.

I quickly set about making the place my own, hanging my pictures and using what I had to make the place more comfortable. Improvisation is a key survival technique so I fashioned a bookshelf out of cardboard I found in a corner of the garden and used my day sack strap as a hanger. I folded the rest of the cardboard under my mattress for better cushioning. The bed still creaked like buggery but I was no longer sleeping almost straight onto metal slats.

Despite the improved conditions, I really felt I'd had enough of prison life by then. Madeleine was eight on 16 June and I'd have given anything to watch her blow out the candles on her cake. Lisa's birthday was on 19 June, the same day my sister Betty was getting married. I'd had to laugh when I'd heard Betty had a life-size cardboard cut-out made of me so that it would look like I was in all the photos. The only full-length picture of me they had was taken at Lewis's passing out parade a couple of years earlier. I had the flu and was well wrapped up so I'd have looked somewhat strangely dressed for a summer wedding. I recorded a message into a visitor's phone to be played at the reception at Salford Rugby Club. It said, '*I am so sorry that I cannot be there on this very special day for you two lovebirds. Unfortunately, I am very busy, as ever, and my current host (Karzai) cannot afford my absence from one of his 'guesthouses'. . . God bless you both and have a fantastic day . . . Love, Billy xxxx'*

In the garden of Pol-e-Charkhi that day, I thought of them all and picked a rose for my cell. Pressing it between the pages of a book, I resolved to keep it for Bear until I got out. Later on, I was able to call her on the mobile phone. We lost the signal twice but when we reconnected, she told me that they now had more than six thousand signatures on the petition they planned to present to Downing Street. 'Brilliant!' I told her. 'Thanks, luv.' Back in my cell, I decided to read some of the comments on the petition that Liz and Lisa had brought in for me and which I hadn't been able to face before. Most of them astounded me.

Owen Dobson, a fellow RMP officer, wrote: '*Having worked and trained alongside Bill . . . including at times of extreme pressure and scrutiny, I feel that I know him well. I have an exceptionally high regard for him – both morally and profession-ally he is as demanding of himself as he is of others. I have seen at first hand his innate sense of justice and of helping those who are vulnerable.'*

Ryan, the sixteen-year-old son of Steve 'Simmo' Simpson, a corporal I'd worked with when I was RSM in Germany, wrote: '*I wasn't even born when my dad served with Billy Shaw but my mum and dad talk about their time in Hohne and my dad has the utmost respect for the man . . . if it was my dad in that place I would never stop until he was free.'*

Perhaps one of the most poignant messages (because she was dying of cancer) came from Major Jane Proctor-Brown, one of my recruits in 1984 at Chichester. She passed out of Sandhurst as a commissioned officer in 1988, and we then served parallel careers. '*Do the right thing!*' she wrote.

Kim and Kev came to see me later that day with the news that my appeal had been set for Saturday, 26 June, which would be four months since my arrest and two months to the day from my conviction. 'There's more good news,' Kev said. 'A team of British prison mentors has moved into the old courthouse next to your wing, so a detail of our lads will be living there. Once they get to know the guards, we'll see if they can try to take you across to watch the odd England match.'

It was all encouraging stuff but I have to admit that back in the privacy of my cell, I had my first panic attack in a while. This was it, then. I'd been persuaded into appealing but if it went wrong and the judges reneged on their promise, I could face a ten-year sentence. Not surprisingly, perhaps, I felt unusually flat and was relieved to be let out later on. In cell No. 1, Anthony did nothing to lift my mood. 'Word travels fast in here,' he warned me. 'Now that people know your appeal is imminent, there'll be added pressure to claim the bounty on your head while there's still time so watch out.'

The following day, 20 June, was Father's Day, when my family usually made a fuss of me. Tim and a couple of friends from G4S turned up with a chocolate cake with 'Happy Father's Day' iced onto it which just about finished me off. I took the cake back to the lads' cell but with no 'sharps' to cut it with Bevan cut it into twelve perfect wedges with a strip of (unflavoured) dental floss. Those little slices lasted us four days and the three of us sat there every afternoon, drinking tea and nibbling on chocolate stickies feeling like millionaires.

Alone in my cell, I counted the days to my appeal and tried to get my head around the idea that I might be freed soon. As before, I knew that even if my appeal was successful I'd be sent back to Pol-e-Charkhi to give the Prosecutor time to consider a counter appeal. But at least I had a chance. Those poor buggers in cell No. 1 didn't know when they'd be getting out and I worried what would happen to them if I was released. Neither had a farthing to their names and had come to depend heavily on my money and the company supplies.

I hadn't had a haircut since they'd shaved it all off in CNJC some three months before and it really needed a tidy-up for my court appearance. 'Hmm,' Bev said when I told him what I wanted. 'You might have a problem. The barber here used to behead people for the Tangos.' I questioned the wisdom of exposing my neck to such a man but with Anthony and a guard to protect me and an assurance that I wouldn't be hurt from Saladin (the head Al-Q man) I decided to risk it. The heavily bearded barber used scissors and hand clippers before shaving my neck with a Bic razor. He was a bit rough pushing my head around but I was otherwise unharmed.

Later that day a sandstorm hit the prison, as often happens during the Kabul summer. Millions of grains of orangey yellow sand blew in through the windows and settled into every crevice of skin and clothing, as well as coating food and toiletries not kept in sealed boxes. As the sand and rubbish swirled in and outside my cell, it reminded me of the terrible sandstorms we'd experienced in Kuwait during the Gulf War. Having taken over control of the border crossings into Iraq,

I'd placed one of my TA sections at an isolated crossing point and gave them their instructions.

'As you can see, our predecessors have dug deep trenches in which to hide vehicles and equipment against potential airstrikes. I wouldn't recommend you use them, however, since the Met Office has warned of imminent sandstorms followed by some pretty torrential downpours. The last place you want to be is in a large open trench that could fill up quickly.' They set to work on their new home and posted sentries before I left to visit other locations. As promised that night, we were hit with storms and rain like I had never seen. Everywhere took a pasting and equipment not tethered down was blown around.

The following morning I revisited all my troops, including the crossing where my TA section was holding the ground. The sight that met me was something to see. All their vehicles and trailers were completely embedded in mud and sludge. Just about every tent and sleeping bag had been blown away and hung shredded on the barbed wire fences along No Man's Land. The entire section was sitting around, looking totally despondent.

'What happened?' I asked the Sergeant.

'There were some terrible storms, Sir,' she replied.

'Yes, I know. I warned you they were coming,'

'We took cover in the trenches but everything just filled up with sand and then mud,' she complained.

The situation was almost comical but I told her to get a grip, post sentries and start digging themselves out. Me and my driver Simon (nicknamed 'Weirdo') helped them gather their equipment and set up their defences again. Thankfully, despite that mishap, they turned out to be a very effective little section.

In Pol-e-Charkhi, I was very grateful that the sandstorm didn't interfere with the television reception because, for the first time, I was invited into the building where the embassy contract boys lived to watch the England vs Slovenia match. The game was good but I barely registered it, so amazed was I to be sitting in a comfy chair watching TV. I was even able to call Liz at half time. 'We're off to No. 10 tomorrow,' she told me. 'We might even get to meet the Prime Minister.' I kissed my medallion and her photo that night before I went to sleep and wished them luck.

The next day brought some less happy news – my appeal had been postponed because Kim needed to have a meeting with Maiwand's lawyer and the judge. Mark Spandler came to see me and brought some letters from home, including an email from Liz who said that David Cameron wasn't available so they'd had to hand the petition to a duty officer at the door. She also sent lots of photos, including the cardboard cut-out of me which made me howl with laughter because I looked like a character from *The Sweeney*.

The next few days brought even more delays and frustrations and I became unspeakably tired of playing the waiting game. I wasn't sure how I'd handle it if I lost, so when the date finally came in for the afternoon of Saturday, 3 July, I was even more desperate to get it over with, either way. Roll on. The closer it got, though, the more anxious I became. Kev had been forced to take his leave and wouldn't be around for my hearing, which I feared might be a bad omen. I missed him sorely and felt as if my right arm had been amputated.

At night I began to have disturbing nightmares that took me back to some of the darkest days of my life, from the headless corpse in Iraq to an accident I was involved in during my time in Malawi. I was with a colleague, Staff Sergeant 'Pop' Larkin in a Land Rover being driven by a Malawian when we came across a ten-year-old boy riding an old bike that was far too big for him. He weaved dangerously along the appallingly maintained road as he tried to dodge potholes. 'Slow down,' I told the driver, but he ignored us, waited until he was right alongside the lad then sounded his horn. Panicking, he wobbled then rode straight into our path. After disappearing momentarily he flew up over the bonnet and landed in a ditch.

'Stop the car!' I shouted at the driver, who'd barely slowed and clearly planned to carry on. 'Stop the bloody car!' I yelled, grabbing the steering wheel. He slammed on the brakes. 'Now reverse!' I half-expected to find the poor lad dead but instead he was ripped to pieces and covered in blood but thankfully had no broken bones. AIDS was rife and I had no gloves so ordered my driver to give me his combat jacket. I used it to wrap around the boy before I lifted him gently into the back of the Land Rover. We drove him straight to what was euphemistically known as the barracks medical centre where the doctor had only iodine and cotton wool. That little boy sat perfectly still and never cried even when the doctor tended to his gashes and grazes.

When he was finished, I wrapped the boy in the jacket again and ordered the driver to take us to his village where his distraught mother had only heard that her son had been knocked down. Lifting the lad from the back, I carried him

287

into their humble shack and placed him on his roll mat where he immediately fell asleep. Using the driver as interpreter, I told her, 'We are very sorry for what happened. The doctor has done what he can and I will be back to check on him, okay?' The next day I scooped up anything I had that I could give the family, including books, pens and stationery, and went back to the village with Pop Larkin. The little boy's face lit up when he saw us and it was humbling to see how much our simple gifts meant to him. His parents thanked us profusely. As we left, and with the squaddie black humour that keeps us all going, Pop turned to me and said, 'They were that pleased to see you, it's almost as if they said, "You can knock down our kids anytime you want!"'

Not all of my dreams had such happy endings. The worst featured the Taliban coming for me in the night. Long fingers or knives would reach for me through the bars of my cell as I slept. The barber would slip in and slice me with a cut-throat razor, or shadowy figures would seep in through the open window and try to smother me with their hands. I'd wake, sweating, in the early hours, fighting off dozens of imaginary assassins. It was time to get the hell out of there.

Twenty-three

In anticipation of what the appeal day would bring, I was up and pacing by the time the guards brought me a prison uniform at 05:00 hrs. To my dismay, it stank of BO and I had to wash it. Two hours later, I put it on damp before the guards fitted me back into chains for the first time in weeks.

Grabbing my 'lucky charms' – my medallion from Knock and a small scrap of pillowcase from Tawqeef, I was led out of my cell. God knows what I looked like with my beard and baggy clothes, still sporting a black eye. 'Break a leg!' Anthony called as I passed their cell. 'Good luck, mate!' said Bevan, his eyes bright. 'God be with you.'

This time, there was no problem getting to the court except that the bus was full and I was the last to be dropped off, so the journey took over three-and-a-half hours. It felt like a bumpy fairground ride I couldn't get off. To add to my pain, the guards never stopped hassling me for money. 'You Westerner. You money!' they insisted. 'Give us!' In the end I gave them what I had to shut them up.

The hearing was to be held back in the original villa where my first case had been held. Helped off the bus, I was greeted by a swarm of people – press, friends and employees. It was a scrum. Maiwand and I were led to the first floor, where we'd have to wait two hours for the hearing at 13:00 hrs.

Kim met us at the door and squeezed my arm. 'I'm not your attorney anymore, Bill,' she said. I was completely taken aback until she added softly, 'You're like family to me now. I'm here today to fight for your release as an innocent man.'

The judge had agreed that the camera crews could come into the court this time along with anyone interested in the case. The clerk kept bringing in extra chairs as more and more people arrived. Defendants, lawyers, the public and the press all sat a few feet from each other sweltering in the heat. My feet were swollen and sore from being in the ankle chains for so long.

The three new judges led by a man named Gul Mohammad came in wearing ties, which Kim told me was a good sign as it implied that they were pro-Christian. Then there was a delay as word came that the Prosecutor couldn't make it. He sent someone in his place, a young man who walked in looking like Elvis Presley in an oversized shiny suit. In any other circumstances I would have laughed.

Within minutes of the hearing beginning, Maiwand's lawyer and father jumped up and began arguing, blaming me for everything. I put my hand up to ask if I could speak and the judge said, 'No. You must wait.' He remained calm through the chaos before calling his court to order. It was like a scene from *Blackadder Goes Forth* and I half expected him to put on a black cap. And so the hours passed noisily. By 16:00 hrs, though, even he seemed worn down by events and he wearily adjourned the case. My spirits plummeted. Kim quickly approached the bench and persuaded him to reconvene the following day. Before I was led away, I made a point of going over to where the judges were sitting to thank them and shake each of them by the hand.

Television crews and reporters from around the world pressed in then to ask, 'How are you feeling, Mr Shaw?' or, 'How do you think your case is going?' Trying to be as diplomatic as possible, I said something like, 'I'd like to thank everyone who supported me.'

'But how confident are you that you'll win?' one persisted.

'Well, obviously I'm not sure at this stage but I sincerely hope that justice will prevail.'

Later that night lying on my bed, the events of the day stormed through my head. I gave up trying to sleep about midnight. Kim had handed me a letter from Lisa in court and I read and reread it, choking myself up every time. After wishing me luck, she wrote of how proud she was of me and what a role model I'd been. She finished with, '*Right, in-depth meaningful stuff said, I hope you have your hearing aid turned up on Saturday and your glasses on! Bring it on! . . . Bear (BBOB) xxxx (Bear Brain of Britain)*' Fired up, I wrote down several bullet points for what to say to the court when the time came. I used the back of Lisa's letter for luck.

By the time I arrived at court at 10:30 hrs on the Sunday I was jumpy as hell but then I spotted Jeff Winder, one of my managers who worked on the Attorney General's contract. He told me that he'd arrived early and wandered into court by mistake. The judge was there taking tea and invited Jeff to join him. 'I told him everything, Bill, like how much work you do for the Afghans and how respected and loved you are. He was very interested. I really think this could go your way today, mate.'

As soon as the hearing began, the judge seemed to be in a fighting mood. He attacked Maiwand personally, questioning his integrity and asking him what he'd done with his share of the money. That sent my co-defendant into space and he continued to blame me for everything until the judge snapped, 'But William doesn't even speak Dari!'

Finally, the judge asked if there was anything I had to say. I rose to my feet and, with Lisa's letter in the one hand that the guards uncuffed, prepared to give possibly the speech of my life. I have been in courtrooms on many occasions during my time in the RMP and I knew how to address the bench with courtesy and respect. Reading through broken glasses that kept slipping off my nose, I spoke slowly and loudly so that everybody could understand. I felt surprisingly calm considering that I was fighting for the next two to ten years of my life.

'Firstly, Your Honour, thank you for giving me the opportunity to explain the unusual set of circumstances in this case,' I began. I told them that there was no dispute that $25,000 was paid because I'd paid it myself. 'However I was cheated and deceived by Mr Eidi Mohammad and person or persons unknown.'

Turning to the young Prosecutor, I said, 'Please can you tell me what is the first piece of documentary evidence in your file?' He stood up to call me a criminal but I told him quite sharply, 'Answer my question!' He sat down then and didn't say another word so I continued. 'I'll tell you what it is – it is my complaint dated January 26, 2010. Ninety-nine per cent of your evidence is what I provided for you, which you have now turned and used against me. This was never what I intended, which was to help your investigation and to explain that we'd been cheated.'

The Prosecutor stood up and objected again, but I was on a roll and barked, 'Sit down!' to a general murmur of approval from my supporters. Then I turned to the judge and said, 'Your Honour, a man of honesty, integrity and strong principles is what you see before you. That is what I am all about. I visited the Prosecutor's office voluntarily many times despite being told that I was a suspect and I never tried to flee. I even went on leave and came back. I wanted to help your system.'

I waited for my words to be translated and then I carried on. 'I should be praised for bringing this matter to the Prosecutor's attention, not punished. The outcome of this trial will be a benchmark for others wanting to report corruption.' My voice began to waver a little but I went on. 'My family have already lost so much by my expressing the truth . . . although I have done nothing wrong and stand here today falsely accused. You asked me what I want out of this trial. I want to be set free and allowed to go back to my Afghan friends and to see my family again, whom I have not seen in several months.'

The judge really seemed to listen to every word I said and when I'd finished, he thanked me very much. Once I sat down, a few friends leaned forward to pat me warmly on the back. Kim then had a final go on my behalf, hammering home about the law and reminding them what their country's legal system had signed up to. 'Someone from the NDS handed the keys of those G4S vehicles to Eidi Mohammad,' she added. 'Someone at the pound opened the gates. Someone let those vehicles out. Yet not one witness has been called by the prosecution and there is not one shred of evidence that is strong enough to convict my client.'

The judge broke for a recess at 11:30 hrs, so that he and his fellow judges could deliberate. Sitting outside the court, I was in an agony of anxiety, barely able to keep still. After more than two hours, the clerk summoned Maiwand to see the judge. Kim immediately objected that we should be allowed in too, so the judge agreed. With the public and press barred, the judge gave Maiwand a pen and paper and told him to write down confirmation that he'd gone into the NDS compound without me. The judge then took Kim and me to one side and said, 'He claims he is illiterate and that someone else wrote his original statement. This way, we'll see if the handwriting is the same.' When he'd got what he wanted, the judge asked us to leave.

It was over an hour later before we were all summoned back inside although it felt more like a week to me. Almost as soon as we sat down the judge began to read the verdict in Dari from the slab onto which I'd rolled my thumb.

This was it then. Straining to hear and leaning towards Kim's interpreter, I heard: 'Eight months in prison, and a $25,000 fine.' There was a huge kerfuffle then as Maiwand began yelling at everyone, as did his father. The judge told them both to shut up and threatened to have them removed.

I closed my eyes and took a deep breath. 'Okay,' I thought. 'I can handle that. Eight months. I've already done four, so just four more to go.' Even if I hadn't been acquitted as I'd hoped, this would mean that I might be home for Christmas. I said as much to Tim and Jeff sat right behind me but one of the television reporters sitting next to them leaned forward and said, 'No! That's not you. That's Maiwand!'

Dear God. What was I going to get then? I sat rigidly waiting for the sentence.

Because of the noise in court I couldn't hear what was being said but could tell that a further proclamation was being made from the bench. Confused, I looked around as everyone jumped to their feet. Kim's face suddenly appeared before mine in the mayhem, her eyes bright. 'You've been acquitted! – Bill! Do you understand? It's over.'

The courtroom erupted with cheers and cries from my friends. Unable to take it in, I sat staring up at her and then I broke down as the media pressed forward to shove cameras into my face. 'How do you feel?' they asked, as if I could begin to explain. An Afghan news crew pushed in and asked why I thought Maiwand had been jailed and I hadn't. I eventually managed to say that I could only respect the court's decision. Ignoring them all then, I pushed my way through the crowd to thank the judge personally. This man had proved to me that there was justice in Afghanistan after all. I hadn't bribed him, and I'd done nothing corrupt or illegal to sway his decision. He was an honourable man working within a dishonourable system and I was so very grateful. Shaking my hand, he smiled and wished me good luck.

I felt such elation then that I didn't know what to do with myself. Tired of all the cameras and microphones I needed to go somewhere quiet to think. But to add to the furore, the young prosecutor announced publicly that he wouldn't contest the court's decision. He made a great deal out of shaking my hand as the cameras clicked and whirred. All the while, I thought, 'We'll see, Elvis.'

The reporters couldn't understand why the guards began

to re-apply my shackles until Kim explained. 'The system here is that the judge has to write up his verdict and send it to the Attorney General. Then it has to be endorsed by the Ministry of Justice once the Prosecutor has agreed not to appeal.'

'But surely Bill's a free man!' one of the reporters protested.

He was right and I suddenly realised how hard it would be to go back to Pol-e-Charkhi and my life as a prisoner.

Just before I was led away through the throng, Kim handed me her mobile phone. I had to press it hard to my ear to hear.

'Oh, Bill!' Liz cried. 'Come home!'

The journey back to Pol-e-Charkhi passed in a blur and before I knew it, I was being led past the rose garden where Bev and Anthony were out exercising. The minute they saw me, they ran over and shouted, 'Bloody well done, Bill! We just heard it on BBC World News!'

Back in my tiny cell I collapsed, physically and emotionally, desperate for it all to end. Freedom was so close I could almost taste it, but I still didn't dare believe it.

The following day, Kev and some of the lads came to visit me before lunch and it was great to see them all, Kev especially. He was gutted that, after all his months of being by my side through thick and thin, he'd been flying back into Kabul at the very moment of my acquittal. To cheer me up, he brought in my old commanding officer from Rheindahlen, Lieutenant-Colonel Kearn Malin, who was in Afghanistan working at ISAF HQ.

'Good to see you, Bill,' Kearn said, shaking my hand firmly, 'especially after such momentous news.' He brought me words of encouragement from the RMP family, as well as some books and magazines. They all seemed so sure that I'd be freed soon that it was hard not to hope so. I told myself that the boxes of supplies they'd brought in with them were only parting gifts to Anthony and Bevan. In a quiet corner of the visiting room, I was able to call Liz on Kev's phone and speak to her without quite so much emotion. 'Not long now, darling,' I said. 'Hang on.'

The next few days were filled with more highs and lows as Kim said the Prosecutor hadn't yet signed the letter to close my case. 'Despite the public announcement by his deputy, he has since stated that he might appeal after all,' she added, dismay creasing her face. She was as angry and upset as I was and promised to see him the next day.

I felt as if I had been kicked in the stomach then. What if he decided to appeal? How long might that take? Another four months? And what if he won this time? Would I even have the same judge, or would the next decide to punish me further? I returned to my cell, sat on the edge of my bed and cried, 'What the hell am I doing here!?' A mosquito buzzed me and I caught it and crushed it in my hand – the first time I'd killed an insect since I'd been locked up. My head seemed void of all the good things that had happened and filled only with an aching dread.

I plugged in my iPod and tried to lose myself in music. But even Freddie Mercury's belting rendition of 'Bohemian Rhapsody' couldn't shake me from my gloom. When I finally fell asleep my nightmares were so bad that I woke up several times to check the bad lads weren't trying to get me. My fears weren't entirely unfounded because the following morning I heard that the Taliban corridor had kicked off after a weapons search and a riot squad had been summoned to storm in if they had to. Because of the upset, I wasn't allowed out into the garden until late afternoon.

By the time Kev and Mark Spandler came to visit me later that day I was almost too depressed to speak. 'I've had enough,' I announced them. 'I'm not sure how much more of this Kabull-shit I can take.'

Mentally, I felt really messed up. I didn't trust anyone anymore. I tried to concentrate on my exercise regime and on watering the garden with Bevan, who tried desperately to jolly me along, but I was beyond anyone's reach. Unless a decision was reached one way or another soon, I honestly wasn't sure what I might do.

The next couple of days I went quite barmy. I'd pack all my stuff up in a small box in case I was freed and then I'd unpack it again. I felt unreasonably tired from the summer heat. The mosquitoes annoyed me far more than usual, as did the ants – a new feature. 'Right now, our Billy, sort yourself out,' I told myself, and then I realised I had said it out loud. How long had I been talking to myself? Unfazed, I carried on, 'You won your appeal and you're going home.' I packed my belongings again and even took all my pictures down. The cell looked horribly bare and I sat on the edge of my bed staring at the walls that had contained me for I couldn't remember how long and wondered how much longer I'd be their prisoner.

By the morning of Thursday, 8 July, I was so low that when the guards appeared to tell me I had a visitor, I almost couldn't face it. Wearily, I sat up, walked down the corridor of my wing and past Anthony and Bevan's cell, without even bothering to say hello. Before I reached the gate, though, it opened in front of me and Kim stepped through, a big grin on her face. She was carrying a freshly pressed shirt on a hanger. Kev was right behind her. Folded in his arms was a pair of my jeans and shoes.

'Come on, Bill,' Kim said, her eyes spilling tears. 'You're going home.'

I watched the words fall from her mouth and shook my head in disbelief.

'It's true, mate,' Kev said, brimming over. 'It's really over.'

Four months, five days had passed since my arrest. It felt more like four years. In total, 128 days of my life had been spent locked up inside three of Afghanistan's most notorious prisons.

My legs didn't seem to want to work properly then, so they helped me back to my cell. Glancing around at my belongings, I grabbed a small box of my most precious belongings and left everything else for Bevan to dole out. As soon as I was dressed in clean clothes, I hurried along the wing to their cell.

'I'm going home, lads!' I cried. 'I'm bloody going home!'

Jumping up and down with joy, they shouted to the guards to let them out. The second the key turned in the lock, they burst out for a group hug. It was so hard to say goodbye to the friends who had made the last term of my imprisonment bearable, but Kim finally took me by the elbow and said gently 'Time to go'. As we left the wing, she added, 'It won't take long but the Commandant wants to see you.' Waiting outside his office was a CNN crew and they rolled their camera as I thanked him with genuine gratitude for his kindness and humanity.

'You are welcome,' he replied, speaking English for the first time. Then he switched back to Dari. 'The Attorney General wants to see William,' he told Kim. When his words were translated, my stomach sank to the floor. Kim protested but the Commandant insisted that the Attorney General still had to endorse my release papers. So, even though I was finally heading out of that place, there was a new and tortuous journey to make. In a convoy of three armoured G4S Land Cruisers, and flanked by two prison guards, I was to be driven across Kabul to the place where – all those months before and in driving rain – I'd first been arrested. This was really twisting the knife in the wound.

Out in the open air, with Kim and Kev at my side, though, I started to feel a little less wobbly. 'It's just a formality,' Kim assured me. 'It shouldn't take long.'

I heard the gates clank shut behind me – just as I'd heard them close on me in Tawqeef what seemed like a lifetime before – and took my first few tentative steps to freedom. Leaving that Afghan prison was not dissimilar to the day I'd left the Army six years earlier and felt equally unnerving. I had no idea what the next few hours and days would bring. Thanks to the company, a reunion with Liz, Lisa, Craig and Lewis in a Dubai hotel lay ahead of me. I knew that I'd eventually be taking the long flight back to Britain to see my beloved 'Moo-Cow' and 'Chunky Monkey', too. Then, Liz and I would go to our house in Spain. Only then, walking Trotsky the dog in the Valenciana hills would I have the chance to reflect on all that had happened and try to figure out what the future held.

But first, I remained a 'prisoner' of the system because when we arrived at the Attorney General's office, we realised it was Thursday and the start of the Afghan weekend. The Attorney General had gone home and so had all of his staff. 'Unless these papers are signed,' one of the Pol-e guards told Kim, 'we will take William back to the prison tonight.'

Big Kev lived up to his name then. 'How are you going to do that, exactly, Sonny Jim?' he said, bristling. 'You haven't got a vehicle, and – besides – we're all armed and you're not!' It was a Mexican stand-off. After many phone calls, a member of staff was finally rustled up and returned to the AG's office to stamp the documents that meant I was officially free.

Although I felt enormous relief, I couldn't completely relax just yet. I knew my ordeal wouldn't be over until I was on a plane heading home. This, of course, couldn't be arranged until I'd been issued with the required exit visa – a process that would normally take at least two weeks, so I'd have to go back to the Anjuman base and wait. Having told Kev not to make a fuss, I slipped back into the compound to sit in my room and sort my belongings, knowing that I probably wouldn't ever be allowed to return. Despite my hopes of sneaking in and out, word quickly got out and one by one, my loyal staff sought me out. Touched by their emotion but still in shock, I just wanted to go somewhere and hide.

Somehow (and to this day I don't know how he managed it) Kev secured my exit visa for two days later – Saturday 10 July. Having said my goodbyes, I climbed into a Land Cruiser which had full diplomatic status and every official document known to Afghanistan. Accompanied by my friends and a full CP team, I was driven along Route Violent for the last time.

The Jalalabad Road was where everything had started to go wrong but I deliberately avoided looking for the spot and kept my mind and my eyes straight ahead.

The tension in my body only eased a little when I finally took my seat next to Kev on board the Kam Air 727 waiting on the runway. That was until three armed members of the Afghan National Police suddenly appeared in the doorway and began walking down the aisle towards us. 'Stay calm, mate,' Kev said, as he watched my knuckles whiten on the arm of the seat between us. 'They do this all the time now; it's just a formality.'

The military policemen with their AK47s strolled through the plane staring at every passenger menacingly. My shirt was stuck to my back with sweat as I sat strapped rigidly into my seat and refused to meet their eyes. I prayed they weren't there to haul me back to jail because I'd sooner have been shot in my seat than be sent back. Kev and I must have lost pounds in weight between us during those anxious ten minutes until the policemen turned around and the stewardess closed and locked the aircraft door behind them.

The plane jerked forward then and headed for the busy runway. After a short turn, its engines fired up and we set off, gathering speed as we rolled bumpily along the pitted concrete. I checked my watch as the wheels left the ground. It was 16:34 hrs. Leaning forward in my seat, I stared out of the window for my last look at the country that had enthralled and appalled me. Lifting up towards the peaks of the Hindu Kush, we flew over that dustbowl of a city that had been my 'home' for over two years.

The plane banked over Tawqeef with its shabby low-rise

buildings nestling in the stinking heart of Kabul. I thought of Sadir and Habibullah, Dr Hussein, the Sri Lankans and Assam, all awaiting trial as they threaded beads or drank *chai*. Bumping through the air currents like a jingly truck on the Jalalabad Road, our plane flew over CNJC with its chiming clock and its caged dog runs where we'd gazed up at planes just like mine. 'Bloody bastards!' Yama was probably shouting up at us at that very moment, shaking his fist.

Then, almost on cue, it wheeled away over the distinctive cartwheel buildings of Pol-e-Charkhi way out in the desert, where my friends would remain locked inside for maybe years to come. It was tea time and Anthony and Bevan would be sitting in their cell, cradling their mugs or listening to the iPod I'd left them; trying to work out how long the money and food I'd given them might last now that the supply chain had broken.

Wave after wave of emotion washed over me as I climbed higher and further away from all the people I'd come to know, from Kim and Azim, from Mr Ghafory and the judges who'd tried my case and from all the lads at Anjuman. I felt relief, joy, sadness, anger and guilt.

None of this should ever have happened. Not to me, or to anyone like me. And certainly not in a country we were trying to help after so many years of strife. All my life I had tried to lead by example, true to my military code. Instead, a horrible example had been made out of me. As I left Afghanistan airspace for good, I felt deeply torn about Queen and country, and how I'd been treated by its consular officials. I reflected on my journey from Salford to Sandhurst, via Bosnia to Buckingham Palace, and finally from Kuwait to Kabul. I forced myself to remember what it meant to be a member of Her Majesty's armed forces and how proud I'd been when the Queen awarded me my MBE.

'Thank you for all you've done, Captain Shaw, and take good care,' Her Majesty had told me with genuine gratitude and warmth as she pinned it to my uniform.

Yes, Ma'am, I will. I'll take very good care of my beloved family and of the precious life that's been given back to me. God save us all.

Epilogue

by Liz Shaw

The day I received the telephone call that Bill had been imprisoned was the day all the colour drained from our lives. After almost thirty years as a military wife, trying not to fear the worst while he served in hot zones around the world, this was news I never thought I'd hear.

How could it be that my 'beautiful man' – that most caring, sensitive father of three who'd spent his life helping others – was incarcerated in some foreign prison charged with corruption? I could never have seen that coming, not in a million years.

After so many months of waiting, I couldn't stand it anymore and flew to Afghanistan. The moment I saw the state Bill was in, I resolved that this wouldn't break us; it would only make us stronger. We wouldn't give up until we had our proud soldier back home. And so the 'Free Bill Shaw' campaign really grew wings. It gave me a reason to get up each morning and helped fill the lonely nights. The campaign was the only thing that kept us all going during those mono-chrome days.

Some colour finally began to seep back into our hearts the day Bill walked into our hotel suite on July 10 – a free man at last. 'Pinch, Punch!' he quipped, before we ran to each other's arms. A little more colour leached in when we got to

Dover where he was overwhelmed by 'Welcome Home' banners and balloons prepared by our smiling grandchildren. The greyness in his face began to fade the day I drove him along the olive-lined road leading to our Spanish villa that he'd dreamt of so often. Alone at last with his 'Lily' he was finally able to relax.

I won't pretend it's been easy, in spite of the counselling he's received. Now that we're on our own, the buck stops with me. To begin with, Bill couldn't sleep with the light off and insisted on keeping the bedroom door open. The sound of any metal clanging against metal would jolt him physically. He cannot bear to see a spider killed, and became soppier than ever about our dog Trotsky. We've always been close as a family but 'Pop's' need to see or talk to the kids every other day or so has become notable.

He lost confidence and often seemed childlike, forgetting his bearings in the most familiar of surroundings. If a song came on the radio that he'd heard in prison, memories would swamp him. We were in a supermarket and when 'Everybody Hurts' came on the Tannoy, he had to flee. A few bars of Steve Harley's 'ransomed heart' song can finish him off completely.

In such emotional turmoil, he couldn't settle to anything and needed constant reassurance. He was always trying to work out what the time was in Kabul so he could guess what Bevan and Anthony might be doing. Guilty that he was free while they were still inside, he asked Kim to do what she could. He named a rose bush after Bevan and still toasts him every sunset. When Anthony was finally released (only to be extradited to Britain on fresh charges) Bill continued to write to him in Brixton prison. And when Michael Hearn, an ex-Royal Signals officer who worked for another PSC, was sent to Tawqeef because of a mix-up over weapons' registration, Bill offered his wife support.

He doesn't like to watch violence or prison scenarios on television, and was very troubled by the plight of the Chilean miners trapped underground for sixty-nine days. He can't stomach any quarrelling, even in jest. Of all things, silence oppresses him the most and he has to fill any quiet moment with sound.

Lost without the routines of work, Bill undoubtedly misses his life on the base, as well as the male comradeship he has always known. He worries about his future and although the company has been so supportive there are times when he feels out of the loop as he – and they – wait to see what he wants to do next. Whatever that is (and he could never go back to Afghanistan), I just want him to be happy.

As the realisation slowly sinks in that he is not only free but will remain so, he has finally begun to relax into our life together. After so many years of living on my own with him far away, it is lovely to go dog walking together, have meals out, and share jobs around the house and garden. Having him to myself without the constant interruption of emails and phone calls from work is such a novelty. We have laughed and we have cried; we have danced by the pool and done all the things he dreamed of doing when he was locked up. Waking up together every morning still feels like a small miracle.

Neither of us will take anything for granted ever again, and we shall always look back on those dark days in Afghanistan with a mix of horror and fear. It has taken well over a year since that grey day when he was arrested, but the sunshine has finally crept back into our lives and with it, the colour of our joy. It is as bright as any orange hanging from our tree . . .

Acknowledgements

There are so many people to be eternally grateful to for their concern and invaluable support during my incarceration. It would be impossible to name them all. If I have inadvertently omitted anyone, I can only apologise profusely.

Special acknowledgements go to Wendy Holden who kindly agreed to take on the task of writing my story with me. Without her help this would not have been possible. She was always there with the tissues. Thanks to Paul Watton, OBE, for introducing Wendy in the first instance.

My incredibly supportive family – Lisa and Marcus, Craig and Rachel, Lewis, Madeleine and Caius – all of whom campaigned endlessly with great dignity. I am extremely proud of their efforts to secure my release. Thanks to my siblings and the whole of the Cowling family for always being there. Kim Motley, my American defence attorney, remained steadfast throughout and would not rest until justice was finally served.

I am indebted to my friends in Afghanistan like Kevin Stainburn, Tim Ward, Wayne Arkley, MBE, Steve Howe, Jeff Winder, Andy Clegg, Lee Townsend and Rob Blackwood, as well as Iliya, Azim and Jamshed, all of whom worked very long hours on my behalf. Nothing was too much trouble in their quest to make my life easier. The G4S team in London – Tina Easton, Charlie Turnbull, Paddy Toyne-Sewell, David de Stacpoole and Nick 'the Greek' Economakis – all of whom were there for the family and worked tirelessly around the clock preparing for every contingency.

Pip Clarkson of PR agency Edwards Harvey guided Liz and Lisa through the unfamiliar and daunting territory of the media world, remaining by their side throughout. Colonel Séan Harris and his wife Nadine, lifelong friends who were so supportive, and Séan was always prepared to go further if my acquittal failed. Warrant Officer Ken Semple (ex-RMP SIB), by far the best copper I have ever known, and who orchestrated the petition for Downing Street and set up the Facebook page. Captain Tony Cooper, MBE, and his wife Pat, as well as Frank and Linda Coughlan – all good friends. Sincere thanks to Charlie Elphicke, MP, and his advisor Stephen Sobey for supporting the case and flying the flag in Dover and Westminster. My agent Alan Nevins for protecting my interests, and Carly Cook from Headline Publishers for her unfailing enthusiasm. Special thanks to the Garcia family – Salva, Amparo and Laura – who so kindly supported Liz in my absence.

To anybody else who helped in any small way with the campaign, added a name to the petition, sent a message, letter, or made the effort to come and visit me, I truly appreciate your support. I could never have got through this without you.